D1125127

CIVILIAN DEVASTATION

Abuses by All Parties in the War in Southern Sudan

Human Rights Watch/Africa
(formerly Africa Watch)

Human Rights Watch
New York • Washington • Los Angeles • London

Library of Congress Catalog Card Number: 94-75427
ISBN 1-56432-129-0

CONTENTS

MAPS

PREFACE

This report is based on a visit to southern Sudan and Sudanese refugee camps in Kenya and Uganda from late June to late July 1993 by a delegation from Human Rights Watch/Africa (HRW/Africa, formerly Africa Watch) consisting of Jemera Rone, counsel to Human Rights Watch, and John Prendergast, a consultant to HRW/Africa. The delegation visited the towns of Nasir, Ayod, Waat, Kongor, Lafon, Nimule, Aswa, and Atepi in southern Sudan, and refugee camps in Uganda and Kenya, and interviewed about 200 victims of the war and other witnesses to the violence. Interviews were also conducted in London, Cairo, Nairobi and Washington, D.C.

HRW/Africa sought to visit Khartoum and other locations in government-controlled Sudan, but was denied permission--at the same time that the government was announcing to the world that everyone was free to "come and see for yourselves." The government initially granted Ms. Rone a visa and agreed on a date for the visit in June 1993. At the last minute, the government asked to defer the visit until July, and then cancelled that visit as well, also at the last minute, without any mention of a future date. The Sudan Embassy in Washington, D.C. even announced in its U.S. publication that HRW/Africa was about to visit. Since it cancelled the July 1993 visit, the government has abstained from any contact with HRW/Africa.

In contrast, HRW/Africa encountered few problems entering the areas of Sudan controlled by the two rebel factions. HRW/Africa met and discussed its human rights concerns with several people in the leadership of SPLA-Nasir/United. Such high-level meetings were not granted by SPLA-Torit, however.

This report is based primarily on the field work of Jemera Rone and John Prendergast. It is based on eyewitness reports where possible, although the eyewitnesses are generally not identified for safety reasons. Because of the preference for first-hand accounts, this is not an exhaustive account of violations during the war in 1991-93. For instance, the tragic situation in the Nuba mountains in south Kordofan is not covered in this report, but was reported in our publication "Sudan: Eradicating the Nuba" (September 9, 1992). The information in this report, however, is fairly representative of the types of abuses that occur throughout the south in the war.

The report was written by Jemera Rone with the help of John Prendergast and edited by Karen Sorensen, research associate of HRW/Africa. HRW/Africa would like to acknowledge with thanks the informed comments of Dr. Douglas H. Johnson of St. Anthony's College, Oxford, England and Dr. Andrew N. M. Mawson of Amnesty International, London, England, on the draft report. We are grateful for the assistance of many others who have asked to remain anonymous.

GLOSSARY

Anya-Nya
the southern Sudanese rebel army of the first civil war, 1955-72

Anya-Nya II
rebel south Sudanese forces who, together with former members of the Sudanese army, formed the SPLA in 1983; also, some of those forces that defected from the SPLA later in 1983 and became a militia force of Nuer in Upper Nile province supported by the Sudanese government; several Anya-Nya II groups over the years were wooed back to the SPLA

EEC
European Economic Community

Hunger Triangle
A name adopted by relief organizations in 1993 for the area defined by Kongor, Ayod, and Waat, in Upper Nile province, where hunger was especially acute

ICRC
International Committee of the Red Cross

Murahallin
Arab tribal militias

NGO
Nongovernmental Organization

NIF
National Islamic Front, the militant Islamic political party which came to power in 1989 after a military coup overthrew the elected government

Nuba
The African people living in south Kordofan's Nuba Mountains; some are Muslims, some Christians, and some practice traditional African religions

OFDA	Office of Foreign Disaster Assistance, within U.S. Agency for International Development
OLS	Operation Lifeline Sudan, a joint United Nations/NGO relief operation for internally displaced and famine and war victims in Sudan which began operations in 1989. It serves territory controlled by the government and by the SPLA. Much of its work in southern Sudan is through cross-border operations conducted by OLS' Southern sector based in Nairobi.
PDF	Popular Defence Force, a government-sponsored militia
RASS	Relief Association of Southern Sudan, the relief wing of SPLA-Nasir
Red Army	SPLA military unit composed of minors
SPLA	the Sudanese rebel army formed in 1983 headed by Commander-in-Chief John Garang; in 1991 it split into two factions
SPLA-Nasir	the faction of the SPLA that broke away from John Garang's leadership in August 1991, led by Riek Machar and based in Nasir, Upper Nile
SPLA-Nasir/United	same as SPLA/United, used here to refer to the rebel movement led by Riek Machar after March 27, 1993
SPLA-United	the name that SPLA-Nasir and other SPLA dissidents adopted after they united on March 27, 1993
SPLA-Torit	the faction of SPLA that, after the August 1991 division, remained under the leadership of John Garang, based in Torit, Eastern Equatoria

	province, until that town fell to the government in July 1992; also known as SPLA-Mainstream
SPLM	Sudan People's Liberation Movement, the political organization of the Sudanese rebels formed in 1983, of which John Garang is chairman
SRRA	Sudan Relief and Rehabilitation Association, relief wing of the SPLA-Torit
Triple A camps	displaced persons camps in Ame, Aswa and Atepi created in 1992 in Eastern Equatoria and evacuated in 1994 due to government military advances
UNDP	United Nations Development Program
UNHCR	United Nations High Commissioner for Refugees
UNICEF	United Nations Children's Fund
White Army	An informal local self-organized defense force of Nuer in Upper Nile province, also called "Decbor"
WFP	World Food Program

I. INTRODUCTION AND SUMMARY

The civil war that has raged in southern Sudan since 1983 has claimed the lives of some 1.3 million persons, southern civilians.[1] The specific causes of death vary--victims either have been targeted, or they have fallen in indiscriminate fire, or they have been stripped of their assets and displaced, such that they have died of starvation and disease. All the parties to the conflict are responsible for these deaths, including the government and the rebels of the Sudan People's Liberation Movement/Army (SPLM/A, hereafter SPLA), who in 1991 split into two factions, SPLA-Torit and the breakaway SPLA-Nasir. All parties have waged war in total disregard of the welfare of the civilian population and in violation of almost every rule of war applicable in an internal armed conflict.[2]

Sudan is internationally recognized as an economic basket case.[3] In the underdeveloped south, war, flood, drought, disease, and mismanagement have rendered useless ordinary survival strategies and made millions wholly or partially dependent on emergency food assistance provided by the United Nations (U.N.) and foreign agencies-- that is, when the government or rebels do not prevent the civilian population from receiving this relief.

Sudan, with approximately twenty-five million people in nearly one million square miles, occupies the largest land area of any country in Africa.[4] The southern third of Sudan, which occupies a larger land

---

[1]Millard Burr, *A Working Document: Quantifying Genocide in The Southern Sudan 1983-1993* (Washington, D.C.: U.S. Committee for Refugees, October 1993), p. 2.

[2]*See* Appendix A.

[3]Sudan is in arrears to the International Monetary Fund (IMF) in the amount of approximately $1.62 billion, which represents 39 percent of all outstanding arrears to that institution world-wide. In August, 1993, the IMF suspended Sudan's voting rights and on February 14, 1994, voted to initiate compulsory withdrawal proceedings against Sudan.

[4]*See* Sudan map, inside front cover.

area than many neighboring countries, such as Uganda, had a pre-war population of some five to six million. The population of southern Sudan is now estimated at four and a half million. The U.N. estimates that the population declined 1.9 percent in the year of 1993, and that the excess mortality in that year alone was 220,000. This report makes it clear, through one horrifying testimony after another, just how such a large toll could have been reached.

Among the abuses committed by the government in the southern conflict, documented in greater detail in prior HRW/Africa reports but also included here, are:

- indiscriminate aerial bombardment of southern population centers;
- scorched earth tactics against villages around garrison towns, burning and looting the villages and killing, displacing or capturing civilians;
- use of torture, disappearance and summary execution, particularly against residents of garrison towns in order to quash civic opposition to government policies, such civic opposition in Juba to the mandatory use of Arabic in what had been English-language schools, and forcible conversion to Islam;
- restriction of movement of the civilian residents of garrison towns--in Juba, forbidding them from leaving even in times of food scarcity--and placement of land mines and military patrols on the exit routes to enforce the ban on movement;
- killing civilians, pillage of civilian cattle and grain and burning of homes by tribal militias armed by persons and political parties aligned with the government to carry on its counterinsurgency war on the cheap and to "drain the sea" of tribes deemed supportive of the SPLA;
- cruel and inhuman prison conditions;
- lack of due process;
- abducting women and children; and
- severe restrictions on relief efforts by international and U.N. agencies, and impunity given to army officers and others who profiteer on relief food.

Among the abuses committed by the two SPLA factions are:

- indiscriminate attacks on civilians living in the territory of the other SPLA faction;
- pillage of civilian cattle and grain and destruction and burning of homes in the opposing faction's territory;
- taking food from civilians, directly or indirectly, by force or fraud;
- abducting civilians, principally women and children, from the territory of the other faction;
- siege of garrison towns by the SPLA-Torit, including on some occasions using starvation of civilians as a method of combat;
- torture, disappearance, and summary executions;
- holding long-term political prisoners in prolonged arbitrary detention, by SPLA-Torit;
- cruel and inhuman prison conditions;
- lack of due process;
- forcible recruitment, primarily of Equatorians, by SPLA-Torit;
- forced portering or carrying heavy military supplies by SPLA-Torit;
- creation by the SPLA of tens of thousands of "unaccompanied minors"--boys originally brought or lured to Ethiopian refugee camps for educational opportunities, who were then segregated from their families and trained and deployed as soldiers although some had not reached fifteen years old (the minimum age under international law)--and similar practices with boys inside Sudan, by SPLA-Torit; and
- denying unaccompanied minors the opportunity to be voluntarily reunited with their families.

The cumulative effect of the way the war is waged, in total disregard of the rules of war, has had a drastic effect on the civilian population of the south. Their hardship and starvation is the direct result of human rights abuses by all parties.

The year 1993 saw an expansion of international relief efforts in south Sudan for political reasons; the need had existed before, but the government had prevented access until shortly after Somalia was the subject of a U.N. peacekeeping action in late 1992. Approved flight access in cross-border operations to southern Sudan grew from seven to forty-five government and SPLA-held locations between January and December 1993, and another forty isolated locations were serviced by barge and rail convoys from the north. Operation Lifeline Sudan (Southern Sector) (OLS)[5] coordinated from Nairobi, Kenya, provides the umbrella for relief activities for the U.N. and over thirty international nongovernmental organizations (NGOs).[6] About 150 international staff from U.N. agencies and NGOs were permanently residing in twenty SPLA-held areas serviced from the south in early 1994.[7]

At the beginning of 1993, the OLS estimated that 1.5 million southerners were in need of some form of assistance, with 800,000 requiring food assistance. Seventy-five percent of the food-dependent were considered "specially vulnerable," or almost entirely reliant on food assistance, not including the Juba population, which would bring that number to over one million people in southern Sudan who required food assistance.[8]

The U.N./NGO efforts accomplished much in 1993: child malnutrition rates were cut by 60 percent in the most seriously affected areas, and 95,000 children were vaccinated against measles, a major killer when combined with malnutrition. Despite these and other successes, the U.N. found that excess mortality was 220,000 in 1993, a decline of almost 2 percent, compared with a typical growth rate of 3 percent in peaceful African country. About 600,000 people, almost one-sixth of the estimated

---

[5]Operation Lifeline Sudan (OLS) is a joint U.N.-NGO relief operation for the needy internally displaced and war victims in Sudan, under the U.N. umbrella. It began operations in early 1989, working on both sides of the civil war, in government and non-government areas, but only with consent of the parties. In 1991 OLS became a program under the U.N. Department of Humanitarian Affairs. The OLS Nairobi-based southern sector operations are coordinated by UNICEF.

[6]OLS (Southern Sector) press release, "UNICEF and WFP Request Urgent Funding for War-Torn Southern Sudan," Nairobi, Kenya, February 14, 1994.

[7]OLS press release, "UNICEF Preparing for Renewed Emergency in Southern Sudan," Nairobi, Kenya, January 31, 1994.

[8]Office of U.S. Foreign Disaster Assistance (OFDA), "Humanitarian Relief Operations in Sudan: Trip Report, July 1993" (Washington, D.C.: U.S. AID), p. 14.

southern population, were still internally displaced. About 23 percent of households were headed by women, another indicator of impoverishment; in the most seriously affected areas, women outnumber men by as much as three to two.[9]

As for the year 1994, the Sudan government's military offensive again has caused tremendous shifts of population. Food shortages and disease naturally follow each one of these population upheavals; the direct and indirect death toll caused by the fighting in 1994 promises to rival 1993. The needs of the civilian population remain dramatic: the U.N. needs assessment for food and non-food items in 1994 for Sudan was $279 million, most of it destined for the south where more than two million people are estimated to be extremely vulnerable because of the breakdown caused by war, and recent crop failures.[10]

In Eastern Equatoria the Triple A camps, home until February to over 100,000 displaced persons, have been evacuated together with local villagers. These civilians have fled south and east, many to locations that are more difficult to access. The government reported it retook Pageri, which was an SPLA-Torit headquarters, on May 24, 1994, and reached Aswa to the south by May 29. U.N. and NGO staff were evacuated from Nimule south of Aswa on the Ugandan border, since Nimule appeared likely to fall next. In Upper Nile province, clan fighting lasting three months among the Nuer in Nasir caused most of the huts there to be burned to the ground and its population of 30,000 to move to Malual, Maiwut and Jikawo. About 10,000 of these people were said to be en route to Ethiopia where they would become refugees. The unaccompanied minors who lived in Nasir were scattered.[11]

None of these military changes mean that the war will come to a military conclusion, since the SPLA still controls most of the hinterland. These substantial government gains, however, mean that the numbers of vulnerable have risen and delivery of assistance to them is made more difficult.

---

[9]OLS press release, "UNICEF Preparing for Renewed Emergency in Southern Sudan," Nairobi, Kenya, January 31, 1994.

[10]OLS (Southern Sector) press release, "UNICEF and WFP Request Urgent Funding for War-Torn Southern Sudan," Nairobi, Kenya, February 14, 1994.

[11]OLS (Southern Sector), "Weekly Update," Nairobi, Kenya, May 31, 1994.

The basic principle of African relief operations has been to define, usually according to nutritional status, the most vulnerable groups within a population and to target them with the minimum necessary food, water and shelter to sustain life. The problem in Sudan and other areas of Sub-Saharan Africa is that one is not dealing with a temporary emergency involving a normally robust and self-sustaining population which can eventually resume its former life. A process of sustained asset transfer which has taken place, particularly in Sudan and other faminized countries, is synonymous with the spread of mass impoverishment. Relief operations may, to varying degrees, help keep people alive but, at best, this is all they do. The way such programs are conceived and resourced means they are usually unable to tackle the process of resource depletion (war and looting) which is equated with recurring famine.[12] These are human rights problems; the devastation of southern Sudan and its peoples can only be halted if the rules of war are obeyed, or if the war itself comes to an end.

Food and sustenance play an important role in internal conflict. They are both weapons and goals. In this situation the donor/NGO system can exercise a good deal of influence, some of it unintentional but nevertheless unavoidable. The donor/NGO safety net has been drawn into the effective partitioning of Sudan,[13] in part because the Sudan government was actively hostile to and neglected the welfare of those civilians it deemed to be aligned with its enemy. The U.N./NGO cross-border relief operation into southern Sudan represents a means of slowing population displacement from and deaths in SPLA territory, making it more difficult or even impossible for the government to force a military conclusion. Similarly, the provision of emergency relief to garrison towns under government control means that the SPLA's ability to capture those towns through siege and starvation of the civilian population is significantly reduced.

---

[12]Mark Duffield, "NGOs, Disaster Relief and Asset Transfer in the Horn: Political Survival in a Permanent Emergency," *Development and Change* 24 (1993): p. 145.

[13]Mark Duffield, "The Emergence of Two-Tier Welfare in Africa: Marginalization or an Opportunity for Reform?" *Public Administration and Development* 12 (1992): p. 151.

International relief food thus has become an important element in the subsistence economy of southern Sudan. As a result, it is wrongly siezed upon as an asset to be taxed, confiscated, expropriated, or otherwise taken for the war effort by the government and the armed factions as well. The relief community is laboring against enormous logistical, environmental, financial and military odds to deliver a fraction of what the devastated southern population requires. U.N. agencies and NGOs involved in Sudan deserve praise for their active concern for civilian welfare, especially so where the parties to the conflict seem not only to have neglected the civilians but also to have targeted and stolen from them.

All parties to the conflict prey on the civilian population. They are sophisticated enough, however, to realize that when it comes to international assistance intended for starving civilians, the armed parties cannot confiscate the aid outright. They devise schemes that are little more than theft.

Armies that steal food from civilians violate the rules of war. So do armies that try to direct the movement of the starving civilian population to strategic military locations, where the armies can be reap the benefit of food and other assistance intended for civilians. While increased vigilance and tighter controls may deter some combatants from some forms of stealing, such controls in and of themselves will not cure the problem. The predatory practices of all parties must be confronted by the international community and the practices deterred through concerted international pressure.

The donor countries and the U.N. should warn the parties to the conflict that their indiscriminate killing, food diversion, looting, burning of civilian property, and other actions that weaken the capacity of the civilian population to become self-sufficient, are violations of the rules of war and will not be tolerated. These practices have already jeopardized the reception of the parties at the international level.

The international community should insist that, if the parties are to fight, they fight within the boundaries set by the rules of war and cease to prey on the civilian population. The international community should not be satisfied until the parties not only acknowledge that such practices are abuses and pledge to refrain from them, but also take firm disciplinary action against troops and officers who offend.

The current internal armed conflict, aside from its asset-transfer aspects, is predominantly a regional war of the north against the south and other marginalized areas such as the Nuba Mountains. The first civil war (1955-72) was also a regional war; it was less destructive and ended with an autonomy agreement for the south concluded in Addis Ababa, Ethiopia. Peace lasted only eleven years.

The role of Islam in Sudan, and Sudan's identification as an Arab or African state, are questions that have been open since independence in 1956. Elements of religion are present in this conflict because, since the military coup in June 1989, the Sudan government has been an Islamic fundamentalist state, run from behind the scenes by the National Islamic Front (NIF). Southerners are not, for the most part, Muslims but practice traditional African religions; a minority of the southerners are Christians.[14] Both the traditional African religionists and Christians have resisted the attempts of the central government--whether the present one, the prior democratic one (1986-89), or the 1983 attempt of the Nimeiri military dictatorship (1969-85)--to apply Islamic law, or *shar'ia*, to the south.

Although a majority of the Sudanese population is Muslim, the NIF's view of Islam is not shared even by a majority of the Muslim population of Sudan. The fundamentalist NIF government won less than 20 percent of the vote in the last free elections in 1986. The NIF differs considerably from the two main traditional political parties that developed over the decades in Sudan, which were based on Sunni Muslim religious and regional sects and families. These traditional parties failed to resolve the north-south issues and related issue of the role of Islam in the state and society.

To solidify control of government and enforce its vision of an Islamic state, the NIF and its allies engaged in serious human rights violations, such as torture, summary executions, and repression of all civil liberties, to stamp out the substantial political parties and civic organizations that were accustomed to play a role in Sudanese politics, even under dictatorships. Popular movements, engaging in strikes and street demonstrations, almost without bloodshed overthrew two military governments in 1969 and 1985. The NIF since 1989 has built up a police state, dismantled the civil service, and dismissed professional soldiers,

---

[14]The Encyclopedia Britannica, *World Data Annual 1993*, says that in 1980 73 percent of the Sudanese population was Sunni Muslim, 9.1 percent Christian, and 16.7 percent practiced traditional beliefs.

replacing them with NIF party loyalists, making NIF overthrow by any popular movement much more difficult.

These serious human rights problems led the U.N. Commission on Human Rights to appointment a Special Rapporteur for Human Rights in Sudan, Gáspár Biró, on March 10, 1993. He visited Sudan twice in 1993 and published a final report on February 1, 1994,[15] in which he concluded, among other things, that two provisions of the Sudan Penal Code are "radically opposed" to the International Covenant on Civil and Political Rights and the Convention on the Rights of the Child, both of which Sudan has ratified. The two provisions are *hudud* offenses[16] and *gisas*, or the institution of retribution.[17]

The Attorney General and Minister of Justice of Sudan attacked the Special Rapporteur, calling the legal conclusions "blasphemous" and claiming that Mr. Biró was a promotor of "satanic morality." The Attorney General told the U.N. Commission on Human Rights that the report was an "attack on the fundamental principles of Islamic penal law."[18]

---

[15]U.N. Economic and Social Council, Commission on Human Rights, Fiftieth Session, "Situation of human rights in the Sudan, Report of the Special Rapporteur, Mr. Gáspár Biró," E/CN.4/1994/48 (Geneva: United Nations, February 1, 1994), pp. 15-16.

[16]*Hudud* offenses are specific crimes for which the Koran provides specific punishment. They include theft, highway robbery, fornication, drinking alcohol, unproven accusation of fornication, and apostasy. For instance, highway robbery must be punished by amputation or death by crucifixion. *See* Abdullahi An-Na'im, *Toward an Islamic Reformation* (Syracuse, New York: Syracuse University Press, 1990), chapter 5.

[17]*Gisas* is retribution for bodily injury including murder. The punishment is at the discretion of the victim or the deceased's relatives, and may be forgiveness, monetary compensation (*diya*) or retaliation in kind. *Ibid.*

[18]"Sudan criticises the author of a rights survey for blasphemy," *The Guardian* (London), March 8, 1994. Khartoum's government-sponsored press denounced Biró as "worse than Rushdie," and organized demonstrations in protest of the report. "Sudan cites higher authority," *The Economist* (London), March 5, 1994.

Elements of race are also present in the conflict. Although a majority of Sudanese are Muslims, Arabs are not the ethnic majority.[19] Those who have fought the central government with the SPLA have included non-Arab Muslims, such as the Nubans from the centrally located Nuba Mountains, not geographically part of southern Sudan but part of the central or transition zone of Sudan. About half of the Nubans are Muslims, but they too have been military targets of the government. Their considerable suffering is not detailed in this report, in part because it has been well covered in other reports by HRW/Africa and other human rights groups.[20]

The south is predominantly inhabited by African peoples, compared to the rest of the country where the majority claim Arab descent. The majority of southern peoples are Nilotes (Dinka, Nuer, Anuak, and Shilluk). The Dinka are the largest single ethnic group in Sudan. The Nuer are the second-largest group in the south. There are numerous non-Nilotic Equatorian tribes, related to others in Central Africa, but their total numbers are smaller than the Nilotes.

Many southerners have fled to the capital of Khartoum to escape the war, only to meet severe racial discrimination, forcible displacement

---

[19]The Encyclopedia Britannica, *World Data Annual 1993*, gives the ethnic composition in 1983 as Sudanese Arab 49.1 percent. Of the southern groups, Dinka were 11.5 percent of total Sudan population, Nuer 4.9 percent, Azande, 2.7 percent, Bari 2.5 percent, Shilluk 1.7 percent, Latuko 1.5 percent. The Nuba were 8.1 percent and the Fur 2.1 percent; these groups are located in the transition zone and west. "Other" was 9.5 percent. The two most frequently-spoken languages are Arabic and Dinka, and Sudan has fourteen minor languages which are further divided into some 100 sub-languages. Of these languages nearly half are found in southern Sudan.

[20]Africa Watch, "Sudan: Eradicating the Nuba," vol. 4, issue no. 10 (New York: Human Rights Watch, September 9, 1992); Amnesty International, "Sudan: the Ravages of war: political killings and humanitarian disaster," AI Index: AFR 54/29/93 (London: Amnesty International, September 29, 1993), and "Sudan, Patterns of repression," AI Index: AFR 54/06/93 (London: Amnesty International, February 19, 1993); African Rights, "The Marginalized Peoples of Northern Sudan" (London: African Rights, March 1993); Sudan Human Rights Organisation, *Sudan Human Rights Voice*, vol. 2, issue 5 (London: Sudan Human Rights Organisation, May 1993).

and crowding into subhuman living quarters by the government,[21] and state-supported attempts to convert them to Islam.

The war has not affected all parts of the south with the same intensity at the same time. In the late 1980s, northern Bahr El Ghazal was the area of greatest suffering, inflicted by tribal Arab militias supported by elements within the government. Their brutal raids on the Dinka of Bahr El Ghazal contributed to famine conditions. After the split in the rebel movement in August 1991, the scene of most intense battle shifted to Upper Nile province. The primary fighting was conducted not against the government but by one SPLA faction against the other for the next two years. Many observers believe that the strife between the two SPLA factions claimed more civilian lives than did the government army.

The suffering was intensified by the government's disruption of the U.N.-led relief effort and its yearly offensives launched to take advantage of the factional fighting that seriously weakened the SPLA's effectiveness. The government recaptured a string of SPLA-held towns in 1992, winning significant ground for the first time in years. The factional fighting in Upper Nile nevertheless continued and spread to Equatoria, claiming lives both directly, through indiscriminate fire and deliberate killing, and indirectly, through war-caused hunger and disease.

Violations of the rules of war are largely to blame for the estimated 1.3 million deaths of southern Sudanese in the first ten years of the current civil war. The lives of millions of civilians have been reduced to surviving by means of international handouts because the manner of combat practiced by all parties not only destroys their families but also robs them of the means of self-sufficiency and rips apart the survival strategies they customarily employ during times of food scarcity. Even before the war, subsistence in the flood-prone marshes periodically subject to drought was never easy--pastoralism with some farming has been and remains the most viable economy. Yet this economy has been crippled because civilians' cattle and grain are looted, whole areas are displaced time and again, and many civilians are unable to settle anywhere long enough to plant or replace their herds.

In this report, we wish to bring attention to the abuses not only of the government but also of the SPLA factions. We note that the

---

[21]Africa Watch, "Sudan, Refugees in Their Own Country: The Forced Relocation of Sqautters and Displaced People from Khartoum," vol. 4, issue no. 8 (New York: Human Rights Watch, July 10, 1992).

government's abuses and repression are not excused by anything the
SPLA factions have done, and vice versa. The government continues to
commit gross violations not only of the rules of war in the south, but also
in the Nuba mountains, and to violate the basic human rights of some
twenty million Sudanese outside the war zones. Unfortunately, its gross
violations continue as amply documented before.

We note that the SPLA claims the widest jurisdiction over the
reduced (4.1 million) population of the south; the government's reach in
the south, despite captures of towns and encouragement of tribal militias,
is not long. Most of the territory and people of the south are under the
control of the SPLA factions, if they are under the control of any
authority, and they have been for several years.

Since our last major report on Sudan in 1990,[22] the SPLA split
into two and sometimes more factions. Until the split, it was difficult to
find rebel insiders or witnesses willing to discuss SPLA abuses. The split
itself generated more violations of the rules of war as each SPLA faction
turned its guns on the civilian base of the opposing faction, and
victimized civilians complained to us throughout the areas we visited.

The leaders of the SPLA factions must address their own human
rights problems and correct their own abuses, or risk a continuation of
the war on tribal or political grounds in the future, even if they win
autonomy or separation.[23] As one member of a small Equatorian tribe
said to HRW/Africa with disgust after he had fled village burnings,
looting, and summary executions by the SPLA-Torit, "And these are the
ones who want to rule us in the future!"

Short of an end to the war, only the elevation of respect for
human rights and humanitarian law to the top of the agenda of all parties
will prevent the extinction of millions more southern Sudanese. The
political leadership of the entire Sudan--north, south, east, west, transition
zone, and in exile--must immediately assume responsibility for the
survival of the southern peoples by exercising its moral and other
authority to stop the continuing victimization of civilians in this war.

---

[22]Africa Watch, *Sudan: Denying the Honor of Living: Sudan, a Human Rights
Disaster* (New York: Human Rights Watch, March 1990).

[23]For an assessment of the political possibilities, *see* Francis M. Deng, "The
Sudan: Stop the Carnage," *The Brookings Review* 12 (Washington, D.C.: Winter
1994): pp. 6-11.

Outsiders involved in the Sudan must insist on an end to human rights abuses as a primary means of preventing the obliteration of southern Sudanese.

HRW/Africa therefore recommends that the U.N. Security Council, among other things, institute an arms embargo on the warring parties in Sudan, with special attention to bombs and airplanes used by the government to attack civilian population centers. We also recommend that the Security Council authorize a contingent of full-time U.N. human rights monitors to observe, investigate, bring to the attention of the responsible authorities, and make public violations of humanitarian and human rights laws. The monitors should have access to all parts of Sudan. They should be based in southern Sudan because the conflict is at its most extreme there.

Creating a contingent of human rights monitors to observe human rights and humanitarian law abuses in the field in southern Sudan is an appropriate step for the U.N. to take now as it expands and develops its protection to and assistance of internally displaced persons. The twenty-four million displaced persons worldwide now exceed the almost twenty million refugees.[24] The internally displaced are similar to refugees except that they have not crossed an international border and therefore do not benefit from the same assistance or protections afforded refugees. Therefore, they are in many respects more needy.

In 1991, the U.N. Commission on Human Rights drew attention to the needs of internally displaced persons.[25] A report on refugees, displaced persons and returnees was submitted to the U.N. General Assembly, suggesting that the Commission on Human Rights might consider creating machinery for addressing the human rights aspects of internal displacement to enable it "to deal with existing problems in this area with the necessary degree of urgency and in a concrete manner, bringing them to the attention of the international community and trying

---

[24]James Rupert, "World's Welcome Strained By 20 Million Refugees," *The Washington Post*, November 10, 1993, quoting Sadako Ogata, U.N. High Commissioner for Refugees.

[25]U.N. Commission on Human Rights, Resolution 1991/25 (Geneva: U.N. Economic and Social Council, March 5, 1991).

to generate the cooperation of all interested and concerned Governments."[26]

The Human Rights Commission appointed a special rapporteur on internally displaced persons, Francis Deng, a Sudanese born in southern Sudan. The Commission on Human Rights has issued his preliminary report;[27] his work and that of others on this issue is continuing.[28]

One chief example of U.N. concern for the internally displaced is the Operation Lifeline Sudan (Southern Sector), since 1989 in the forefront of U.N. efforts for the displaced through cross-border operations directed from Nairobi, Kenya. OLS serves the displaced inside southern Sudan and thus helps prevent their mass starvation within Sudan and a larger flow of refugees to countries bordering on Sudan. This operation does not address the rules of war abuses committed by the parties, nor provide protection to the displaced.

The U.N.'s growing concern with the human rights problems of internally displaced persons could be addressed more readily in southern Sudan than perhaps anywhere else in the world. Human rights monitors could utilize an already-existing OLS logistical system provided for the delivery of relief supplies, yet the monitors could operate separately and would not burden those U.N. and NGO staff concerned with the emergency food operation. U.N. human rights monitors could be incorporated into the same program for personal security already

---

[26]U.N. General Assembly, "Report on Refugees, Displaced Persons and Returnees, prepared by Mr. Jacques Cuenod," E/1990/109/Add.1 (New York: United Nations, June 27, 1991).

[27]U.N. Economic and Social Council, Commission on Human Rights, "Further Promotion and Encouragement of Human Rights and Fundamental Freedoms, including the Question of the Programme and Methods of Work of the Commission, Alternative Approaches and Ways and Means within the United Nations System for Improving the Effective Enjoyment of Human Rights and Fundamental Freedoms, Analytical report of the Secretary-General on internally displaced persons," E/CN.4/1992/23 (Geneva: United Nations, February 14, 1992).

[28]See Roberta Cohen, "Strengthening United Nations Human Rights Protection for Internally Displaced Persons" (Washington, D.C.: Refugee Policy Group, February 1993), pp. 5-8.

provided to the rest of the OLS and NGO staff operating in southern Sudan.

Such monitors would be able to investigate abuses and report on them, thus raising the profile of abuses in the conflict. Increased U.N. reporting would lead to greater sensitivity on the part of the rebel forces, which would be an enormous benefit to the millions of people living under rebel jurisdiction. More attention paid to the government abuses would prevent the government from denying that such atrocities, particularly indiscriminate fire and scorched earth campaigns, occur. Coverage of abuses by all sides would illustrate to the parties that one is not being singled out and that all must conform to human rights and humanitarian law, no matter what their enemy's abuses.

The use of human rights monitors in this conflict could provide U.N. decision-makers with a prototype for deploying monitors in other conflicts, without committing the U.N. to equivalent action elsewhere.

There is already U.N. recognition of the severity of the human rights problems in Sudan: a special rapporteur was appointed to review human rights conditions in the country, and his reports indicate the need for more human rights attention to the Sudan, including attention to abuses committed during the armed conflict. Under the circumstances in Sudan, human rights concerns should not be deferred until the end of the conflict. The war has been particularly long-standing, lasting from 1955-72 and 1983 until the present, or twenty-eight of the last thirty-nine years. Its solution is not imminent and active combat is the rule of the day, subjecting the civilian population to new abuses of human rights and the rules of war every year, as this report illustrates. Human rights monitors, by regularly documenting and reporting on abuses in a manner that is beyond the capacity of nongovernmental organizations, would focus the attention of the parties and the world on the need for reform and respect for human rights.

Field human rights monitors could be hired specifically for Sudan to work under the supervision of the special rapporteur for Sudan, under the supervision of the High Commissioner for Human Rights, or under a separate and temporary human rights structure created by the Secretariat as in El Salvador and Cambodia pursuant to peacekeeping arrangements. The Centre for Human Rights has deployed monitors recently in the former Yugoslavia, where the conflict continues, and has opened a field office in Cambodia from which staff gathers human rights information for the reports of the special representative of the U.N.

Human Rights Commission. Although there is not an armed opposition nor an internal armed conflict in Haiti, U.N. human rights monitors are being deployed there.

We recommend that the United States, the United Kingdom, and other concerned countries fully support these recommendations, and, while continuing to pressure the Sudan government to improve human rights and humanitarian access, also pressure the SPLA factions to improve their human rights performance. The government and the SPLA factions should be put on notice that the international community considers improvements in the following areas to be top priority: 1) due process, 2) political detention, torture and summary executions, 3) death penalty, 4) attacks on civilians, 5) means of acquiring food, 6) recruitment, particularly of minors, and 7) voluntary family reunification.

The Sudan government, because of its human rights performance, receives little foreign aid. That should continue until substantive improvement has taken place and until the human rights performance of the SPLA factions is significantly improved, there should be no consideration given to any assistance to the SPLA factions by any government.

Nongovernmental organizations play a vital role in the delivery of food and non-food relief to the needy in south Sudan. They, too, should use their influence to persuade the parties to conform their conduct to international standards of humanitarian law and human rights.

The devastation of the civilian population in southern Sudan is the fault of all the parties to the conflict. They have waged war in complete violation of the most minimal rules of war. The international community, including neighboring countries, donor nations and the U.N. should play a meaningful role in bringing pressure to bear on the parties to cease their violations, in the interest of the survival of the southern peoples.

Upper Nile

II. BACKGROUND

During the period prior to independence in 1956, southern Sudan was administered separately from the north by the British under the Anglo-Egyptian condominium government[1] which had ruled Sudan since the beginning of the twentieth century. The language of instruction in southern schools was English,[2] and customary law was applied, with Christian missionary work encouraged and Islamic missionaries banned. Some Europeans and Christians looked to this separate administration to create a barrier to further Arab or Muslim penetration of Africa.

Armed conflict between north and south Sudan started in 1955, before independence. The conflict was punctuated by an autonomy agreement in 1972 that ended the first civil war between southern separatist forces and the central government, then headed by President Jaafar Nimieri, a military dictator. Members of Anya-Nya, the guerrilla army of southern Sudanese, were to be integrated into the national army, the local police, the prison service, and the wildlife service.[3]

By 1983, when the second civil war began, the autonomy agreement had been broken numerous times by the government. One such violation involved dividing the south into three regions, enabling the central government to deal separately with each and to play them off against each other on a tribal basis. The government also asserted control over the two most valuable natural resources of the south and all

---

[1] The Anglo-Egyptian Condominium government was a hybrid form of shared sovereignty created to acknowledge former Egyptian claims on Sudan and to accomodate British interests. Egypt itself was under British protection at the time. Egypt and Great Britain acted together to reconquer the Sudan from the Mahdist independent nationalist government (1885-98). While the bulk of the reconquest army was Egyptian, it was led by British officers. P.M. Holt & M.W. Daly, *A History of the Sudan*, 4th ed. (London: Longman Group UK Ltd, 1988), pp. 117-18.

[2] It was not until the Arab-Israeli war of 1967 that the language of instruction in northern Sudan was changed from English to Arabic.

[3] Douglas H. Johnson and Gerard Prunier, "The Foundation and expansion of the Sudan People's Liberation Army," in *Civil War in the Sudan*, ed. M.W. Daly and Ahmad Alawad Sikainga (London: British Academic Press, 1993), p. 119.

Sudan—the waters of the Nile and oil—while failing to live up to promises to develop and educate the south.[4]

The second civil war was built on the shoulders of the first. The SPLM/A was formed in 1983 in Ethiopia from Anya-Nya II groups and Sudan army mutineers from the 105 Battalion stationed in Bor, Upper Nile, who escaped to Ethiopia, where they were joined by others.[5]

The SPLA experienced political divisions almost immediately. John Garang, a former Anya-Nya I guerrilla who became a Sudan army officer and received an American education, emerged as a leader. He advocated a united secular Sudan. Many Anya-Nya II leaders sought the Anya-Nya I objective of secession or self-determination; they were attacked in Ethiopia by Garang's supporters and his Ethiopian government army allies. Ethiopia was then governed by dictator Mengistu Haile Mariam. There were shootouts and even military clashes between contending Sudanese factions, and John Garang de Mabior emerged as the chairman and commander-in-chief of the SPLA. The dissidents who did not escape to Sudan were either killed or detained in SPLA prisons in Ethiopia and Sudan.

The Sudan governments and political parties aligned with the governments tried to tribalize the first and second civil wars by using local rebels to fight guerrillas in neighboring territories. In the mid-1980s the remaining Anya-Nya II dissident officers and troops, mostly Nuers, formed a government militia also called Anya-Nya II. It rallied Nuers in its native Upper Nile province against the Dinka as represented by Garang's SPLA. Many Nuers, however, remained with the SPLA despite

---

[4]The Jonglei canal through Upper Nile was planned to channel the waters of the Nile ultimately to populous Egypt. It was not finished because of the war. The main oil field was near Bentiu, Upper Nile. The two major oil fields in southern Sudan are said to have proven reserves of about 250 million barrels, none of which has been drilled yet due to the war. U.S. Department of Commerce, International Trade Administration, "Foreign Economic Trends and Their Implications for the United States," FET 92-36 (Washington, D.C.: U.S. Department of Commerce, August 1992).

[5]The Sudan army traditionally had recruited heavily from among impoverished southerners. In previous centuries slave soldiers were common in East Africa. *See* Douglas H. Johnson, "The Structure of a Legacy: Military Slavery in Northeast Africa," *Ethnohistory* 36 (Winter 1989): p. 72.

government efforts to portray the war as a tribal clash of the Dinka against everyone else.[6]

The Anya-Nya II attacked SPLA recruits as they were being marched from west to east, from Bahr El Ghazal to Ethiopia for military training in SPLA bases there. Anya-Nya II also prevented the SPLA from returning to Bahr El Ghazal in any large numbers.[7] According to one authority, "The Anya-Nya II was, between 1984 and 1987, one of the most serious military obstacles to the supremacy of the SPLA."[8] While a government militia, Anya-Nya II committed abuses against civilians believed to be aligned with the SPLA. The Sudan governments made no effort to curtail or punish these abuses.[9]

The SPLA undertook a policy of trying to win over Anya-Nya II, with some success. Commander Gordon Kong Cuol of Anya-Nya II led his men into an alliance with the SPLA in late 1987, and other Anya-Nya II forces followed suit, leaving a few Anya-Nya II with the government.[10]

---

[6]Johnson and Prunier, "Foundation and Expansion," pp. 125-29. Garang was a Bor Dinka and many of the old Anya-Nya recruited into the SPLA were Equatorians resentful of what they saw as Bor Dinka dominance, even of the 1972-83 autonomous southern regional government. Among the pastoralists of Upper Nile, the Bor Dinka had the advantage of having a Christian Missionary Society (CMS) school located in Bor, one of the few schools in the province. The Bor Dinka took advantage of this educational opportunity to escape from the poor economic possibilities offered by the Bor environment.

[7]Johnson and Prunier, "Foundation and Expansion," p. 128.

[8]Alex de Waal, "Some comments on militias in the contemporary Sudan," in *Civil War in the Sudan*, ed. M.W. Daly and Ahmad Alawad Sikainga (London: British Academic Press; 1993), p. 150.

[9]Africa Watch, *Denying the Honor of Living*, pp. 78-80.

[10]Johnson and Prunier, "Foundations and Expansion," p. 130.

ETHIOPIAN REFUGE

Regional politics gave the southern rebels the opportunity to build up a large professional army. Mengistu, then dictator of Ethiopia and a client of the U.S.S.R., backed the creation of the SPLA and provided not only for refuge for hundreds of thousands of Sudanese refugees who streamed into Ethiopia, but also for military bases where the SPLA could train its recruits on hardware coming from the Soviet bloc. The rebels' political movement, the Sudan People's Liberation Movement, adopted the Marxist rhetoric of the day, but the SPLA dominated the politics, which were focused not on socialism but on Sudanese north-south issues and especially on the military goal of capturing territory from the Sudan army.

Sudan and Ethiopia have had a long history of funding and facilitating each other's dissidents for purposes of mutual retaliation and attempted deterrence.[11] Rebel Eritreans fighting for the separation of Eritrea from Ethiopia were aided by the Sudanese government. Southern Sudanese rebels were assisted by an Ethiopian monarch (deposed in 1974) and then by Ethiopian Marxist military officers.[12] Both governments not only lost or delegated control of large parts of their territory to the rebels they sponsored, but confronted drought, famine, and massive refugee flows over periods of years.

There was also an overlay of Cold War allegiances. The Sudanese government was until the early 1970s aligned with the Soviet Union. In 1971, an attempted coup by the Sudanese Communist Party pushed Sudan President Nimieri into a closer alliance with the West.

Ethiopia was aligned with the West until the overthrow of Emperor Haile Selasse in 1974 eventually brought a group of junior Marxist officers into power in 1977. The Ogaden War (1977) was the excuse for the Soviet Union to switch its patronage from Somalia to the more populous Ethiopia, which had much better developed facilities for

---

[11]Lemmu Baissa, "Ethiopian-Sudanese Relations, 1956-91: Mutual Deterrence through Mutual Blackmail?" *Horn of Africa*, III-V (Washington, D.C.: October 1990-June 1991): pp. 1-25.

[12]Sudan permitted Eritrean, Tigrean, Amhara, and Oromo rebels to open offices and operate from its territory and Ethiopia permitted the SPLA the same. Cross-border attacks between Sudan and Ethiopia were not uncommon.

communications and naval access. The Soviets backed the Mengistu regime until it was overthrown in 1991.

From 1989 until the fall of the Mengistu regime in Ethiopia in May 1991, the SPLA made major advances throughout the south, taking the towns on the Ethiopian border and numerous towns in Upper Nile (Nasir, Akobo, Waat, Bor), Bahr El Ghazal, and Equatoria (Torit, Kapoeta, Nimule, Kajo-Kaji, Kaya, Yambio). By mid-1991, the momentum was solidly with the SPLA, which controlled most of the south with the exception of major garrisons such as Wau (Bahr El Ghazal), Malakal (Upper Nile), and Juba and Yei (Eastern Equatoria). The SPLA's border access to Ethiopia, Kenya, Uganda, and Zaire was enhanced and OLS erratically supplied food and other humanitarian supplies to areas under government and SPLA control from 1989.

The SPLA's momentum came to a halt after the May 1991 overthrow of the Mengistu regime, when an eight-year patron-client relationship between Mengistu and the SPLA was destroyed overnight. The SPLA lost its military bases, principal supply lines, and main supplier of military goods.

The SPLA evacuated its bases and refugee camps in Ethiopia within a matter of days or weeks after the fall of Mengistu, and escorted hundreds of thousands of Sudanese refugees back into Sudan, where little provision had been made for them.

Once inside Sudan, the refugees' fortunes rapidly changed. The relief they had become accustomed to receiving in Ethiopia was not provided; what came to them was little and late, since the relief community had to negotiate often unsuccessfully with the hostile Sudan government over security and permissions.

In mid-1991, before the 271,000 Sudanese refugees in Ethiopia made their hasty repatriation to Sudan, the U.N. had warning that a disaster was impending. A later study criticized the U.N., concluding that "the OLS did not prepare adequately for the inevitable suffering that such a move would entail."[13] By mid-1991, 130,000 repatriates had been

---

[13]Alastair Scott-Villiers, Patta Scott-Villiers and Cole P. Dodge, "Repatriation of 150,000 Sudanese Refugees from Ethiopia: The Manipulation of Civilians in a Situation of Civil Conflict," *Disasters* 17 (1993): p. 206. This study concludes that the returning refugees were pawns in Sudan's civil war, manipulated by governments, military forces and the media, and that the international community failed to deal effectively with their plight.

registered in Nasir, 100,000 in Pochala, and 10,000 in Pakok, all just inside the Sudan border.[14] In July 1991, just before the August Nasir-based rebellion within the SPLA, about 90,000 refugees from the Itang SPLA camp in Ethiopia were in the Nasir and Sobat basin areas of Upper Nile.[15] The OLS response was late and inadequate. Food relief did not reach Nasir until five weeks after the returning refugees started arriving in Nasir.[16]

At the same time, the exodus from Ethiopia disrupted the fragile subsistence economy of the Sobat basin and Ethiopian border in southern Sudan, which limped from battle to famine to flood and worse. Itang had served as a commercial substitute for the Arab traders in the Sobat basin; these traders, before 1983, had been the sinews of the southern Sudanese commercial economy. The Itang trading network, with surplus goods flowing from the refugee camps to the Upper Nile border and Sobat valley areas, collapsed overnight, and nothing took its place. The sudden appearance of hundreds of thousands of repatriated refugees with little international support put an additional strain on the SPLA and tribal relations.

The Uduk, a small Sudanese tribe who fled with the rest of the Sudanese refugees from Itang to Nasir, encountered such harsh conditions in Sudan in mid-1991 that they returned to Ethiopia as refugees in 1992, making this their fourth or fifth mass migration in the short period of three or four years, their numbers diminishing with each move, placing them at the top of the list of Sudanese groups most likely to disappear.[17]

---

[14]Scott-Villiers, "Repatriation of Sudanese Refugees," pp. 207-210.

[15]*Ibid.*, p. 210.

[16]*Ibid.*, p. 211.

[17]In 1989 the SPLA attacked and overran an Oromo (Ethiopian) refugee camp in the Yabus valley of Sudan. The Oromo Liberation Front (OLF) in turn in January 1990 attacked and destroyed the Sudanese refugee camp at Tsore, near Assosa, Ethiopia. This camp housed 42,000 refugees, of whom 28,000 were Uduk who were driven from Blue Nile province in 1987 after the Rufaa Arab militia targeted them as suspected SPLA supporters. The Uduk refugees fled Tsore and several were shot dead by the OLF on the way; crossing into the

SPLA SPLIT IN 1991

The SPLA until 1991 had quelled several internal efforts at dissent with the help of Mengistu's army and internal security apparatus. With Mengistu's fall, the SPLA leadership became instantly vulnerable to more division. By the end of 1990, two senior commanders in the Upper Nile operational area, Lam Akol and Riek Machar, had been raising questions about the democratization of the SPLA command council, and by March 1991 their relations with Garang deteriorated.[18] Garang had concentrated SPLA forces in Equatoria for a major wet season assault on Juba, leaving Machar's forces in Upper Nile lightly protected and vulnerable to government forces from either Malakal to the west or from Ethiopia to the east. Complicating matters were the huge numbers of refugee returnees streaming into the Sobat basin and eastern Upper Nile towns. They faced an aerial bombing campaign and continuous interruptions in the supply of international humanitarian aid to the area by the Khartoum regime.

On August 28, 1991, scarcely three months after Mengistu's fall, the three commanders of northern Upper Nile, based at Nasir--Riek and Gordon Kong Cuol, both Nuers, and Lam Akol, a Shilluk--called for the

---

Sudan at Yabus Bridge, the Uduk refugees together with some SPLA troops were bombed by the Sudanese air force. When the refugees retreated into the hills they were shelled. Over the next few months they straggled into the Itang refugee camp in Ethiopia, where they were marginalized and many died. They fled Itang with the rest of the Sudanese refugees in May 1991 when Mengistu fell, and were kept in Nasir by SPLA-Nasir, which refused them permission to leave despite the serious food shortages in Nasir until mid-1992, when they then numbered 11,500. They moved to a nearby area of Upper Nile but were subjected to such banditry that they returned in July 1992 to Itang refugee camp in Ethiopia, a difficult journey during which more died. When Itang was attacked by hungry Nuer, the Uduk fled to Gambela, with more dying on the trek. There were then about 10,000 Uduk refugees. Wendy James, "Uduk Asylum Seekers in Gambela, 1992: Community Report and Options for Resettlement," prepared for United Nations High Commissioner for Refugees (Geneva and Nairobi: UNHCR, 1992), pp. 16-22.

[18]Douglas H. Johnson, *The Southern Sudan: The Root Causes of a Recurring Civil War* (Oxford: manuscript pending publication, August 1992), p. 67.

overthrow of Garang and broke with the main body of the movement.[19]
Joining them were the Upper Nile SPLA barracks at Ayod, Waat,
Abwong, Adok, Ler, and Akobo.[20] The stated goals of the breakaway
group, known as the Nasir faction after the town where their main
garrison was based, were of democratizing the SPLA, stopping human
rights abuses, and reorienting the SPLA's objective from a united secular
Sudan to independence for the south.

Many commanders remained loyal to Garang, who was not
overthrown. The SPLA remained split, roughly along tribal lines,
especially after the Nasir forces (mostly Nuer) massacred many Dinka
civilians in an effort to capture Garang's home territory of Bor. The
massacre touched off one of the most violent periods of inter-factional
and inter-tribal fighting in southern Sudan's history. It exacerbated a
desperate situation for the civilian population and led directly to the
creation of the "Hunger Triangle," a pocket of famine from Ayod to
Kongor to Waat, so named in 1993 when the U.N. and other relief
operations were finally permitted access to the needy in this area of
intense factional fighting.

FAMINE CREATION

Armed conflict and deliberate government strategies have largely
been responsible for the long history of famines in Sudan; famine can be
regarded as an outcome of a political process of impoverishment resulting
from the transfer of assets from the weak to the politically strong.[21]
Four specific groups are chiefly responsible for the famines that have
taken so many Sudanese lives during the second civil war; three of these
groups have been vehicles for state policies and have been utilized as
proxies by the government to attack the SPLA and its supporters at a

---

[19]Johnson and Prunier, "Foundation and Expansion," p. 139.

[20]*See* Upper Nile map, facing Chapter IV.

[21]Duffield, "NGOs, Disaster Relief and Asset Transfer."

relatively low cost to the government and without putting too much military recruitment pressure on the north.[22]

First of the groups were the government-aligned militias of Anya-Nya II, the *murahallin*[23] and others. Their task was to attack and plunder other civilians and take their reward in the form of looted cattle. They also harassed and looted famine migrants. While the Anya-Nya II had a political agenda of building a separate state independent from the north, and had sharp political differences from their fellow tribesmen in SPLA, the murahalin never had a political agenda.

Second was the army, which supported militias, isolated some garrison towns from the surrounding areas by forcibly preventing civilians from fleeing besieged towns, created and maintained artificial scarcities of food in these towns, and actively obstructed relief efforts.

The third group contributing to famine was traders connected with the military. Because the army had sole control over the movement of commodities in garrison towns, some officers used this control as an opportunity to extract maximum profits in times of scarcities they helped to create. One egregious example was in Wau in 1987.[24]

Fourth was the SPLA. Three elements in its military policy were responsible for creating famine conditions: the siege of government-held towns, including obstruction of relief; the raiding, destruction and looting of villages; and the forced requisitioning of food from rural people. The SPLA policy began to change in early 1988, toward greater encouragement of relief efforts, probably because the SPLA realized that it would be unable to operate effectively in areas that had been depopulated and, as the SPLA controlled larger and larger territories, it realized the benefits of allowing relief to reach both sides. As detailed below, however, the SPLA has not abandoned its famine-creating practices and has in some respects intensified them.

---

[22]Alex de Waal, "Starving Out the South, 1984-9," in *Civil War in the Sudan*, ed. M.W. Daly and Ahmad Alawad Sikainga (London: British Academic Press; 1993), pp. 165-72.

[23]Arab tribal militias called murahallin were formed by tribes in the Baggara federation of cattle-keeping nomad tribes in northern Sudan close to the border of south Sudan.

[24]De Waal, "Starving out the South," p. 171.

The manner in which the government waged war through its three groups was instrumental in creating famine out of the war. Their actions were made possible by a central government policy which openly or tacitly encouraged them,[25] and which, in turn, was made possible by the attitudes of the Sudan's donors and creditors, who were largely uninterested in the threat or reality of famine in the south. The attitude of the donors, however, began to change since 1988, with the creation of the OLS, with more attention paid to the desperate plight of southerners.

The raiding, displacement, and asset destruction did not affect all parts of southern Sudan simultaneously but created a situation of extreme instability at times in which ordinary economic activities and survival strategies became impossible. Even peaceful areas had their fragile economic and environmental balance destroyed after experiencing deluges of displaced relatives and others looking for food.

Although raiding occurred long before the civil wars, and often was settled by negotiations between tribal leaders and payment of compensation where agreed, the practice changed in the second civil war when the raids became part of a larger political game in which negotiations for local compensation were not relevant. The objective became to take without compensating, to win war booty, and to impoverish the other side. The result was extraordinary impoverishment of the civilian population, resulting in periodic famines and large numbers of civilian deaths.

In 1989, an agreement with the Misseriya Arab militia and the SPLA put a stop to most of the government-funded Misseriya raiding that had occurred from 1984-88 and caused the famine of 1987-88 and the large-scale migration from northern Bahr el Ghazal.[26] The negotiations were successful because in 1988, SPLA units established a *cordon sanitaire* along the Bahr el Arab (Kir River), the border between northern and

---

[25]At the same time as famine occurred, the Sudan government did its best to invoke sovereignty and use bureaucratic obstructions to keep relief food from starving southerners. The government, although heavily indebted and internationally ostracized, nevertheless "skillfully maniputed donor countries to keep control over humanitarian programmes." Francois Jean, ed., *Life, Death and Aid, the Medecins Sans Frontiers Report on World Crisis Intervention* (New York: Routledge, 1994), 18.

[26]*Ibid.*

southern Sudan, ensuring that without negotiations the cattle-owning Baggara tribes (including the Misseriya) could not have access to dry lands for their cattle.[27] After this agreement, trade between the Dinka of Bahr El Ghazal and the Baggara was reestablished, with the Baggara having access to dry season pasture in the Dinka areas and the Dinka having relative freedom of movement in and out of southern Kordofan and southern Darfur.

HISTORICAL BACKGROUND OF THE HUNGER TRIANGLE

The outside world was given a closer look at the mechanics of famine creation in 1993 when the government finally allowed relief agencies access to areas of the Upper Nile where the faction fighting had been fiercest. The fighting continued even as the relief agencies were attempting to bring assistance to the remaining civilians, whose resources were severely depleted.

As many of the testimonies of abuses in this report come from survivors of fighting in the Hunger Triangle (Ayod-Kongor-Waat) in Upper Nile, a closer look at this particular area is merited.[28] The plight of civilians in the region shows just how destructive to civilian life violations of the rules of war can be, far beyond the killings, which were not inconsiderable.

For centuries, the harsh clay plains environment of the Upper Nile region in the Sudan has forced its Dinka and Nuer inhabitants to survive through mixed cultivation and herding. Agriculture alone was unreliable, due to the combination of erratic flooding, unreliable rainfall and clay soil. A millennium ago this led to the development of a mainly pastoral economy, in which the pastoralists move their cattle following the water as it dries up, until they come to rest on the *toic*.[29]

---

[27]Johnson and Prunier, "Foundation and Expansion," p. 132.

[28]*See* Upper Nile map, facing Chapter IV.

[29]Toic is the river-flooded grassland along the rivers, which in the dry season becomes pasture. In Upper Nile there are four main vegetation areas: permanent swamp, river-flooded grasslands or toic, rain-flooded grasslands, and relatively flood-free land where the villages are built and cultivation undertaken. In the wet

The economies of the various ethnic and political Upper Nile groups are linked together and form a wider regional system that enables each group to survive the limitations of its specific geographical area. The groups use a variety of networks of exchange, some based on kinship obligations, some on direct trade. Through these networks, the peoples of the region have enjoyed regular access to distant resources, crossing political and ethnic boundaries.[30] As the historian Douglas H. Johnson has written:

> We should recognize that people go where the food is, that in this region lines of kinship frequently follow and strengthen lines of feeding. Social ties . . . were, and still are, the main way in which the Nilotic people survive and recover from the natural catastrophes which are endemic to their region.[31]

In times of shortage, they drew on each other's reserves, even if there was only a surplus in relative terms.[32] One tactic they employed was to raid both cattle and grain, especially during the nineteenth century, when raiding was more common than in the current century. Trade in cattle and ivory was yet another link between the Dinka and Nuer. Intermarriage was another: by the time of the great floods of 1916, the southern Dinka were used to marrying their daughters to the Nuer in times of need, in spite of intermittent periods of conflict, and there were

---

season, or during a flood, the rivers rise, the rains fall, and the toic is flooded. The months of April-November are the wet season in Upper Nile. Two or three crops of sorghum are sown during the rains. During the dry season cattle are moved away from the villages in stages, following the water as it dries up and exposes new pastures, until they come to rest on the toic. Douglas H. Johnson, "Political Ecology in the Upper Nile: The Twentieth Century Expansion of the Pastoral 'Common Economy,'" *Journal of African History* 30 (1989): p. 465.

[30]*Ibid.*, p. 463.

[31]*Ibid.*, p. 484.

[32]*Ibid.*

already a number of Dinka women living among the Nuer in marriages mutually recognized by both peoples.[33]

The SPLA split of 1991, while not tribally motivated, drove a military and political divide between these groups in Upper Nile. In addition, the places of greatest SPLA factional fighting of 1991-93 were in the Duk Ridge and Kongor,[34] which in the past produced food surpluses but because of the fighting could no longer be a bridge in the hunger gap.

One of the main problems coinciding with the war in the 1980s was environmental: rainfall declined, followed by floods in 1988 and later in Upper Nile. For instance, the area of Waat (Lou Nuer) suffered particularly from drought during the planting seasons of the late 1980s. The area around Duk Faiwil and Pok Tap (Nyareweng Dinka) was relatively flood- and drought-free. The Lou Nuer therefore came in large numbers of family groups in 1988-90 to the Nyareweng Dinka, many of them seeking out the same Dinka individuals to whom the Lou Nuer had provided shelter during the floods of the 1960s.

In 1991, when Lou crops were destroyed by floods and Lou herds devastated by disease, they would have again turned to the Nyareweng for assistance, but for the SPLA faction fighting. By then the SPLA-Nasir and Anya-Nya II of Ayod had attacked the Duks and Kongor and wrecked the area, forcing many Nyareweng Dinka to flee with nothing. The Lou Nuer therefore were not able to seek refuge with their Nyareweng Dinka

---

[33]*Ibid.*, p. 480. The Gaawar Nuer were approached by southern Dinka in times of need by the end of the first decade of the twentieth century. For a time they refused grain and insisted that the Dinka bring girls for marriage if they wanted cattle. The Gaawar Nuer paid a lower rate to the Dinka than was customary among the Nuer but higher than most Dinka could afford among themselves, so there was an economic incentive for intermarriage on both sides. *Ibid.*

[34]The Duk Ridge -- a series of sandy knolls now occupied by the Gaawar Nuer from Mogogh to south of Ayod, the Ghol Dinka at Duk Fadiat, and the Nyareweng Dinka at Duk Faiwil -- was frequently productive throughout the first half of the century. By far the most productive land south of the Duk Ridge was in the area of Kongor, which has dark soil, but lies in a depression, subject to much flooding. The area of permanent habitations and cultivation is protected by banks round all the villages, offering some security from the seasonal floods. Johnson, "Political Ecology in the Upper Nile," pp. 469-70.

contacts because Nyareweng Dinka were destitute and simultaneously seeking assistance for themselves.

Thus the brutal conflict in the Hunger Triangle tore open the customary safety nets and exposed hundreds of thousands to hunger, disease and death.

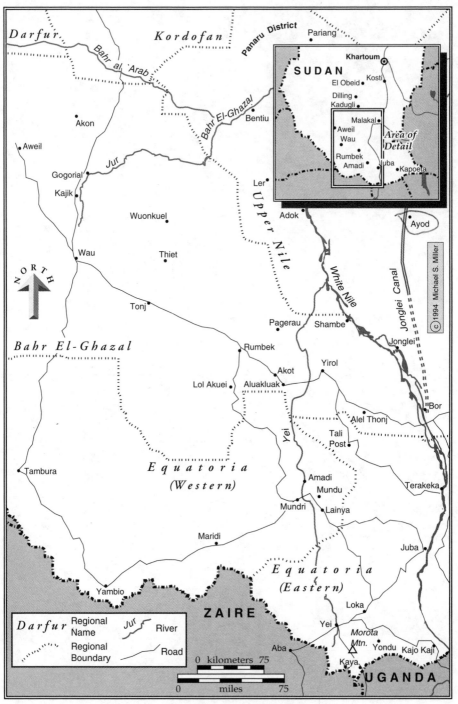

Darfur

Kordofan

Panaru District

Pariang

Bahr al 'Arab

Bahr El-Ghazal

Akon

Bentiu

Aweil

Jur

Gogorial

Kajik

Wuonkuel

Ler

Adok

Wau

Thiet

Upper Nile

Tonj

White Nile

Pagerau

Shambe

Bahr El-Ghazal

Rumbek

Jonglei

Akot

Yirol

Lol Akuei

Aluakluak

Alel Thonj

Bor

Tali
Post

*Equatoria
(Western)*

Yei

Amadi

Tambura

Mundu

Terakeka

Mundri

Lainya

Maridi

Juba

*Equatoria
(Eastern)*

Yambio

Loka

ZAIRE

Yei

*Morota
Mtn.*

Yondu

Kajo Kaji

Aba

Kaya

UGANDA

Darfur Regional
Name   *Jur* River

Regional
Boundary   Road

0 kilometers 75

0   miles   75

Jonglei Canal

©1994 Michael S. Miller

Ayod

Area of Detail:

Khartoum

SUDAN

El Obeid   Kosti

Dilling

Kadugli

Malakal

Aweil

Wau

*Area of
Detail*

Rumbek

Amadi   Juba   Kapoeta

NORTH

Western Equatoria & Bahr El-Ghazal

III. VIOLATIONS OF THE RULES OF WAR BY GOVERNMENT FORCES

The Sudan government has engaged in widespread violations of the rules of war during the period of 1992 to early 1994, indiscriminately killing southern civilians, burning their villages, and indiscriminately bombing and shelling their population centers. Its forces also tortured and killed detainees in southern garrison towns. In Juba alone those disappeared after government arrest in 1992 number over 100; they are all presumed dead.

GOVERNMENT ABUSES DURING THE 1992 DRY SEASON OFFENSIVE

The 1992 government dry season offensive was characterized by serious violations of the rules of war that usually accompanied government military campaigns: killing civilians, burning villages, and indiscriminate aerial bombardments and shelling.

The Khartoum regime's offensives on several fronts in 1992 dealt the SPLA its heaviest military losses in years. The SPLA-Torit lost many population centers it had controlled in Equatoria and Upper Nile provinces, including Torit, Kapoeta, Pochalla, Pibor Post, Yirol, and Bor. The government's gains were made possible because in August 1991 the SPLA had split into two factions--known as SPLA-Torit and SPLA-Nasir-- and engaged in faction fighting (*see* Chapter IV).

Following the split, the government did not attack areas controlled by the SPLA-Nasir faction, nor did the SPLA-Nasir faction undertake any offensives against the government, with the possible exception of the attack on Malakal in October 1992.[1]

---

[1]The SPLA-Nasir took credit for this attack, which appeared later to have been largely the initiative of a Nuer prophet.

In summary, there were four prongs to the 1992 government offensive.[2] The first crossed from Ethiopia to the Sudanese border town of Pochalla, captured it on March 9, 1992, and went on to take Pibor Post on April 23. The second was an advance south from Malakal to capture Bor on the White Nile on April 4. The third prong started in Wau, Bahr El Ghazal, in the direction of Tonj, and captured Yirol on April 11 and Shambe on April 14;[3] Tali Post was captured by the government-supported Mandari militia in May. Another column from Wau proceeded north to open the rail routes closed between Wau and Aweil since 1986. A fourth government contingent came out of Juba, the regional capital of several hundred thousand people, heading south to relieve the besieged garrison of Yei, one of the only garrison towns in Equatoria in government hands.[4] These troops, instead of going to Yei, crossed the Nile in an effort to take Torit, and were bogged down in fighting at Ngangala. They took that outpost in mid-April and Lirya in mid-May, Kapoeta on May 28 and Torit, until then the headquarters of the SPLA-Torit, on July 13.[5]

The SPLA-Torit kept Juba under heavy siege and made two serious incursions into Juba proper in June and July 1992, although it did not succeed in taking Juba. In the course of defending against the SPLA-Torit, the government forces committed many abuses, including torture, summary executions, and forced displacement of the civilian population of Juba.

As part of its strategy, the government frequently denied access to U.N. and international relief agencies seeking to alleviate the hardship caused by the conflict. Starting in March 1992, the government ordered

---

[2]*See* Sudan map, inside front cover; Upper Nile map, facing Chapter II; Western Equatoria and Bahr El Ghazal map, facing Chapter III; and Eastern Equatoria map, facing Chapter IV.

[3]Millard Burr, *Sudan 1990-1992: Food Aid, Famine, and Failure* (Washington, D.C.: U.S. Committee for Refugees, May 1993), p. 26.

[4]*Ibid.*

[5]*Ibid.*, p. 26-27. Torit had been heavily defended for months but the SPLA-Torit evacuated the town in June 1992 before it fell to the government in order to concentrate SPLA forces on capturing the larger town of Juba.

relief personnel to leave many southern locations, refused permission to airlift supplies to starving civilians, staged attacks by Toposa militia on relief convoys around Kapoeta, and for months denied permission to truck food and non-food items into most of the south.

In March 1992, the government expelled the International Committee of the Red Cross (ICRC), which had sustained about 100,000 recent repatriatees[6] in Pochalla. Beginning in April 1992, coinciding with its dry season offensive, the government also revoked permission for OLS relief flights to areas under SPLA-Torit control. After a delay, permission was given on April 21, 1992, to the OLS to deliver food to Akobo, Waat, and Nasir, all towns under SPLA-Nasir's control.[7] On May 19, 1992, the government announced that all relief flights to all destinations in the south could be resumed, ending a six-week ban on flights to the war zone.

Despite what the government said about resumption of relief flights, however, the OLS remained frustrated in its attempts to deliver food to all the needy populations. The OLS was cut off again, then permitted to resume flights to Nasir and Waat in August 1992, but not to any other locations because either the SPLA or the government of Sudan did not approve these other locations as flight destinations.

Government Offensive from Ethiopia into Eastern Upper Nile in 1992
The Sudan government took Pochalla on March 9, 1992, after several unsuccessful attempts which included indiscriminately bombing a camp for repatriatees. After moving from Pochalla to Pibor Post, the government troops killed civilians, burned huts, and looted cattle in outlying villages.

---

[6]Repatriatees are refugees who have returned or repatriated to their country of origin.

[7]United Nations, OLS, SEPHA Bi-Monthly Report no. 16 on OLS Emergency Operations in Southern Sector for the Period 19 April to 5 May 1992, Nairobi, Kenya, p. 1. These areas had not been attacked by the government, but those displaced from the government attack on Pochalla were flooding into Akobo, and tens of thousands of repatriated refugees in Nasir continued to remain in precarious condition.

The SPLA had held Pochalla, in Anuak territory, since 1986.[8] Within a few weeks after the fall of Mengistu, Pochalla had grown from a small border town to the overnight home of about 100,000 Sudanese who fled their Ethiopian refugee camps. Most of this population fled from Fugnido. The SPLA moved its military base from Ethiopia to Pochalla, locating it one and a half hours east of the repatriatees' camp, on the road that led from the border. The repatriatees were assisted by the ICRC.[9] When they had been there several months, early one morning the Sudan government and Ethiopian forces started shelling from the direction of Ethiopia. A woman repatriatee told HRW/Africa she believed that the shells were aimed at the repatriatees' camp, over the heads of the SPLA. The SPLA shelled back. At the first shelling, the civilians scattered to the bush. The shelling lasted until noon, and then the Sudan government and Ethiopian forces pulled back.

The second attack, which occurred about a month later, started with an artillery barrage, with shells landing in the center of the repatriatees' camp. At 10 A.M., a plane dropped bombs, appearing to be targeting the smoke from burning cattle dung near the camp. Six bombs killed people and cattle. Others were wounded. The civilians stayed outside Pochalla until midnight. After a week, a plane returned to bomb again, prompting the civilians to begin to leave the area entirely.

Many repatriatees walked to Kapoeta with an SPLA escort. They stayed together in large groups, afraid of being killed if they traveled alone. The journey was terribly long and difficult; the road was flooded and there were attacks by Toposa militia. Many repatriatees went hungry and others drowned or were killed by animals. A woman repatriatee told HRW/Africa that it took months for her group of about 12,000 former refugees to reach Kapoeta, which they accomplished in about January 1992.

By the time of the successful government attack on Pochalla in March 1992, the 100,000 repatriatees from 1991 had been reduced in number by several such evacuations, some well publicized. When it expelled the ICRC in March 1992, the government accused it of helping to recruit children into the SPLA and of giving logistical support to the rebels. The accusation, which was not true, arose from the humanitarian

---

[8]Johnson and Prunier, "Foundation and Expansion," p. 130.

[9]*ICRC Annual Report 1992* (Geneva: ICRC), p. 50.

assistance given by the ICRC to repatriatees fleeing Pochalla. Among them were several thousand unaccompanied minors, at whom, some believed, the government attacks were especially aimed. (*See* Chapter IV.)

Advancing from Pochalla, government forces on April 23, 1992 captured Pibor Post, held by the SPLA since March 1987. A Murle man in his early twenties was in his home village of Kondago outside of Pibor Post when government forces entered the village after the capture of Pibor Post.[10] He was planting in his garden, away from the house, when the army entered at 4 P.M., shooting "indiscriminately." He and others fled two hours into the forest as soon as they heard the shooting. The next day, they sneaked back, but returned to the forest when they saw the army was still there. They returned the next day to find that the army had left, after burning down the huts and killing many villagers. Among the dead were thirty-two children who were burned inside a hut, apparently gathered there by the army in order to burn them along with the hut. Four of this man's children, ages five, six, seven, and eight, and his brother's children were killed.[11] Other villagers were shot.

The army looted most of the cattle, either looting or shooting one hundred of the witness's 113 cows. "Everything but the trees was burned," he said, including a large African Inland church, also used as the school, and a Catholic church. Because the army burned and looted all their food, this man and others left the village that same day and walked west into SPLA-controlled territory.

---

[10]This man said that earlier some Murle residents in Pibor Post were sent by the government to the village to meet with the chief (sultan). The Murle of Pibor Post, who allegedly were given money by the government representatives, came three times to meet with the chief and ask him to call a meeting of the people and tell them they had to "learn the Koran." The chief refused.

A month after this refusal, the chief, Nam Korok, and two helpers were taken away by the army to Pibor Post. One helper, who escaped and ran back to the village, told the people that they had been taken to the army compound where the other two were killed. After that everyone was afraid to go to town.

[11]He had three other children of whom one died en route to the displaced persons camp; of seven, only two survive.

Government Offensive from Malakal South in March/April 1992

In a separate prong of the government offensive on SPLA population centers, motorized army troops advanced south from Malakal and passed through Duk Fadiat in Upper Nile, wreaking havoc on Dinka (but not Nuer) villages as they proceeded.[12] Tens of thousands of southern civilians were displaced between March and May 1992 during this offensive.

A Dinka religious leader who lived in the Duk Fadiat area said that a government convoy passed through that outpost in March 1992. The army burned the houses on the road but did not sweep beyond the road. The civilians fled to the toic, the river-flooded grassland. The army did not search out cattle, but they took the cattle they found and kept advancing south. The witness went to the toic because there he could find food, fish and roots, to eat. "There was no food in Duk because of the fighting in 1991," he said. They all eventually went to Ayod.

By March 1992, Kongor had been nearly deserted for several months, but the government in March 1992 nevertheless destroyed the few civilian structures left standing after the devastating SPLA-Nasir raids of a few months earlier. According to a Dinka chief from Kongor, a government army truck convoy from Malakal to Bor passed alongside the Jonglei canal, made a short detour through Kongor, stayed in Kongor only a few hours, then returned back to the canal. During that time the government troops destroyed the cement buildings, including a dispensary, schools, the rural council office, and others. There were only a few people living in Kongor at the time. "Here was a no-man's land, only hunger," the chief said. A married couple, Dau Deng and his second wife, Achol Ajak, were killed by an army tank during this incursion into Kongor: the tank pursued them between Kongor and Panyakur.

Bor, which is strategically located on the White Nile, frequently was subjected to government aerial bombardment. It was captured by the government on April 4, 1992. A twenty-eight-year-old Bor civilian man who was wounded in the attack on Bor said that the day before Bor fell, at about noon, a government Antonov plane circled and bombed.[13] He

---

[12]*See* Upper Nile map, facing Chapter II.

[13]An Antonov is a Soviet-made plane. After an attempted coup by the Sudan Communist Party in 1971, the Sudan government switched its allegiance to the West and received no further from The U.S.S.R. military supplies.

and many others ran to the bank of the White Nile for shelter. Some people were bleeding, he said.

The next morning, at about 11 A.M., an artillery attack on Bor commenced from the Malakal road. The residents of Bor "were surprised the enemy was so close," he said. As he was running away from the artillery, out of Bor to the south, he heard the sounds of fighting between the SPLA and the government. The SPLA had apparently advanced into Bor from its base outside Bor to engage the government troops.

On his way out of Bor, the witness was hit by government artillery fire. There were no SPLA troops in the vicinity. The shell that wounded him killed his older sister, his six-year-old brother, and another man. Three other women were wounded as well by the same shell. The fifty cows he had managed to save from the 1991 SPLA-Nasir attack were looted by the army.

A combined relief operation directed by the U.N. delivered substantial food relief within the first six weeks following the SPLA-Nasir 1991 raids on Bor and Kongor, but the situation degenerated quickly, with feeding centers reported to be "not coping at all" with the 58 percent of children said to be severely malnourished. International relief staff left Bor on March 18, 1992, following the advice of the Sudan Relief and Rehabilitation Association (SRRA)[14] in view of the impending government attack; the feeding program for 6,000 children was abandoned. Other international staffers similarly left Malek on March 31 and arrived in Jemeiza, seventy-five kilometers south of Bor, where they reestablished a supplementary feeding program for 5,000 malnourished children in three centers and 7,000 others in villages in the area and started distributing dry rations to the displaced.[15]

After the government occupied Bor, it burned the villages of Baidit, Mathiang, Moreng, Molek, and Anyidi in April and May 1992; the villagers fled the government.

The further battering of Dinka civilians pushed tens of thousands of them west to neighboring Dinka tribes in Bahr El Ghazal. In July 1992 groups of Bor and Twic (Kongor) Dinka were arriving daily in Aguran,

---

[14]The SRRA is the SPLA-Torit relief wing.

[15]SEPHA Bi-Monthly Report No. 14 on OLS Emergency and Relief Operations in the Southern Sector for the Period 21 March to 5 April 1992, p. 1.

after a 150-kilometer journey of ten to twenty days; many reported the death of infants en route.[16]

An assessment of the Bor area in late 1992 revealed that it was almost deserted although it had once been heavily populated. Many civilians from surrounding areas arrived daily in Bor in late 1992 seeking food and other assistance. The Sudan government, in control of the town, permitted their free movement. However, no agreement could be reached between the government and rebels to permit relief agencies to cross the lines around Bor to deliver food to the needy where they lived.[17]

---

[16]Fighting subjected the civilians to continual displacement. Two Dinka chiefs from Wernyol north of Kongor in Dinka territory first fled the SPLA-Nasir raids in September 1991, wandering twenty days with their followers south to Jemeiza, bypassing Bor. They ate wild leaves and fruits until, fifteen days later, the U.N. arrived with relief food.

"The U.N. then was not like now. It was very good, they brought food without stopping, in good quantities and useful items. This U.N. now [July 1993] is very irregular here," a chief told HRW/Africa.

The two chiefs did not plant in Jemeiza because it was still the dry season. "When the rains were near," or in April 1992, the government took Bor. This group of displaced left Jemeiza, because 1)it was on the main road and could be reached easily by the government from Bor, and 2) when the rains started, the road to Jemeiza and Bor would become impassable for U.N. vehicles. They waited fifteen days and no U.N. trucks came. They ate wild fruits and leaves. It started to rain. These displaced took the seeds the U.N. gave them and began to walk back home.

They were right to fend for themselves by moving; they did not know it but the international staff who had set up a feeding camp in Jemeiza were evacuated on April 8, 1992, and after that the U.N. could not reach the displaced anywhere in this area. SEPHA Bi-Monthly Report No. 15 on OLS Emergency and Relief Operations in the Southern Sector for the period 3 April to 21 April 1992, p. 1.

This group walked for twenty days to reach the area of Panyakur near Kongor, then went back north to Wernyol during the wet season of 1992, and planted the U.N. seeds. They were in Wernyol during the second SPLA-Nasir attack in July 1992.

[17]OLS (Southern Sector), "1992/93 Situation Assessment," February 1993, Nairobi, Kenya, p. 13-14.

Government and SPLA-Nasir Attacks in Bahr El Ghazal in 1992

Bahr El Ghazal was formerly the most densely populated area of all southern Sudan, with the population of the floodplain area of Aweil and Gogrial in 1976 estimated at 1.5 million.[18] The area was, however, suffering from widespread destruction of crops by flooding in 1992 and a poor harvest in 1991, also due to flooding. Flight permission to the area was suspended by the government of Sudan in early 1990 and was only reinstated in December 1992, leaving the area, far from international borders, also far from international purview.

Government abuses during an offensive in Bahr El Ghazal in 1992 included burning villages, looting, and killing civilians. During the campaign, the government won back control of several strategic towns from the SPLA-Torit and disrupted the relative calm that had prevailed in Bahr El Ghazal for a few years.

Government troops and Popular Defence Force (PDF) militia proceeded from the government garrison town of Wau in March 1992, and destroyed a string of villages across Bahr El Ghazal province, reaching Rumbek garrison in early April.[19] The SPLA-Torit engaged government troops at the Na'am River Bridge on the Rumbek-Yirol road and at Allau cattle camp. The government forces withdrew to the north, burning many more Dinka villages, including Luel, Paloc, Pandit, Kap, Mageir, Markur, Yali, Mangar and Aromniel. The government finally captured Yirol on April 11 after bombing it. Shambe, a Nile port for southern Bahr El Ghazal and an important crossroads for the SPLA's supply system, fell on April 14, also after bombing.[20]

A thirty-year-old Dinka woman then living in Yirol town said that government forces bombed Yirol one week before they attacked. When they entered the town in the early hours of the morning, she was in her hut, or tukl. She heard firing and ran outside, where she saw random

---

[18]*Ibid*, p. 20. Others note that the 1983 census for Aweil area council was 691,309 and for Gogrial area council 322,734, totalling 1,214,043. This census was disrupted, however, and its figures are often rejected by southerners.

[19]*See* Western Equatoria and Bahr El Ghazal map, facing Chapter III. The attacked villages included Abiem Nayar, Nyangakoc, Manyiel, Citgok, Makuac, and Pagor.

[20]Burr, *Food Aid*, p. 26.

shooting. "Anyone was shot--men, women, children," she said. "Some of the soldiers burned houses with people in them." The soldiers captured many people; some were taken away, others were executed.

Three of this witness's daughters and two sons were killed in the attack. Two of her children survived, but a young daughter later died when running from another attack near Mundri in Western Equatoria. Her family's cattle were all raided from a nearby cattle camp.

From Yirol, the Sudan Army set out, with tanks and troop carriers, to round up cattle and set fire to villages in a radius of twenty kilometers from Yirol. A relief worker noted that previously government troops had not systematically set fire to villages in this area. This time, however, the destruction was systematic. At least fifteen villages were affected.[21]

The Dinka woman and her relatives escaped Yirol to hide in the forest around Aguran. They saw smoke from the burning villages, from which people escaped and joined her group in the forest.

U.N. and NGO presence in Bahr El Ghazal and thus information on these attacks was quite limited because of the flight ban on destinations in that region and its inaccessibility by road during the rainy season. What began to emerge, however, was that the government's scorched earth campaign was again producing vast numbers of displaced.

The 1992 dry season campaign occurred at a time when many civilians had returned to the villages from the grazing grounds to prepare the land for cultivation. Although part of the motivation for the scorched earth campaign may have been to prevent the SPLA-Torit from having any cover under which to sneak up on Yirol, the extent of the burning greatly exceeded that need. It also drastically weakened the capacity of the civilian population to survive, forcing many of them to move south.

About 90,000 Dinka who lived north and northeast of Rumbek were displaced by tribal clashes, and about 50,000 living in Yirol were displaced by the intensive fighting preceding the government's recapture of the town on April 12. Many were gathering around Aluakluak between Rumbek and Yirol, as were others displaced from the Bor/Kongor area.

---

[21]These villages included Abiem, Panabier, Lualthiep, Alakec, Banylom, Nyang, Manyang, Tit Agau, Nyatiba, Goltoin, Geng Geng, Wunapoth, Arwau, and Pakeu.

At that time, relief agencies estimated that Aluakluak had a population of 150,000.[22]

Indiscriminate Government Bombing and the Capture of Kapoeta and Torit in 1992

Prior to the capture of Kapoeta and Torit in Eastern Equatoria, the government engaged in indiscriminate bombardment of the two towns. In the course of the government capture of Kapoeta and afterwards, the army and militia killed civilians; many were targeted deliberately because they were Dinka.

Kapoeta, captured by the SPLA on February 25, 1988, was retaken by the government on May 28, 1992, in a surprise attack in which the Toposa militia played a key role because of their knowledge of the terrain. The government had provided guns and ammunition to the Toposa so they could fight the SPLA and the Lotuko tribe, a longstanding Toposa rival. The SPLA then armed the Boya against the Toposa.[23] In early 1991, the SPLA reached an agreement with local Toposa, but the move was not entirely successful.[24] A witness told HRW/Africa that the Toposa militia in 1992 "frequently raided the town, taking goats and cattle. They would kill to get livestock."

Indiscriminate Bombing of Kapoeta

The government indiscriminately bombed Kapoeta on March 13, 1992, killing several civilians. The fact that Kapoeta was a seat of local administration for the SPLA-Torit did not convert the entire town into a legitimate military target. Nor was the relief warehouse, described below, a legitimate military target.[25]

---

[22]OLS (Southern Sector) Bi-Monthly Situation Report no. 20, June 21-July 3, 1992, Nairobi, Kenya, p. 8.

[23]Johnson and Prunier, "Foundation and Expansion," p. 135.

[24]*Ibid.*, p. 140.

[25]To be a legitimate target, such a warehouse would have had to be dedicated to military use, and this warehouse held civilian relief supplies. *See* Appendix A.

A man who witnessed the bombing said the attackers used an Antonov plane. He was working in a hut next to a relief food warehouse by the river at 11:30 A.M. when he heard the plane approaching. People scattered, and several were killed. He saw the body of a thirty-year-old man and later attended his burial.

Twelve shells were dropped near the relief warehouse, which he thinks was deliberately targeted. The twelve craters left by the bombs were deep enough for him, a Dinka man about six feet six inches tall, to stand in; the craters were "in a line" outside the warehouse, a large brick building with a zinc roof, which was damaged. Also damaged was a nearby one-story hotel.

The same plane circled around and made a second run on Kapoeta. It dropped bombs on the airstrip and wounded three people, one a driver whom he knew personally.[26]

An elderly woman in Kapoeta also saw two bombing runs that day; in one, three bombs fell in one place killing five women, and in the other, three men, forty cows, and twenty goats were killed. The dead were Toposa civilians. She saw the bodies--one of the women had her head blown off, and one of the men was cut almost in two at the waist.

The government bombed irregularly. There would be two or three months or one week off, then it would start again. There was no pattern. "They would let people forget then bomb randomly," she said.

Targeted Killings of Dinkas

Because the May 28 attack on Kapoeta surprised the SPLA-Torit, it could not properly organize an evacuation. In the hasty flight, some of those left behind when the government and militia entered were tortured and killed.

Government soldiers differentiated in their treatment of various tribes: the Toposa-speaking civilians were kept alive, as were the Nuer and those from Equatorian tribes, such as the Boya, Lotuko, and Acholi.

---

[26]The airstrip would be a legitimate military target if it were used for military purposes by the SPLA-Torit. This airstrip was used predominantly if not entirely for the civilian relief effort.

The Dinka were singled out for punishment.[27] Many were captured, tied, shot, and thrown inside houses which were set on fire. The aunt and uncle of a nineteen-year-old Dinka boy were killed this way, as well as their four children.

Elijah Dau, a Dinka and financial comptroller of Kapoeta for the SPLA, had remained behind with two of his four wives. He was killed, allegedly shot by the Toposa militia at about 4 or 5 P.M. on May 28 while trying to surrender. Kir Monychol, a graduate of the University of Cairo, was killed with his wife Chuti Deng, chair of the Kapoeta Women's Affairs Committee, and three others who were intercepted by the Toposa militia outside of Kapoeta, according to one who survived this attack.

The nineteen-year-old Dinka above, who did not flee fast enough, was hidden by his Toposa schoolmate friends. The attack on Kapoeta seemed to him to last about five hours. After the government shelling stopped, from hiding he saw the Toposa militia entering, followed by the army in military vehicles and tanks. The Toposa shot people "indiscriminately," he said, and the army shot mainly at men. Both government troops and militia looted. Only the houses at the outskirts of town were burned, leaving the houses in town standing for Toposa militia use. This boy remained in hiding ten days, then escaped.

The government raided villages around Kapoeta after seizing the town, including Bunao village, the Norwegian Church Aid (NCA) mission, two hours from Kapoeta, and Khor Mashi village, a displaced center one and a half hours from Kapoeta where many took refuge after Kapoeta fell. Inhabitants of both villages were accused of harboring the SPLA, and government soldiers reportedly killed civilians in both places, and burned all the houses in Khor Mashi and Bunao.

People fled Kapoeta in two directions: on the road south to Kenya, or west to Torit. A woman witness told HRW/Africa that she and her children fled at 4 A.M. and arrived three hours later in Khor Mashi, then traveled farther. Her strength began to give out, however; her feet were badly blistered and she fell down as she escaped, wounding her left upper arm, where she bears an ugly scar. She was hot and exhausted. She said that her skin peeled off, "on my arms, buttocks; my tongue split, too."

---

[27]Many Dinka came to Kapoeta after it was taken by the SPLA in 1988; some participated in the administration and were among the top military officers, which caused resentment among the locals. The Dinka were not native to this area.

She saw many lying on the ground, dead, because they had no water and they had to pass through a desert area outside Kapoeta, where there was "no river and no water, just small trees without leaves." A car picked her up and took her and her children to Torit Hospital. She was there for two days and then was evacuated to Aswa Hospital, where her recuperation took two and a half months.

Indiscriminate Bombing of Fleeing Civilians
Even after Kapoeta was retaken, the government air force chased the fleeing civilians, bombing them on the road south to Kenya. Although most of the Kapoeta evacuees reached Narus to the south on May 28, the SPLA advised them not to stay because they feared the government troops would reach Narus. The civilians and SPLA evacuated Narus about 7 P.M. The next day, May 29, the column of refugees started reaching Lokichokio, Kenya at 9 A.M. It was so long that its end was not visible from Lokichokio. The end of the column was bombed that day at a Toposa village where some of the slower people were resting; reportedly one was killed and three injured. Between 20,000 and 22,000 Sudanese left Narus to seek refuge in Kenya, including 12,500 unaccompanied minors.

To the west of Kapoeta, Torit, which was captured by the SPLA on February 27, 1989[28] and became its capital thereafter, was recaptured by the government on July 13, 1992. The SPLA did not put up any resistance to the recapture because at the time the SPLA-Torit was concentrating all its military efforts on the larger city of Juba, which it entered on June 7 and July 6, 1992.

En route to Torit, the government first recaptured the town of Lirya on the road from Juba to Torit on May 12; by that date, the SPLA had begun the evacuation of Torit.[29]

---

[28]Johnson and Prunier, "Foundation and Expansion," p. 137.

[29]SEPHA Bi-Monthly Report no. 17 on OLS Emergency Operations in Southern Sector for the period May 5-20, 1992, Nairobi, Kenya, p. 1. The last three nongovernmental organizations, Health Unlimited, New Sudan Council of Churches, and Norwegian Church Aid, evacuated their staffs on May 15. By that time, the general population largely had evacuated the town and so had SPLA/SRRA non-essential personnel. *Ibid.* All U.N./NGO buildings appeared to have been looted by departing civilians and SPLA military personnel before the

Not all the civilians left that month. According to a Pari civilian still there at the time, a week or more before they took Torit government troops shelled the town from a distance of several miles while repairing a bridge. The shelling went on every day that week, usually for two hours at a time, he said. When those left in Torit heard the shelling begin, everyone "hit the ground" to avoid shrapnel.

During one incident, three boys and their two fathers, relatives of this Pari man, died when they were hit by a shell that landed five meters away from him.

GOVERNMENT ABUSES
BEFORE AND DURING THE BATTLE FOR JUBA, 1992

Juba, the former capital of and largest city (estimated population 287,000)[30] in the southern region, has been under siege by the SPLA-Torit since 1986.[31] Located in Eastern Equatoria on the West Bank of the White Nile, its population, which before the second civil war in 1983 was about 150,000, has since been augmented mostly by displaced Equatorians from outside Juba who fled to Juba when their resistance to the SPLA-Torit failed.[32]

This section focuses on abuses committed by the government in Juba in 1991-92. The information is supplemental to the considerably detailed work already done by Amnesty International on the government's repression of the population of Juba and on the population's civic resistance.[33] Abuses committed by the SPLA-Torit

---

government forces entered Torit.

[30]Census, 1991, cited in internal report of a relief agency working in Juba, dated August 25, 1992.

[31]Africa Watch, *Denying The Honor of Living*, p. 70.

[32]*Ibid.*

[33]Amnesty International, "Sudan: Deaths and detentions: the destruction of Juba," AI Index: AFR 54/26/92 (London: Amnesty International, September 23, 1992); Amnesty International, "Ravages of war."

before, during, and after the battle for Juba are included in Chapter IV, below.

Abuses During the 1991-92 School Strike and Civic Struggle

In the course of suppressing civic resistance to its policies of forced Arabization and Islamization, the government arrested and brutally treated student demonstrators and leaders.

The struggle began in May 1991, when the government announced proposed new laws to change the language of instruction in the south from English to Arabic and to make compulsory the study of Islam.[34] The students in Juba organized themselves and held workshops and seminars in protest. The Young Christian Student Movement passed resolutions against the change in language of instruction, which, they protested, would have an adverse effect on their academic careers.

In August 1991, the laws were passed, and on September 9, 1991, a school boycott of primary, intermediate, and secondary schools took effect in Juba. A peaceful student march to the office of the minister of education in Juba was stopped by the police, who ordered the students to disperse. The students tried to negotiate with the police, who after an hour started to use tear gas and electric prods to disperse the crowd. Some students were arrested. The next day the students attacked the office of Dawa Islamia, the Islamic missionary organization supporting the curriculum changes. Arrests of students continued.

---

[34]According to Amnesty International,

> The issue of Arabic as the language for teaching in secondary and higher education is politically sensitive in Sudan. Historically, English is the language of government in southern Sudan and is the medium of instruction in most southern educational institutions. Tuition in English is regarded by many southern Sudanese intellectuals as protecting their cultural identity in relation to Muslim northern Sudan. Steps to Arabicize the educational system started in 1991 when the government announced that all school-leavers seeking university places would be required to pass an examination in Arabic. Since 1972 southerners had been exempted from this requirement. Southerners argue that the requirement discriminates against southern students gaining university places.

Amnesty International, "Urgent Action, Sudan," AI Index: AFR 54/25/92, London, July 31, 1992.

Five days later, a new state governor was appointed who ordered the release of the students; they were videotaped before release. He issued an order establishing a governing student body as an alternative means of registering student complaints.

On September 22, 1992, while the school boycott continued, the secondary school students assembled at Juba Commercial Secondary School and elected representatives, who drew up a list of demands and made an appointment to meet the governor and the Council of Ministers the next morning. At the meeting, the students presented their demands and the governor responded that he would make the changes that fell within his jurisdiction but that other matters would have to be referred to the central government, including stationing armed Popular Defence Forces in schools[35] and on Juba university grounds.[36]

The main student demands related to a regional curriculum, the language of instruction, and the teaching of religion. The students objected that textbooks contained information about the north that was not "practical or useful to the south." They thought it highly unfair that mid-year exams would be held in Arabic, not in English as before.

The students called off the boycott, with the ultimatum that it would be resumed on October 10 if matters were not resolved.[37] On October 14, a committee of three persons appointed by the governor to resolve the crisis in Khartoum informed the student representatives that their complaints had been accepted and that there was no further need to boycott classes. The students asked for the commitments in writing. When they received nothing, the boycott resumed.

Students Arrested and Beaten

At the end of October 1991, as the boycott held fast, the minister of education announced the dissolution of the governing student body. At

---

[35]To the complaint about armed Pakistanis in the Popular Defence Force, the minister of education said that the Pakistanis were there on a religious mission. The students replied that in such a case uniforms and guns were not indicated.

[36]University classes had been transferred to Khartoum in 1990, but the majority of the student body did not make the transfer.

[37]The secondary school academic year is April to March.

midnight, three student leaders were arrested; they were interrogated by security authorities and released three days later. Other arrests followed.

At least one student was arrested at home during this period with an arrest warrant issued by the governor; his house was searched, although the authorities had no search warrant. They took him to state security headquarters, made him take off his shirt, and beat him on the back with a leather whip, to make him "give in." He was beaten during interrogation and also in his cell, where he was held in isolation. After two days of interrogation concerning church and political leaders allegedly behind the movement, he was released; he was kept under close surveillance.

From time to time during November 1991, security authorities would force some students to announce on the radio that they had dropped their complaints and were ordering the other students to go back to classes.

Escaping Students Tortured by Military Intelligence

In November 1991, the government announced that the schools in southern Sudan were to use Arabic rather than English as the language of instruction.[38] By the end of that month, seeing the intransigence of both sides, some students started to leave the country on foot. Those who were intercepted by the army were taken to military intelligence headquarters and tortured.

A BBC broadcast on December 25, 1991 of interviews with students who had fled Juba and reached Uganda on foot inspired more to try to escape, including a group of about twenty-eight students who left for Uganda on January 8, 1992. They found a guide to assist them in traveling through the military posts and the land mines outside Juba. He recommended that they break into two groups; one group, waiting in the bush eight kilometers south of Juba near an army headquarters, was left behind in the confusion.

Because some in the group had already attempted three or four unsuccessful escapes, they proceeded without a guide. After moving five more kilometers, they were surrounded by the army and ordered to stop. Although they were unarmed and complied with the order, the army shot at them, and they fell down, most escaping injuries. A boy and a girl in

---

[38]Amnesty International, "Urgent Action: Sudan," AI Index: AFR 54/14/92, London, April 6, 1992.

the group, however, disappeared at that point and have not been seen since. The other twelve were captured; three were young women. All were taken to the military intelligence headquarters in Juba. The nine boys were packed into one room with twenty-one male students arrested earlier, four of whom, unbeknownst to the others, were informers.

The next morning the male captives were ordered by the soldiers to get in the "Hindi" position, which involved putting one's head on the floor with straight legs and lifting the hands, arms locked, behind and over the back. From this position they were kicked in their hands and neck by the soldiers, who referred to this as their "breakfast."

Three boys were called to the office and told to bring their documents. All were beaten and had their documents taken. One was questioned about why he wanted to go to Uganda and why he did not use legal means. He explained that he had secured a visa but that transport from Juba was difficult.[39] He had applied to fly on a relief plane to Nairobi, but while waiting for that permission, his visa expired and the authorities would not renew it.

During questioning, an interrogator lashed this student and banged his head against the wall, asking him about the role of the U.N. in helping the students flee to Uganda. The interrogator claimed that the U.N. kept vehicles near Kajo Kaji to take the students to Roman Catholic Bishop Taban, who would take them to Uganda. The student detainee denied this. The interrogators made him lie on the floor on his back, already wounded from lashing, and lashed him several minutes more.

The next day, everyone in the cell received minor beatings from the various soldiers who passed by. The numbers of male detainees in the cell increased gradually to sixty-five. On the following day, Sunday, twenty students were removed from the overcrowded cell and put in a makeshift cell, a trench with logs covering the top. Since it was Sunday, the students asked for and received permission to pray. The guards gave them back one of the Bibles they had confiscated and allowed a Mexican nun to enter the army base to pray with them. Priests brought food for the students and the soldiers.

On Monday, a second lieutenant, Ibrahim Salam, became annoyed when he heard a student detainee singing a hymn. According to

---

[39]Visas or travel permits are required by the government to enter or leave the besieged city of Juba; they are hard to secure for those without government connections.

this twenty-three-year-old student, this lieutenant called him into an office, alone. The lieutenant took out a display of torture tools (pin, pliers, whip, cocked pistol, red peppers in a bag) and placed them on a table, and told the student to remove his jacket, saying, "We're in a state of emergency. If I kill you now like a dog, no one will question me. Which of all these things do you want me to use?" The student refused to select any torture instruments. The officer, in an effort to force the detainee to admit that he was a student leader and SPLA-Torit agent and that the U.N. was behind the student movement to Uganda, made the detainee lie on his face on the floor, and beat him. He also tightly tied each of the boy's fingers and punctured his fingertips with the needle, making blood spurt out. He also made him stand an arm's length from the wall, leaning against the wall; and he beat the detainee's outstretched arms and head.

The student passed out. When he opened his eyes he saw by a wall clock that he had been unconscious for three hours. He was ordered to leave the office but was unable to move. Then he was told to put on his jacket, but he could not. The officer nevertheless forced the jacket on him; it became bloody.

The student crawled to the veranda, sat down, and moved slowly down the steps to the trench. He lay face down without talking to the other prisoners. It was hard for him to eat and when the guards came to count the prisoners at 6 P.M. he could not stand up. He asked for permission to sleep outside the trench, and a soldier agreed and gave him two blankets and a pillow.

The next day, his jacket was stuck to his wounds. The same officer who had tortured him tore the jacket off his back, reopening the wounds. A nurse at the base took pity on the victim and surreptitiously gave him antibiotics. An informer saw him take a pill and informed that the prisoner intended to commit suicide. The wounded student was again interrogated, although he was in a weak state, and forced to turn over the medicine.

One night, he was taken in a car to the bank of the White Nile. His hands were tied behind him and he was ordered to get out of the car and kneel facing the river. The soldiers cocked a gun behind his ear and told him "This is the last moment you have. Do you want to change your statement?" He had already decided they were going to kill him so he did not change anything. They kicked and threatened him some more but did not shoot him.

On the night of January 19, 1992, the student was driven to the White House, a notorious torture center and death row. The captors showed him around the building with a flashlight. "Have you seen the fate of the others? You will face the same thing if you stick to your statement," they said. They tied his legs and arms behind him with a rope around his chest. They attached a metal hook to the rope in front of his body and pulled him up to hang from the ceiling. His head was thrown back. For two minutes, "things became very difficult," he said, then they lowered him down and finally took him back to the base.

The next day he was shown an "order of execution" for himself. He was taken to kneel on an outcropping of rock over a valley with a small stream. "Say your last prayers," the soldiers told him and hit him with a rifle butt. Three soldiers cocked their rifles. "All will open up with their rifles. That is how we kill people. Have you finished your prayers?" After a little more of this, they took him back to his cell.

The church put pressure on the army because of the reports of torture that were leaking out of the base. Military intelligence then ordered the beatings to stop, about fourteen days after the arrest of the student whose torture is described above. The student overheard a military intelligence officer tell the torturer, "The investigation is finished and I do not want to see any unnecessary beatings." The interrogation of all but a few had already been completed by then.

Thereafter, they were not beaten. The student group, by then six girls and fifty-nine boys, was transferred to police jurisdiction on January 22, 1992, where they had "fine treatment, no harassment." The boys were kept in two big dormitories and even given games to play. All the students were released on February 6, 1992, on condition that a relative be a guarantor. The relative was to be photographed, and if the student "went missing," the relative would be responsible. The student was told by security authorities upon his release that they could not allow him to leave Juba because he was "dangerous." The authorities also tried to recruit him after he returned home.

Arrest of Priests Followed by Police Shooting at Demonstrators, Killing One

Following these events, the government targeted for arrest Catholic clergy. When demonstrations were held to protest the arrests, the police used excessive force in countering the demonstration, shooting into the crowd and killing one student.

In March 1992, the head of the Catholic schools and another priest were summoned by the police to explain why the Catholic schools had not been reopened; the student school boycott of government schools was still in effect. Two priests, Father Constantino Pitia and Father Nicholas Abdallah, were arrested on March 10 and flown, without any notification to church authorities, to Khartoum on March 15.[40]

Juba civilians demonstrated on March 15, 16, and 17, to protest the arrests of the priests. On March 17, teargas was used to disperse the crowds. A fourteen-year-old boy, Francis, who was at the head of the crowd, died when the soldiers shot into the crowd. His body was carried to the church by the demonstrators. For his funeral the next day, the funeral route, seven kilometers from the church to the school, was lined with tanks and heavily armed soldiers. The government also deployed prison warders, wildlife police, intelligence agents, and police. Marchers were ordered to disperse in ones and twos; they were warned that larger groups would be shot at. The priests who were present agreed to obey the order, and the crowd dispersed.

The two detained priests were released in April 1992 after twenty-six days in custody. They returned from Khartoum to Juba in early May and were met by a large group of supporters at the Juba airport.[41]

GOVERNMENT ABUSES FOLLOWING JUNE-JULY 1992 SPLA-TORIT ATTACKS ON JUBA

During the summer of 1992, SPLA-Torit made two military incursions into Juba, on June 7 and then again on July 6, and nearly

---

[40]Amnesty International, "Urgent Action: Sudan," April 6, 1992.

[41]"Juba Welcomes Freed Priests," *Sudan Update*, vol. 3, no. 18 (London: May 20, 1992), p. 4.

captured the city. Each incursion was followed by a wave of retaliatory killings, disappearances, and arrests of civilians, soldiers, police, army, wildlife, and prison forces, according to a wildlife warden and others.

The SPLA-Torit, calling its incursion "Operation Jungle Storm," entered Juba from the south at 5 A.M. on June 7. It claimed to have occupied the headquarters of the Southern Military Command for three hours and captured the BN116 Artillery Unit before it withdrew the same day.[42]

There was heavy shelling by both sides and attacks on residential areas. The fighting produced at least 198 war wounded, who were taken over the border by land to the ICRC hospital in Lokichokio, Kenya. In Juba, local ICRC staff and the Sudanese Red Crescent assisted the victims and transported hundreds of wounded to hospital and distributed medical supplies sent in by the ICRC.[43]

During those days, the Juba government could not tightly control the movement of the civilian population, and it was estimated that some 50,000 people left Juba for the safety of Mundri, Kaya, Kajo Kaji, and Aluakluak.[44]

The SPLA-Torit launched a second surprise attack on July 6, 1992, re-entering Juba using the streams and inlets of the White Nile and remaining a few days, according to a wildlife warden who was there. The SPLA-Torit occupied key military areas and was forced to withdraw only after ten days of heavy fighting.

The government claimed that the attack followed an infiltration by SPLA-Torit elements in civilian clothes. A government source said the infiltrators killed a large number of government troops and innocent civilians, but that eventually the garrison regained the initiative and

---

[42]SPLM/A, *County* (Nairobi, Kenya), June 8-9, 1992 (publication of SPLA-Torit).

[43]*ICRC Annual Report 1992*, p. 51.

[44]SEPHA Bi-Monthly Report no. 19 on OLS Emergency Operations in Southern Sector for the period June 7-22, 1992, p. 2.

drove out the infiltrators.[45] Relief agencies received reports of about 500 civilian casualties from the July 1992 fighting, which were largely the result of shortages of food and medicine.[46]

Summary Executions, Disappearances, Arrests, and Mass Displacement

These two thwarted SPLA-Torit attacks were followed by crackdowns by Juba government forces, including killings, disappearances, and arrests.

According to Amnesty International, the day after the June SPLA-Torit assault, forty soldiers providing air defense at Juba Airport were extrajudicially executed by the government.[47] In the next days, security authorities reportedly arrested over eighty southern Sudanese soldiers, policemen, prison guards, and paramilitary guards in the Department of Wildlife, suspected of being SPLA-Torit collaborators or sympathizers.[48] It was reported that, following the attacks, security authorities also arrested people in responsible positions, such as customs officials, technicians, church workers, youth leaders--in short "anyone who may be suspected of being sympathetic to the SPLA-Torit or opposed to the Islamic government."[49]

The highest level arrest was that of Retired Maj. Gen. Peter Cirillo, former governor of Equatoria, taken from his house in Juba at gunpoint to Khartoum because his younger brother, Maj. Thomas Cirillo,

---

[45]Statement by H.E. Mr. Abdel Aziz Shido, Minister of Justice and Attorney General, Republic of the Sudan, on agenda item no. 114 (c) at the 48th Session of the General Assembly of the United States, New York, dated November 24, 1993, pp. 6-7.

[46]OLS (Southern Sector) Bi-Monthly Situation Report no. 21, June 21-July 3, 1992, p. 2.

[47]Amnesty International, "Ravages of war," p. 19.

[48]Amnesty International, "Destruction of Juba," p. 1. It appeared that some southern Sudanese members of the army, prison guard, police, and wildlife forces had helped the SPLA-Torit plan the raid from within Juba, and defected or fought alongside the SPLA-Torit.

[49]Africa Faith and Justice Network, "Maryknoll Sisters' Report on War-Torn Juba," Nairobi, Kenya, September 5, 1992.

defected to the SPLA-Torit during the attack with some of his troops.[50] Maj. Gen. Cirillo was released in Khartoum several months later, in February 1993.

On the night of June 23, 1992, seven southern Sudanese soldiers reportedly were extrajudicially executed.[51]

The SPLA-Torit entered Juba for a second attack on July 6, 1992, through the suburbs, including Lalogo. Over the next ten days, heavy fighting took place in and around the suburbs of Lalogo, Kator, and Rejaf West. The army regained control, although the SPLA-Torit continued to shell targets inside the city.[52] The army ordered the evacuation of Lalogo and Kator on July 11 and the next day burned down these and other areas, leaving 100,000 civilians squatting without shelter in the old center of Juba, at the height of the rainy season.

On July 16, a group of forty southern Sudanese soldiers serving in the government army reportedly were extrajudicially executed, accused of collaborating with the SPLA.[53]

In the course of regaining control, the army made a large sweep through the town. Soldiers forced their way into private homes, searching for SPLA-Torit combatants. During the searches, many civilians were beaten and many possessions looted. An unknown number were arrested, including some who were later released. Amnesty International was informed that at least 200 civilians were killing during these operations.[54] After the army sweep, relatives were too frightened to remove the bodies and "many were left unburied for several days."[55]

Amnesty International documented 230 men arrested by the government in Juba between June and August 1992 but never accounted

---

[50]Amnesty International, "Destruction of Juba," p. 1.

[51]*Ibid*, p. 2.

[52]*Ibid*.

[53]*Ibid*., p. 3.

[54]*Ibid*., p. 2.

[55]*Ibid*.

for; many of them were prominent Juba civilians.[56] In April, 1993, Amnesty International confirmed the death of Camillo Odongi Loyuk, a retired southern Sudanese army officer who was arrested in Khartoum in June in retaliation for the attack on Juba. He was tied spread-eagled to the window bars of a room, where a rope with a sliding noose was tied around his testicles and tightened if he moved. He was beaten to death. The government denied responsibility and maintained that Loyuk was free.[57]

Government Execution and Disappearance of International Aid Employees

Among the many who were executed and disappeared by the government in the aftermath of the SPLA-Torit July 1992 attack were several relief workers. U.S. AID employees Andrew Tombe and Baudoin Tally were arrested and later executed. Two other U.S. AID employees, Dominic Morris and Chaplain Lako, were arrested in August 1992 and have disappeared.[58] Two U.N. employees, one Michael Muto Alia, the highest-ranking United Nations Development Program (UNDP) representative in Juba, were arrested and disappeared. One European Economic Community (EEC) employee, Mark Laboke Jenner, admittedly was tried and executed.

After the June attack, U.S.AID handed over the care of its Juba compound to Tombe and Tally, two U.S.AID southern Sudanese employees. During the attack the following month, government forces entered the compound and commandeered all the vehicles. When Tombe and Tally tried to stop them, they were arrested. The U.S. Embassy inquired about the arrests and was first told that the Khartoum government had no information. The U.S. request to travel to Juba to investigate was stalled on security grounds.

The Sudan government later claimed that Tally had disappeared and that Tombe had been arrested and he confessed. It said the case had

---

[56]Amnesty International, "Patterns of repression," p. 8.

[57]Amnesty International, "Urgent Action Report: Sudan," AI Index: AFR 54/14/93, London, April 30, 1993.

[58]U.S. Department of State, *Country Reports on Human Rights Practices for 1992* (Washington, D.C.: GPO 1993), p. 256.

been investigated and that Tombe was tried on August 15, 1992,[59] "by a competent court of law which convicted and sentenced him to death. It was proved that he used the communication equipment available to him to direct the artillery of the SPLA-Torit in bombarding the city and was justly punished for his treachery."[60] The government claimed that the defendant's actions had led to hundreds of casualties and that his execution was unjustly characterized as an extra-judicial killing "ignoring the fact that there is a constitutional government authority in a city which was then under siege by an enemy, and an act of treachery can only be dealt with by court martial, and in accordance with the rule of law."[61]

The government has never established, however, what rule of law it applied and whether any trial was held, much less one that comported with elementary notions of due process. The record of this trial has never been produced. The government referred to unspecified evidence from unnamed witnesses and a confession that was never released. It failed to specify the venue of the trial, the participants, or the judicial procedures applied.[62]

The Sudan government orally informed the U.S. that Tally was also executed, but did not provide any further information. No oral or written information whatsoever has been provided to the U.S. government regarding its two other disappeared employees, Lako and Morris, last seen in Sudan army custody in Juba.[63] Sudan, responding to U.S. diplomatic protests, "ordered a judicial enquiry into that incident. The commission of inquiry is headed by a judge of the High Court who is yet to submit his report," wrote the Sudan government in November 1993, a year and three months after the event. "Delay is due to the continuous requests for information of persons alleged to have

---

[59]"Embassy Khartoum honors 2 Foreign Service nationals who were executed," *State* magazine (Washington D.C.: U.S. Department of State, February 1994), p. 3.

[60]Shido to General Assembly, November 24, 1993, p. 7.

[61]*Ibid.*

[62]"Embassy Khartoum honors 2 who were executed," *State* magazine.

[63]*Ibid.*

disappeared after the incident. That report would be distributed to interested governments and organizations on completion."[64]

HRW/Africa awaits the report, but we must assume after such a lengthy delay that it will never be produced. It appears to us that it was never the intention of the government to produce such a report, but simply to engage in delaying tactics.[65]

Two Sudanese employees of the UNDP were arrested in Juba during the period after the July 1992 attack and disappeared. It is suspected that they also were executed. Despite repeated requests, the government did not provide any information about them until November 1992, when the Juba authorities told the U.N. that one of the men, Michael Muto Atia, was arrested on July 31, 1992, and was awaiting trial in Khartoum. The authorities in Khartoum, however, said he had "disappeared."[66] The fate of the other man, an unnamed driver, is unknown.

Mark Laboke Jenner, a Sudanese employee of the EEC in Juba, was executed in mid-August 1992. Sudanese officials say that he was sentenced to death by a military court for treason, but there has been no independent confirmation that he had received any trial, let alone a fair one.[67]

Government Accountability for Killings and Disappearances

Following the two SPLA-Torit attacks, the government received so many complaints of summary executions that it bowed to pressure and

---

[64]Shido to General Assembly, November 24, 1993, p. 7.

[65]Meanwhile, the government, apparently oblivious to the irony, criticized the U.N. special rapporteur's interim report because his investigations were not completed within a few months, ignoring the fact that the government's investigation into one incident has lingered over a year.

[66]Amnesty International, "Ravages of war," p. 18.

[67]Amnesty International, *Annual Report 1993* (London: Amnesty International, 1994), p. 271.

established a committee in November 1992 to "investigate the incidents in Juba town in June and July."[68] This committee has proved useless.

When the U.N. special rapporteur inquired about the results, the committee revealed that it had not visited Juba until April 1993, ten months after the events in question, and only for four days. The committee felt another visit was required, which would not take place "soon" due to a "shortage of fuel for air transport." The committee did not have any answer regarding the sentences pronounced by the special military courts reportedly set up in Juba after June 1992.[69]

The U.N. special rapporteur in September 1993 asked for an accounting of 230 persons allegedly arrested in Juba between June and August 1992.[70] In its November 1993 written reply to the special rapporteur, the government repeated that it had arrested and tried "some" infiltrators, did not mention the fate of the 230 persons, and referred only to the trial and execution of one person, Tombe who had been an employee of U.S.AID.[71]

The government continues to ignore requests for an accounting of the arrests and disappearances of persons last seen in custody following the battle for Juba. In the vast majority of the 230 cases of disappeared following arrests in Juba in this period compiled by Amnesty International, the authorities have failed to provide any information at all. The disappeared remain missing[72] and are presumed dead.

---

[68]Amnesty International, "Ravages of war," p. 19.

[69]U.N. General Assembly Forty-eighth Session, Agenda item 11K (c). "Human Rights Questions: Human Rights Situations and Reports of Special Rapporteurs and Representatives, Situation of human rights in the Sudan, Interim report on the situation of human rights in the Sudan," prepared by Mr. Gáspár Biró, Special Rapporteur of the Commission on Human Rights, A/48/601 (New York: United Nations, November 18, 1993), p. 10.

[70]*Ibid.*

[71]Shido to General Assembly, November 24, 1993.

[72]Amnesty International, "Ravages of war," p. 19, and later information.

Detention and Deportation of Clergy

On July 31, 1992, the Catholic archbishop of Juba, Paolino Lukudu, and Fathers Immanuel Jada, James Oyet, and David Tombe were summoned to a meeting with Mohammed al-Mahdi, chief of security, for the purpose of interrogating Father David Tombe. On August 2, Father Tombe was taken to the main barracks, where he was mistreated, then to Khartoum, where he was held incommunicado until February 1993.[73]

On August 16, 1992, an order was given to all Catholic and Protestant expatriate missionaries to leave Juba for Khartoum within twenty-four hours, later extended to fifteen days. The archbishop met with security authorities to avoid the deportation but had no success. On September 4, four Protestant missionaries left for Nairobi.[74] Five Comboni sisters and six Comboni fathers were escorted to the airport by security authorities and flown to Khartoum following a written order that they be removed for their own protection.[75] All remaining foreign missionaries were deported from Juba on September 5, 1992. Expulsion of foreign missionaries hit hard because there were never enough Sudanese priests and nuns to minister to the Catholic population of Juba, and because of the role they played in relief and in reporting on government abuses.[76]

---

[73]Amnesty International, "Ravages of war," p. 17. The government did not provide answers to inquiries about Father Tombe for several months, and it was presumed he was dead.

[74]Comboni Mission News, Rome, September 5, 1992, quoted in "Foreign Missionaries Expelled," *Sudan Update*, vol. 3, no. 25 (London: September 9, 1992), p. 1.

[75]*Ibid.*

[76]A communique from two Catholic bishops of New Sudan Council of Churches, Bishop Paride Taban of Torit and Bishop Joseph Gasi Abangite of Tombura/Yamibo, noted:

> The departure of the missionaries is going to deprive the helpless civilians of Juba town of very much needed help and at least moral support . . . . It is our belief that the missionaries are being evacuated in order to remove any undesirable witnesses to the atrocities being committed against the innocent

Forcible Displacement of Civilians into Inadequate Conditions

After the July 1992 attack, the Juba government forcibly displaced over 100,000 civilians living there,[77] herding them from their homes to the city center and crowding them into unsanitary and inadequate locations, or leaving them exposed to the elements in open spaces. It also burned the homes and crops left behind by the civilians, all in violation of the rules of war. Furthermore, it refused to allow the civilians, who were in desperate conditions and entirely dependent on erratic international relief, to leave Juba.[78]

On July 11, the army ordered the evacuation of Lalogo (the displaced persons camp and the village) and Kator neighborhoods and burned them and other areas the next day, forcing their inhabitants to

---

civilian population of Juba town at the hands of government troops . . . . It is true that a few missionaries had asked to be evacuated from Juba because of poor health and the shock of the atrocities they had witnessed. The majority of the missionaries, however, freely decided to remain in Juba town.

Ibid.

[77]Some relief agencies estimated that some three-quarters of the population of Juba were displaced (which might be as many as 200,000 people), and that the rest of the population was confined to their houses.

[78]Refusing to let starving civilians leave Juba is not a new government tactic. When fighting started between SPLA and government forces in October 1989, the government stopped relief aid flights to Juba. The army consistently denied the displaced the right to return to their villages after that, even though the arrival of relief supplies was very insufficient and erratic and dependent on government whim. Burr, *Genocide*, p.40.

squat without shelter in the city center.[79] Most displaced from Kator, Lalogo, Jebel Kujui, and Tong piny camps lost their shacks.[80]

The destruction of housing appeared to be in retaliation for alleged support for the SPLA-Torit in those areas (which the rebels had passed through) as well as an effort on the part of the army to create "free fire" zones in which to attack SPLA-Torit guerrillas attempting to enter Juba. Crops were also destroyed. A witness noted that "the maize crop, at a milky stage, and the dura [sorghum], at the flowering stage, were all cut down by the army on July 14 and the fields were mined."[81]

This massive displacement of up to three-quarters of the Juba population[82] occurred while the army prevented civilians from leaving Juba. "Afterward there was no freedom of movement in Juba. People would be killed if they tried to move," one civilian said. The army reportedly mined routes out of Juba to prevent people from leaving.

The displaced were forced to live in completely inadequate conditions as squatters in and around the concrete buildings comprising the old commercial and administrative center of the city.[83] They were squeezed into an area of about twenty-five square kilometers, about one-quarter of the whole urban area.[84] Conditions were reportedly sub-

---

[79]Amnesty International, "Destruction of Juba," p. 2. One observer noted that during the fighting, some of those in the displaced camps on the outskirts of Juba fled their homes for the relative safety of buildings in the city center to escape rebel bombardment. Didrikke Schanche, "Food Stocks Exhausted for 350,000 in Beseiged [sic] Juba," Reuters, Nairobi, Kenya, August 7, 1992.

[80]The U.S. Committee for Refugees said that this forcible displacement started "well in advance of the SPLA attacks; displaced camps and neighborhoods were destroyed and the population packed into an area one-quarter its previous size." Burr, *Food Aid*, p. 27.

[81]Quoted in "Crops 'Destroyed,'" *Sudan Update*, vol. 4, no. 1 (London, September 22, 1992), p. 2.

[82]OLS (Southern Sector) Bi-Monthly Situation Report No. 22, July 21-August 5, 1992, p. 2.

[83]Amnesty International, "Destruction of Juba," p. 1.

[84]Burr, *Food Aid*, p. 27.

human: hunger, thirst, disease, lack of shelter, and fear were daily battles, according to the foreign missionaries who witnessed this before their expulsion:

> [T]housands of people are living as squatters under makeshift plastic coverings, each family in a space no bigger than 8 x 5 feet. Thousands of others have fled to the banks of the Nile River or sought some protection behind walls of buildings. Others are jammed into one- or two-room houses of relatives. Every church and school compound and other public properties are crowded with these squatters. Water and sanitation facilities, even in the best of times, have never been adequate in the town, and under these circumstances became an unimaginable horrible situation . . . the people, plagued by mosquitos, have been living in these sub-human conditions for almost two months. They are unable to return to their own homes because in many cases these have been burned and demolished by the army for what the army claims to be military, strategic reasons. Even where the houses are still standing, the people are afraid of harassment, brutality, and arrest by government soldiers, especially at night.[85]

Other reports confirmed these descriptions, adding that the majority of displaced persons were exposed to the torrential rain of the season and afflicted with the cold and humidity of the night. Most slept on a mat or blanket, but some lay on the bare ground.[86]

Since stores were closed, people had to rely exclusively on relief, and many thousands were reported to be fleeing to Yei, Mundri, and

---

[85]Africa Faith and Justice Network, "Maryknoll Sisters' Report on War-Torn Juba."

[86]Nils Carstensen, "Southern Sudan - Report on a Forgotten Crisis," Danchurchaid (Copenhagen, Denmark), September 16, 1992, p. 4.

Kajo Kaji areas,[87] despite the double ring of land mines around Juba
and other hurdles such as army and SPLA patrols. Indeed, one agency
reported that in only twenty-four hours on July 14-15, about 1,000
people displaced by the Juba fighting arrived in Kajo Kaji seeking relief
and saying that more people were following behind them.[88]

By late August 1992, families from Malakia, Atlabara, Nimeera,
and Buluk neighborhoods started to return to their homes, and people
from Kator, Kassava, Mayo, and Nyakura were waiting to move back.[89]

Law on Forced Displacement

Forced displacement of the civilian population for reasons
connected with the conflict is prohibited under article 17, Protocol II,[90]
which makes only two exceptions: the immediate safety of the civilians
and imperative military reasons.[91]

The term "imperative military reasons" usually refers to
evacuation because of imminent military operations. The provisional
measure of evacuation is appropriate if an area is in danger as a result
of military operations or is liable to be subjected to intense bombing. It
may also be permitted when the presence of protected persons in an area
hampers military operations. The prompt return of the evacuees to their
homes is required as soon as hostilities in the area have ceased. The
Sudan government bears the burden of proving that its forcible relocation

---

[87]OLS (Southern Sector) Bi-Monthly Situation Report No.21, July 4-20, 1992,
p. 2.

[88]*Ibid.*, p. 9.

[89]Report of relief agency working in Juba, dated August 25, 1992.

[90]Protocol II of 1977 Additional to the 1949 Geneva Conventions. *See*
Appendix A.

[91]Protocol II, Article 17 --
> The displacement of the civilian population shall not be ordered for
> reasons related to the conflict unless the security of the civilians involved
> or imperative military reasons so demand. Should such displacements
> have to be carried out, all possible measures shall be taken in order that
> the civilian population may be received under satisfactory conditions of
> shelter, hygiene, health, safety and nutrition.

conforms to these conditions. It appears that its displacement of civilians went far beyond what was necessary for military operations, and was accompanied by extensive property destruction.

Even if the government were to show that the displacement and destruction were necessary, it still has the independent obligation to take "all possible measures" to receive the civilian population "under satisfactory conditions of shelter, hygiene, health, safety, and nutrition." All available evidence points to the conclusion that the government completely failed to take any measures to provide for civilians. Indeed, the government destroyed civilian housing and crops without any apparent military necessity, in punishment for alleged collaboration with the SPLA-Torit.

If the government will not provide for the civilians it dislocates, in the alternative either it must have recourse to international relief actions[92] or it should let the population engage in self-help and depart for safer areas outside the besieged city. If it can or will do none of the above, then it is under an obligation to adopt another military strategy-- not one that displaces over 100,000 civilians and provokes mass destitution, disease, and death.

Prohibition on Targeted, Land Mine Attacks on Civilians

The land mines ringing Juba directed at the civilian population constitute a violation of the rules of war. Making civilians the targets of land mines or any other weapon is forbidden in customary international law.

Following the SPLA November 1988 call on residents to abandon Juba, the army embarked upon an extensive campaign of planting land mines around the town and gave general warnings that they would not

---

[92]*See* Protocol II, article 18 (2):

If the civilian population is suffering undue hardship owing to a lack of the supplies essential for its survival, such as foodstuffs and medical supplies, relief actions for the civilian population which are of an exclusively humanitarian and impartial nature and which are conducted without any adverse distinction shall be undertaken subject to the consent of the High Contracting Party concerned.

permit civilians to leave.[93] Other efforts to contain civilians in Juba included capturing and returning persons attempting to leave and punishing them, including with torture.

Civilians are not legitimate military targets, even if they are attempting to leave a city. The would-be escapees are not taking part in the hostilities at the time of their escape; indeed, most of those in flight very much want to be far from the hostilities.

While some of the government land mines may be directed at SPLA attackers, it is clear that they serve the forbidden other purpose as well: containing civilians. Indeed, if the civilians were permitted freely to leave Juba by road or air, they would not be faced with the danger of encountering government land mines on small paths.

GOVERNMENT ABUSES IN 1993

Scorched Earth Campaigns: Bahr El Ghazal

In late 1992 and 1993, the government continued to launch attacks on the main population centers of Bahr El Ghazal, including the Yirol, Rumbek, Gogrial, and Aweil areas, inflicting civilian casualties, and burning and looting civilian property.

In mid-January 1993, government forces from the Wau garrison attacked Karic village in Rumbek County early in the morning, according to an elderly Dinka resident. They surrounded one side of the village and began shooting wildly. The soldiers looted the houses and the grain storage buildings, using vehicles to load the groundnuts, sorghum, and sesame, and then burned the buildings.

The army stole all fifty-eight head of cattle that belonged to one witness. Most of the villagers similarly lost their cattle. Government soldiers also took this witness' three daughters (ages seven, nine, and eleven) and three sons (ages eight, fourteen, and fifteen). He still did not know what had happened to them months later. Numerous people were burned alive in their huts during the attack, many of them still asleep at the time.

---

[93]Africa Watch, *Denying the Honor of Living*, pp. 76-77. The government gave no specific warning about which areas had been mined. These land mines were in a different location from the SPLA ring of mines, and were well within the "security cordon" of Juba, the area under army control.

When the army left, the witness returned to Karic to find nothing left. Even the wells were destroyed. He, his two wives, and seven remaining children then had to eat leaves and roots to survive, he told HRW/Africa.

The government destroyed a well in the area of Aliam Toc I, east of Rumbek, that had been one of the few functioning wells left in the area, according to a medical worker.

Prior to 1992, leprosy had been under control for ten years due to the work of the Comboni sisters who ran three leprosy centers in Bahr El Ghazal: Pagarau near Yirol, Kuel Kuac, and Aqile. Pagarau was overrun by the government in 1992; the patients were killed and the healthy relatives who lived with them were kidnapped. Kuel Kuac and Aqile were not taken by the government, but there are no more services at any of the three centers. The lepers from the three centers were dispersed, and now do not receive aid or medical attention. A medical professional who used to work with the lepers estimated that there were in mid-1993 between 1,000 and 2,000 lepers in the Lakes Province of Bahr El Ghazal, including in Yirol, Rumbek, and Tonj; he believed this constituted a leprosy epidemic.

A U.S. State Department cable describes operations by the government in northern Bahr El Ghazal in late 1992 and in February-March 1993. According to this source, two military trains, each with about 3,000 troops mostly from former Arab tribal militias incorporated into the PDF, traveled from Babanusa in Southern Kordofan to Wau in Bahr El Ghazal. The first train was preceded by foot soldiers who allegedly killed or captured civilians in their path, burned houses, fields, and granaries, and stole thousands of cattle. The second train left in March 1993 carrying horses for the soldiers, who in five days allegedly killed a large number of civilians between Manwal Station and Aweil and captured several hundred women and children. The soldiers burned granaries and fields and looted cattle, causing many to starve to death later. When the soldiers reached Meiram, they were said to have raped scores of displaced southern women.[94]

Some villages in Bahr El Ghazal have been attacked in retaliation when government vehicles run over SPLA mines, according to this cable.

---

[94]U.S. Embassy, Khartoum, Sudan, cable released May 12, 1994, in Washington, D.C..

Troops usually burn the first village they find in such cases and kill its inhabitants for their supposed collaboration with the mine-layers.[95]

Government forces, especially the PDF, were alleged to routinely steal women and children in Bahr El Ghazal. Some women and girls were said to be kept as wives,[96] others were believed to be shipped north for forced labor on Kordofan farms, and still others were alleged to be "exported," mostly to Libya, where their fate is not known. The cable noted that there are instances of government authorities in Wau and Aweil freeing kidnapped women and children.[97]

Since the government recaptured Yirol on April 11, 1992, that town has been used as a staging base for raids on adjacent civilian areas controlled by the SPLA-Torit, causing tremendous displacement in Lakes Province in Bahr El Ghazal. A villager reported that his family was forcibly displaced from Panliet village by one of the army's 1993 forays from Yirol town.

Church officials alleged that government forces inside Gogrial town frequently raided and burned peripheral villages eight to ten miles around the town to form a "no-man's land" between the government and SPLA-Torit territory. Church sources calculated that several government expeditions destroyed 200 villages along the main roads. Most of their inhabitants either rebuilt or moved to remote areas to protect themselves from further incursions. Livestock was looted by the army and militias, and little was left for the civilians. Schools and bush markets were frequently hit by army ground forces and air bombardments.[98]

---

[95]*Ibid.*

[96]In this practice, which is not new, the kidnapped woman becomes part of the family, with second-class status. Among some southern Sudan peoples, the girl children are valuable because at marriage a dowry is paid to their fathers, usually in cattle. Girl children thus can enrich a family. Similarly, kidnapping women for wives relieves the kidnapper of paying the dowry price and these women can bear girl children.

[97]*Ibid.*

[98]Reports compiled by the New Sudan Council of Churches (NSCC) and the Diocese of Rumbek, Nairobi, Kenya, May 1993, pp. 3-8.

Church sources also reported that a government offensive was launched in northern Aweil district on March 18, 1993, killing hundreds of civilians and razing several villages to the ground.[99] Government soldiers were said to consider the villagers of Aweil district to be SPLA sympathizers or combatants and often targeted them, regardless of sex or age. In March, 1993, villagers went into Aweil, seeking food that they believed had arrived on a train from Babanusa. Government troops captured thirty-two villagers inside Aweil and tortured them, cutting their testicles with scissors and cutting off their ears; ten escaped, including one who was severely injured, and twenty-two were killed, according to church sources. Two of those killed were Deng Mojok Kuol and Garang Ateng Akuei, both from Gaal village, fourteen miles from Aweil town.[100]

In the government garrison town of Wau, thirty-seven people suspected of collaborating with the SPLA were summarily executed by government forces in March 1993, including Ugok Ukello Muodic and Bol Theme Akec, according to a former resident.

Government-supported militia used Wau as a base for raids and burnings of nearby villages. In 1992-1993, government troops burned villages along the railway line.[101] It is estimated that many civilians were killed during the attacks. The surviving residents were displaced to the Akon area. Troops also looted many cattle, sheep, and goats as well as sesame, groundnuts, and cereals; they burned grain storage buildings, according to the same former resident.

Attacks on Civilians: Bor

In late January 1993, government-supported Mundari militia between Jemeiza and Mongalla in Eastern Equatoria attacked civilians fleeing Bor, making their way south to the displaced persons camps near Nimule. Reportedly three people were killed. In February 1993, the government attacked the village of Kolnyang near Bor and robbed cattle from civilians displaced from Jonglei. In early 1993, the New Sudan

---

[99]*Ibid.*, p. 8.

[100]Reports compiled by NSCC and the Diocese of Rumbek, May 1993, p. 8.

[101]These included Wunlit, Aulwic, Lol Akuei, Gaal, Wargeng, Ametnyang, Kajik, Alel Thonj, and Wuonkuel.

Council of Churches charged that the government imprisoned, tortured, and buried alive four members of the Episcopal Church of Sudan in the Bor area: Rev. Peter Lual, evangelists Matthew Duol and Paul Kon, and layman Joseph But.[102]

Indiscriminate Government Bombing in 1993

A frequent government weapon is aerial bombardment of SPLA strongholds which the government cannot hope to reach overland. "The wide open spaces of southern Sudan, with scanty cover, make air superiority the key to controlling the ground," noted one reporter.[103]

The planes and bombs used in these air raids are notoriously inaccurate. Apparently, in many raids little effort is made to actually hit military targets and bombs land several kilometers away from possible targets. Frequently the bombs hit civilian population centers, either accidentally, in which case the bombing is indiscriminate, or deliberately. On at least one occasion in 1993 and another in 1994, aerial campaigns hit displaced persons camps housing tens of thousands, caused civilian dead and wounded, and so terrorized the people that they deserted the camps.

Mundri, in Western Equatoria, half of whose estimated population of 30,000 was displaced Bor Dinka, was bombed twice by government planes in late November 1992, and repeatedly in February 1993. One such bombing occurred on or about February 4, 1993, at 10 A.M. A Catholic priest in Kaya, 383 kilometers away, received a radio message about the bombing at 5 P.M. that day. He arrived in Mundri two days later. Two men and two women were killed; they were already buried by the time he arrived. He was told that twelve bombs had been dropped which hit Mundri, Lowei and Amadi.

Mundri was being rebuilt when it was bombed again on February 24, when the priest was present. Twelve consecutive bombs were dropped at 12:30 P.M., killing three women and two men. One of the men was killed when a bomb fell on a mango tree ten meters from where he was sitting in a doorway. Two women were killed by another bomb, which

---

[102]New Sudan Council of Churches letter to Pope John Paul II, Nairobi, Kenya, February 15, 1993, p. 1.

[103]Mwambu Wanendeya, "Sudan air terror sets off exodus of refugees," *The Sunday Times of London*, February 20, 1994.

landed one meter away from a shallow shelter where one of the women was hiding. A third woman and a second man were killed when another bomb fell on their hut. Five were injured, and houses were set on fire.

On February 6, 1993, the government bombed the market of the Eastern Equatorian outpost of Kajo-Kaji.[104] The market was the most populated civilian area in town. Seventeen civilians were killed, including six children, four women, and one teenage girl. Ten were seriously wounded. A witness to the incident, a thirty-three-year-old man from a nearby village, said that twenty-four were injured. He remembered that the government had bombed Kajo-Kaji four times from 1991 to 1993.

U.S. member of Congress Frank R. Wolf, on his third trip to Sudan, visited Kajo Kaji shortly after the February 6 bombing. He made the following statement about the extent of the destruction he found:

> I saw first hand recent damage in the town of Kajo Keji on the western bank of the Nile where the Khartoum government bombed the crowded town market square, killing and injuring many. The Khartoum government conducted high altitude bombing on this village when there was no military presence. I saw bomb craters where they hit huts and destroyed the market place. I visited what was termed a hospital but what was in reality a filthy, rat-infested place where the injured were gathered. One woman, injured in the air-raid, had shrapnel still in her head. She had no hope and little chance for tomorrow. When it seemed conditions were as bad as they could be, they got worse.[105]

---

[104]Kajo Kaji in Eastern Equatoria is 216 kilometers from Kaya, although the good road between the two runs through government-controlled Yei. (Yei is a government garrison almost entirely deserted by civilians today.) Kajo Kaji is on the West Bank of the Nile across from the Ugandan border town of Moyo. The 1983 census for Yei area council was 340,599, which included Yei town (27,214) and Kajo Kaji rural council (96,063). Many small Equatorian tribes inhabit the area: Kakua, Pojulus, Mundri, Arocaya, Lovaro, Kalico, Makaraka, Kuku, Bari, and others.

[105]Statement by U.S. Rep. Frank R. Wolf, Congressional Delegation to the Horn of Africa, February 5-February 12, 1993 (Washington, D.C.: undated).

On February 24, the Kajo Kaji market was bombed again several times.

Also in February, a bombing run on Amadi, north of Yei, killed cattle. The bombings, even when they do not kill civilians, are frightening, and they prevent people from remaining and cultivating in areas where bombing occurs. SPLA commanders have ordered bomb shelters to be built, but civilians say there are not enough of them to protect the population.

In February, March, and April 1993, government planes bombed in the mountainous area of the Didinga tribe in Eastern Equatoria, south of Kapoeta and Torit along the Ugandan border. In the February bombing, which occurred at about 10:30 A.M. near Lotukei, witnesses said that two planes were aiming at the SPLA base in Lotukei, five miles away, and "in the course of the attack, some bombs fell on homes." The ten-year-old niece of a witness was killed in the play area outside her hut. The bomb left a crater larger than a hut (about ten by fifteen feet) and blasted out all the trees in the surrounding area. Others who were wounded at the same time were taken to Kenya for medical treatment.[106] The planes made two runs, one in the morning and another in the afternoon. Twelve bombs were dropped in each.

The second bombing took place on March 17, 1993, at about 3 P.M., also in Lotukei. Twelve bombs were dropped on an old well used by both SPLA soldiers and civilians. Some thirty people were injured in the bombing; some were SPLA and others were civilians, although the witness who saw the event did not know the number in each category. About twenty houses near the well were set on fire by the bomb.

The third bombing was in April, 1993, in Chukudum. A man on the nearby mountain saw and heard the bombing from his position of safety. He said that the bomb did not hit the large SPLA base in Chukudum, but fell on the tukls about two kilometers away. When the plane left, the witness and others inspected the damage and were told of injuries.

Government Offensive in Western Equatoria from July-August 1993

Beginning July 26, 1993, the government launched its largest offensive since the dry season campaign of March 1992. It was a two-pronged offensive, with aerial bombing in the areas between Yei and

---

[106]The ICRC runs a hospital for the war wounded in Lokichokio, Kenya, on the Sudan border.

Morobo in Eastern Equatoria, as well as in Kaya on the Ugandan border. The bombing intensified on August 3.[107] The government had not launched a dry season (November to April) campaign in the 1992-93 period, apparently preferring to watch U.N. developments in Somalia and the intense fighting in Upper Nile between the SPLA factions.

The first prong of the offensive was unsuccessful. In mid-July, 1993, some 5,000 government troops in armored vehicles from the garrison town of Juba moved towards Nimule, an SPLA-Torit-controlled town close to the Ugandan border. The government troops were repulsed.

The second prong started on July 24, opening a second front with movement of troops from the garrison town of Yei towards rebel-held Kaya. An aerial campaign was part of this renewed offensive against the SPLA-Torit, ultimately aimed at cutting off the rebel road and supply line from Uganda.[108] By mid-August, the government had retaken Morobo, a strategic crossroads town on the Juba, Yei, and Kaya roads, and cut the supply lines for relief efforts as well as for the SPLA from Uganda to Bahr El Ghazal and Western Equatoria.

The U.N. High Commissioner for Refugees (UNHCR) appealed to the government on humanitarian grounds to suspend all military activities in the area, to no avail. The relief organization Africa Action in Need (AAIN) was daily sending food to 70,000 displaced people in towns in Western Equatoria, and non-food supplies to many more. The offensive made it impossible for AAIN to bring in food and supplies and it estimated that the offensive would put a total population of about 750,000 at great risk of starvation.[109]

The immediate result of the July, 1993, bombing was that approximately 75,000 people were internally displaced, 27,000 fled across

---

[107]New Sudan Council of Churches, Press Release, Nairobi, Kenya, August 9, 1993.

[108]Julie Flint, "Anti-Rebel Offensive Creates Sudanese Refugee Crisis," *The Guardian* (London), August 10, 1993, p.1.

[109]Sam Kiley, "Famine fear in Sudan as army attacks the rebels," *The Times of London*, August 12, 1993, p. 1.

the border to Uganda, and 1,000 went to Zaire,[110] according to the UNHCR. An outbreak of measles in a refugee transit center in Uganda killed fifty-seven refugees, thirty-eight of them children, almost immediately.[111] Some 20,000 of the internally displaced, mostly Dinkas, went north and east to Dinka areas and were reported to be arriving in Akot.[112]

During the second week of August, 1993, after the government took the town of Morobo, government planes bombed the surrounding areas to break an SPLA siege of Morobo. Government planes bombed the outskirts of Kaya on August 7; those fleeing reported that the government had bombed and shelled the displaced camp.[113] Thereafter the SPLA-Torit began to urge civilian populations to move east to Kajo-Kaji.[114]

Relief workers who toured Kaya a few days later observed that the town and the U.N.-run camp nearby at Yondu were deserted and had been looted.[115] Yondu had been established in 1992 for the mostly Dinka displaced people who were streaming in from the Bor and Yirol areas. They crossed the Nile around Jemeiza and continued westward past Aluakluak and Mundri to the Kaya area. Because there was not enough room for them in Kaya, they were resettled at Yondu, a former Ugandan

---

[110]Mark Huband, "Thousands Flee new Fighting in Famine-Racked Southern Sudan," *The Washington Post*, August 18, 1993, p. A27.

[111]UNHCR press release, "Over 100,000 Sudanese Refugees Flee to Uganda," Nairobi, Kenya, August 25, 1993.

[112]OFDA, "Sudan Civil Strife/Displaced Persons, Situation Report no. 6," September 10, 1993, p. 6.

[113]Robin Denselow, "Boy soldiers fail to shift rebels in weary Sudan," *The Guardian* (London), November 2, 1993, p. 1.

[114]Mark Huband, "Thousands Flee new Fighting in Famine-Racked Southern Sudan," *The Washington Post*, August 18, 1993, p. A27.

[115]Julie Flint, "Anti-rebel offensive creates Sudanese refugee crisis," *The Guardian* (London), August 9, 1993, p. 1. Later information indicated that SPLA-Torit troops under the command of Commander Pitia were responsible for the looting.

refugee camp about fifteen kilometers north of Kaya. Since access for relief overland from Uganda was relatively easy, the area became a magnet also for the displaced from Mundri and Aguran.[116] A November 1992 U.N. World Food Program (WFP) assessment reported the presence of 10,000 displaced at Yondu.[117]

Seven months later, they were displaced again and Yondu was deserted.

Bombing in Late 1993

Thiet, in Bahr El Ghazal, attracted thousands of displaced persons in search of food who were fleeing what they called Nuer militia in early 1993.

There were tens of thousands of displaced who depended on this relief program and airstrip. A journalist visiting the area in June 1993 reported that many were displaced from the Lon Arik area, where Nuer tribesmen had killed over ninety and displaced thousands.

> Most of the survivors trekked on foot to Thiet, believing that they would find food, shelter and medical care. A few found little. The majority found none....
>
> What was billed as "the last convoy" to beat the rains left Kaya at Uganda/Sudan border in March. After avoiding Sudan government controlled towns and land mines on the roads, only nine out of the original 23 trucks managed to reach Thiet on 2 May. Thirteen got stuck in the mud or broken down in various parts of the route. One got blown up by a land mine, killing the driver.
>
> Thiet district's normal population of 150,000 is now well over 200,000 and increasing daily, due to expectations

---

[116]OLS (Southern Sector) UNICEF/WFP Bi-Monthly Situation Report no. 29, November 6-21, 1992, p. 2.

[117]OLS (Southern Sector) UNICEF/WFP Bi-Monthly Situation Report no. 30, November 22-December 6, 1992, p. 4.

that the World Food Programme will either fly supplies
into Thiet town or carry out aerial drops.[118]

On November 12, 1993, a government squad of MIGs buzzed the town,
and then an Antonov airplane dropped fourteen bombs next to the
airstrip of Thiet, where a large group of civilians had gathered at a
feeding center. Three civilians were wounded[119] and the relief team
then working there was evacuated.

The cumulative impact of government scorched earth campaigns
and bombing in 1993, plus poor harvest, plummetted areas of Bahr El
Ghazal to near disaster by 1994. An epidemiological survey in Akon in
April 1994 revealed that an alarming 45.5 percent of the under fives were
malnourished.[120]

In Loa in Eastern Equatoria, on November 23, 1993, three
persons were reportedly killed, including two children, and at least fifteen
injured when government planes dropped two bombs on the marketplace.
Two other bombs exploded close to a Christian mission.[121] The
government also bombed the area of Chukudum again, on December 20,
1993.

INDISCRIMINATE GOVERNMENT BOMBING
IN THE 1994 DRY SEASON CAMPAIGN

The result of the government's 1994 dry season campaign and
indiscriminate aerial bombardment in Equatoria was to kill and injure
civilians and to so terrorize the surviving inhabitants of three large
displaced persons camps, Ame, Atepi, and Mundri, that they deserted the
camps; over 100,000 were displaced in the month of February, 1994. The

---

[118]Jacob Akol, "Agony continues," *New African* (July 1993), p. 20.

[119]U.N. Commission on Human Rights, "Situation of human rights in the
Sudan, Report of the Special Rapporteur, Mr. Gáspár Biró," p. 9.

[120]Medecins Sans Frontiers press release, "Medical aid group says the stage
is set for a new humanitarian disaster in Sudan," New York, May 24, 1994.

[121]*Ibid.*

U.N. Secretary-General expressed his deep concern over the renewed fighting and called on all the parties to cease all hostilities immediately to put an end to the suffering of the innocent civilian population.[122]

Shortly before the 1994 offensive began, the government removed Kajo Kaji, Kaya, Mundri, Maridi and Nimule (in all the area of the offensive in Equatoria) and four other locations from the list of destinations where food aid could be safely delivered by the U.N. Striking out the above named food distribution centers exposed over 200,000 displaced to risk of starvation.[123]

The government had been massing troops in its garrisons at Juba, Wau and Torit for weeks. It appeared to have the capture of Nimule, a White Nile town very near the Uganda border, and Kaya, another Uganda border town, as military objectives, in an effort to cut the SPLA's military supply lines to Uganda. These routes are also essential to the international relief effort to feed millions of needy displaced southerners,[124] including over 100,000 huddled together in three camps at Ame, Aswa and Atepe (called the Triple A camps) on the east bank of the White Nile between Juba and Nimule. The Triple A camps were the single largest concentration of displaced in southern Sudan.[125]

---

[122]U.N. press release, "Sudan 3," EIN/06/94, New York, February 14, 1994. The offensive struck in the middle of a country-wide UNICEF immunization campaign to protect Sudan's 4.5 million children against measles and polio. The regional director of UNICEF appealed for temporary ceasefires to allow the immunization teams to reach 800,000 war-affected children in southern Sudan. A measles outbreak had just claimed fifty-five lives in Juba. UNICEF press release, "Sudan 2: Displaced Sudanese Flee Camps As Fighting Escalates," EIN/05/94, New York, February 8, 1994.

[123]OLS (Southern Sector) Sitatuion Report No. 53, February 1-15, 1994, p. 5; OLS (Southern Sector) press release, "UNICEF and WFP Request Urgent Funding for War-Torn Southern Sudan," Nairobi, Kenya, February 14, 1994, p. 2; Richard Dowden, "Sudan army poised to cut off rebels in the south," *The Independent* (London), February 8, 1994.

[124]Keith B. Richburg, "Sudan Opens Offensive Against Rebels," *The Washington Post*, February 8, 1994, p. A14.

[125]*See* Eastern Equatoria map, facing Chapter IV.

The government also was after Mundri and Maridi, a few hundred kilometers to the west of the White Nile; they sit astride the road to Zaire. Over 30,000 displaced lived near Mundri.[126]

As for the Triple A area, bombs began to fall in January, 1994 on Loa, the site of a Catholic mission and several NGO offices. Loa is located between two Triple A camps, Aswa and Atepi, which were largely Dinka, although many other groups were represented: Uduk, Nuba, Lotuko, Pari, Murle, to name a few.

The expected government dry season offensive did not open, however, until February 4, when the government launched an artillery attack on established SPLA-Torit positions near the front line at Kit, south of Juba. On that same day, Arapi was bombed; the SPLA-Torit reportedly had a headquarters in Arapi, between Loa and Pageri and also in the vicinity of the Triple A camps.[127] No casualties were reported, although some bombs again fell near NGO compounds in nearby Loa.

Shortly thereafter, the Mandari government-supported militia was reported to have attacked the Ame camp; one source said that this nighttime attack on the camp left two women and two children dead and sparked the exodus from this camp[128] that held about 40,000 displaced, largely Dinka survivors of the 1991 Bor massacre. Ame had never before been attacked and although some journalists were unclear how such a small attack could have caused the relocation of tens of thousands of displaced,[129] Ame is very close to the front line at Kit.

A particularly bad bombing occurred on February 7 at Parajok east of Nimule and south of Palataka, near the Ugandan border. According to reports, there were eighteen people killed and twenty-eight injured.

---

[126]Richard Dowden, "Sudan army poised to cut off rebels in the south," *The Independent* (London), February 8, 1994.

[127]*Ibid.*

[128]Keith B. Richburg, "Sudan Opens Offensive Against Rebels," *The Washington Post*, February 8, 1994, p. A14.

[129]Richard Dowden, "Attack forces Sudan refugees to flee camp," *The Independent* (London), February 10, 1994.

The following day, Pageri was bombed, leaving eight dead. About half of the 10,000 people living in Pageri were displaced. The bombing was witnessed by several reporters who "had to dive for cover as a lumbering Soviet-built Antonov military plane dropped four bombs shortly before noon on the village."[130] The bombs on Pageri hit a building containing arms and ammunition which was set off, but the SPLA-Torit denied the locale was a rebel base, claiming that a "military police station" was hit.[131] Pageri was a continued target almost daily between 10 A.M. and 2 P.M. even after it was deserted by most civilians; few houses escaped damage and the few civilians who remained spent the day in the bush, hiding from the bombers.[132]

On February 12, Arapi was bombed again. Former residents of Arapi and of the camps at Ame and Atepi walked five days and fifty kilometers east of Nimule to Laboni, which almost overnight became a displaced persons camp for 70,000. Laboni, reachable through Parajok and just north of the Uganda border, is cold at night and access over a mountain road and destroyed bridges is difficult; the tens of thousands of displaced were stranded without food for five days upon arrival at Laboni.

The displaced abandoned most of their belongings when leaving Ame and Atepi, which, along with the village of Apari, were completely deserted. According to a U.N. relief worker who visited Ame shortly after, "All relief items were destroyed by the attacking forces. Tons of food was

---

[130]Agence France Press news agency, "Government planes bomb village and refugee camp near Ugandan border," Paris, February 8, 1994, reprinted in *BBC Summary of World Broadcasts*, the Middle East, Part 4, in ME/1918 MED/16 [37], London, February 10, 1994; *see* David Chazan, "Khartoum bombers hit divided rebels," *The Times of London*, February 10, 1994. Minutes later the Antonov dropped another two bombs which fell close to Aswa camp but did not cause casualties. *Ibid.*

[131]*Ibid.*

[132]Mwambu Wanendeya, "Sudan air terror sets off exodus of refugees," *The Sunday Times of London*, February 20, 1994.

scattered in the village, and medicines and immunization equipment were destroyed."[133]

Some 10,000 former Ame, Atepi and Apari residents went south to the Aswa displaced camp, the only one of the Triple A camps still operating.[134] Due to the threat of further military activity in the area, the SRRA targeted the displaced population of Aswa camp and the displaced of Pageri, about 37,000 persons, for relocation to Mongali, 18 kilometers east of Nimule.[135]

On March 1, 1994, the bombing moved further south in the Triple A area. Twenty-four bombs fell in and around Nimule and Aswa displaced persons camp. The bombs fell in the town of Nimule, near the bridge, and near the hospital. One killed a twelve-year-old girl in Nimule and a total of nine civilians were injured, five of them near the hospital.

On February 4, the same day the government attacks started in the Triple A area, another front was opened 250 kilometers northwest of the Triple A camps. The Mandari tribal militia launched a ground attack on Mundri[136] and government planes bombed Maridi southwest of Mundri.[137] Mundri, by then deserted, was subjected to a ground attack on February 12 and bombed on February 19 and 20, although no civilians were left there or at the nearby Kotobi displaced persons camp, from which the estimated 30,000-35,000 displaced had fled.

This second large group of displaced fled to Angutua displaced persons camp, twenty-four kilometers southeast of Maridi near the Zaire border. The deserted town of Mundri went back and forth between the SPLA-Torit and the government, which managed to hold on to Amadi

---

[133]UNICEF press release, "Sudan 2: Displaced Sudanese Flee Camps as Fighting Escalates."

[134]OLS (Southern Sector) Situation Report No. 53, February 1-15, 1994, p. 1; OLS (Southern Sector) press release, "UNICEF and WFP Request Urgent Funding for War-Torn Southern Sudan."

[135]Ibid.

[136]Ibid.

[137]See Western Equatoria and Bahr El Ghazal map facing Chapter III.

which it took in February.[138] The SPLA-Torit reported that 281 people had been killed or injured by the government shelling of Mundri.[139]

LEGAL STANDARDS
APPLICABLE TO BOMBING AND SHELLING

Many of the bombing attacks described above were indiscriminate and violated the rules of war.[140] Indiscriminate attacks are defined in Protocol I, article 51 (4), as:

a) those which are not directed at a specific military objective;

b) those which employ a method or means of combat which cannot be directed at a specific military objective; or

c) those which employ a method or means of combat the effects of which cannot be limited as required by this Protocol; and consequently, in each such case, are of a nature to strike military objectives and civilians or civilian objects without distinction.

A further definition of indiscriminate attacks is in Protocol I, article 51 (5)(b), referring to those attacks which may be expected to cause incidental loss of civilian life, injury to civilians, damage to civilian objects, or a combination thereof, which would be excessive in relation to the concrete and direct military advantage anticipated. This codifies the rule of proportionality: an attack which may be expected to cause excessive civilian casualties and damage is a disproportionate attack. The rule reflects a balance between 1) the foreseeable extent of incidental ("collateral") civilian casualties or damage, and 2) the relative importance

---

[138]Julian Bedford, "War 'like football' smiles rebel chief," *The Guardian* (London), February 16, 1994.

[139]Scott Peterson, "Fresh fighting raises fears of Sudan famine," *Daily Telegraph of London*, February 15, 1994.

[140]*See* Appendix A.

of the military objective as a target. No matter what the value of the military objective, it never justifies excessive civilian casualties.

The government has offered several defenses of its practices. With reference to the Kaya attacks in February, 1993, the government denied that the bombings were indiscriminate and that it was aiming at military targets of the armed opposition. This defense was weakened by the government's further claim that there were no camps for displaced persons in the SPLA controlled areas, but only military camps.[141] HRW/Africa joins the Special Rapporteur in dismissing the latter assertion; not only eyewitness accounts told to HRW/Africa researchers but also U.N. and NGO staff more than refute that specious contention. These agencies, working with 150 international staff in twenty SPLA-held areas to feed and assist over one million needy, generated thousands of pages of reports detailing the movement of the displaced inside SPLA-controlled areas of south Sudan.

If the government was aiming at a military objective in Kaya, it did not hit the target but instead hit a market during daytime hours. The circumstances strongly suggest that, if the government was not engaging in the forbidden practice of deliberately targeting civilians, it was engaging in the forbidden practice of using a means of attack which was not capable of being directed at a military target.

Attacks that employ a "method or means of combat which cannot be directed at a specific military objective" are forbidden. The bombing methods used by the Sudan government air force have been described time and again as hand-rolling bombs out the back hatch of Antinovs as they fly at high altitudes.[142] This method or means of attack is the very definition of indiscriminate. If a high-flying plane manages to deliver a hand-rolled bomb out of the hatch and on to a military target, it is simply a matter of luck.

Such complete lack of targeting ability is consistent with accounts of bombs frequently landing two to five kilometers from known military targets. In the case of the bombings in the Didinga area, for example, the

---

[141]U.N. Commission on Human Rights, "Situation of human rights in the Sudan, Report of the Special Rapporteur," p. 9, citing government reply.

[142]Richard Dowden, "Sudan army poised to cut off rebels in the south," *The Independent* (London), February 8, 1994. Attacks have also been made by Chinese-built MiG-19 aircraft strafing roads and villages. *Ibid*.

civilians believed that the Sudan government was aiming at SPLA-Torit military bases in the region, even though they missed such targets sometimes by as much as eight kilometers.

Where the military target is in a non-populated area, the lack of targeting capability would not be a barrier to bombing. When the government attempts to use bombing systems that have no apparent targeting mechanisms in populated areas, however, it clearly is engaged in indiscriminate bombing.

Furthermore, since the attack on the Kaya market as well as the other attacks described above were during the day, the government does not have the excuse that a civilian concentration such as a market was not visible. It is the duty of the attacker to take reasonable precautions to avoid inflicting excessive civilian casualties, and to refrain from attack if such avoidance is not possible.

In early 1994, the government again defended its bombing practices, describing allegations of military offensives on civilians as "completely false and baseless." Instead of maintaining, as they had only a few months before, that there were no displaced persons' camps inside SPLA zones, the government sought to blame the SPLA-Torit and Garang for using civilians as human shields, by locating military bases near civilian concentrations, presumably referring to the Triple A area (Loa) and Thiet (Bahr El Ghazal) bombings.[143]

Whatever the conduct of the SPLA-Torit, it can never excuse the government from launching attacks that foreseeably will cause excessive civilian casualties. Even if the SPLA-Torit deliberately located bases in immediate proximity to displaced persons camps, the government must still adhere to the rule of proportionality and either use precision weapons as a necessary precaution to avoid such casualties, or, if it does not have the means to avoid such civilian harm, refrain from attack.

Finally, several of the attacks described above do not appear to be directed at a specific military objective--a grain warehouse is not a legitimate military objective, nor is a column of fleeing civilians, nor a marketplace. The civilian population as a whole as well as individual civilians are to be protected against attack. Civilians and civilian

---

[143]"Foreign minister denies allegations of government attacks on civilians in south," Radio National Unity, Omdurman, Sudan, February 16, 1994, quoted in *BBC Summary of World Broadcasts*, The Middle East, Part 4, ME/1925 MED/12 [28], London, February 18, 1994.

objectives are not legitimate military objectives and they may not be
directly targeted.

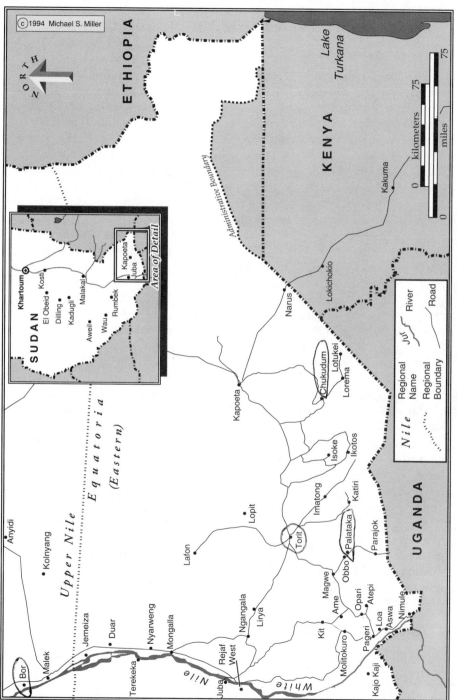

Eastern Equatoria

IV. SPLA VIOLATIONS OF THE RULES OF WAR

On August 28, 1991, two Upper Nile SPLA commanders, Riek Machar Terry Dhurgon, Lam Akol Ajawin, and another SPLA commander, Gordon Kong Cuol, called for the ouster of SPLA Commander-in-Chief John Garang de Mabior. Their garrison at Nasir was joined by the SPLA barracks at Ayod, Waat, Abwong, Adok, Ler, and Akobo, and some Anya-Nya II Nuer militia that for several years had fought on the side of the government. The stated goals of the breakaway group, known as the Nasir faction, were of democratizing the SPLA, stopping human rights abuses, and reorienting the SPLA's objective from a united, secular Sudan to independence for the south.

This strategy backfired in part because of widespread human rights abuses committed by the SPLA-Nasir forces in the 1991 fighting. These abuses introduced more mistrust into already strained tribal relations among southerners.

The fighting between the two factions has persisted for the two and a half years since the August 1991 split; since then it has extracted a higher civilian toll even than the government offensives.[1] The devastating toll is due directly to the way the factions have waged war in violation of the rules of war.

Among the violations of the rules of war committed by the two SPLA factions are indiscriminate attacks on civilians living in the territory of the other SPLA faction; summary executions and disappearances; torture; holding prisoners in harsh conditions; pillage of civilian assets (cattle and grain) and destruction of civilian property (the burning of houses) in the opposing faction's territory; taking food from civilians by force; capturing civilians, principally women and children, from the territory of the other faction; and denying unaccompanied minors the opportunity to be voluntarily reunited with their families by the SPLA-Torit and in 1993 by the SPLA-Nasir/United. Abuses particular to the SPLA-Nasir/United include directing the movement of the civilian population to Yuai in Upper Nile in order to facilitate creation of a military outpost in this front-line position, thus exposing the civilians to military danger rather than taking precautions to protect them. SPLA-

---

[1]Jean, *Life, Death and Aid*, p. 17.

Torit abuses included siege of garrison towns that in some cases amounts to using starvation of civilians as a method of combat; indiscriminate shelling of Juba; holding SPLA political prisoners and Ugandan rebel dissidents in prolonged arbitrary detention; forcible recruitment, largely of Equatorians; forced portering; and the creation of tens of thousands of "unaccompanied minors"--boys originally brought or lured to Ethiopian refugee camps for educational opportunities, who were then segregated from their families and trained and deployed as soldiers.

The total impact of these abusive practices has been to rip apart the safety net the southern Sudanese utilize as a protection from hunger in times of food scarcity in this environmentally precarious region. The safety net consists in the first instance of self-help measures or survival strategies such as sale of assets, primarily cattle, as well as migration to find work, to fish and gather wild fruits, and to call upon the network of relatives and others -- sometimes of different tribes -- who are indebted to the potential famine victim. Where assets have been plundered, and migration is impossible because of renewed tribal animosity or useless because the place of migration has been raided as well, the civilian victims of military attacks must look to other sources of food. One of those sources is the international community. Its efforts to bridge the hunger gap caused by the conflict, however, frequently have been stymied by the same conflict, as all parties take advantage of their armed might to compel civilians to part with their meager rations and not infrequently block relief deliveries with reckless disregard for civilian welfare.

Thus pockets of hunger have persisted and hundreds of thousands have died of food scarcity and disease as a direct result of the factions' brutality and callous disregard for the rules of war and the civilians those rules would protect.

SPLA FACTION FIGHTING
IN UPPER NILE PROVINCE FROM 1991-1992[2]

In September 1991 it was by no means certain which units and areas were loyal to Riek and which to Garang, especially in the border areas along the Duk Ridge in Upper Nile, where there had been

---

[2]*See* Upper Nile map, facing Chapter II.

intermarriage for many generations.[3] The Nasir faction hoped to demonstrate military superiority by taking the Upper Nile home territory of Garang, a Bor Dinka, thereby convincing wavering commanders to switch sides.

From September through November 1991, SPLA-Nasir forces raided a series of villages in the Dinka districts of Bor and Kongor in Upper Nile Province. These raids, in which some 2,000 civilians perished, became known as the Bor Massacre. Many of the deaths occurred as civilians tried to prevent SPLA-Nasir raiders from looting cattle. The raiders killed women and children as well as men, and took other women and children captive.

The widespread killing, looting, and kidnapping, as well as the burning of civilian homes, were clear violations of the rules of war. The Dinka villages and cattle camps that were attacked and looted were not legitimate military targets, and the civilian population and objects in them were not caught in military cross-fire. The attacks often took place in villages where there was no SPLA-Torit or other military presence.

The number of civilians who died of hunger and disease after the raids will probably never be known. However, it was very high in the Bor and Kongor districts, judging from the accounts of the Dinka who fled to the toic (river-flooded grassland) to hide and search for food there. Many children died in the toic after the fighting was over.

The SPLA-Torit launched a counteroffensive against the SPLA-Nasir areas in Upper Nile in early 1992, which continued into the rainy season.[4] These reprisal raids followed the pattern set in the Bor Massacre of violating the rules of war by indiscriminately killing civilians and looting and destroying civilian property.

Killings and Looting During September/October 1991

In the September-October 1991 SPLA-Nasir raids, the attackers proceeded south from Nuer territory to the Dinka administrative center of Kongor, looting and killing as they went. Once in Kongor, they turned back north to Nuer territory.

---

[3]Some of the SPLA units in Nasir wanted to stay loyal to Garang and there were shootouts. The Shillok tribe was divided.

[4]The rainy season in Upper Nile starts in April or May.

On the way to Kongor, they encountered a group of SPLA-Torit soldiers commanded by a Nuer, William Nyoun Bany,[5] which had overrun a small contingent of Nasir loyalists in Kuac Deng (four hours or twelve miles south of Ayod and still in Nuer territory) and taken their cattle. Apparently the factions clashed on September 5, 1991, south of Kuac Deng and the Garang forces occupied Duk Fadiat, a Dinka outpost some thirty-five kilometers south of Kuac Deng.[6]

Much of the faction fighting has been along the Duk Ridge, a series of sandy knolls which run from Mogogh in the north to Ayod and Kuac Deng then to Duk Fadiat and Duk Faiwil.[7] The northern section is occupied by Nuer, the southern by Dinka. The ridge is less subject to flooding than the surrounding area and is planted with sorghum. The Jonglei Canal, whose construction was interrupted by the conflict, runs along the Duk Ridge.

Three days after the clash in Kuac Deng, the two factions fought in Duk Fadiat, where the line between Nuer and Dinka is not hard and fast, and intermarriage is common.[8] A witness told HRW/Africa that both

---

[5]Commander William was the most active Nuer commander in the SPLA and remained loyal to Garang until he also defected one year later.

[6]Although some of the participants in these military events claim to remember the exact dates, all dates are approximate. It is very hard to establish exact dates in general, especially for this period of time.

[7]Johnson, "Political Ecology in the Upper Nile," p. 468.

[8]Dinka tribes in Duk Fadiat (Ghor and Nyarweng) as well as other Dinka who border on the Nuer areas have facial scarrings, parallel markings, similar to those used in the area by the Nuer. One Dinka Christian pastor said that the Dinka in Bor/Kongor discriminated against the Ghor Dinka "because we are marked like Nuer."

These Dinka use the parallel markings because "They are more manly. Only the men have these marks. The men and women of Bor have the same marks," in contrast. The Bor and Twic Dinka have inverted chevron-shaped markings on their foreheads common to the Mundari from whom the markings were adopted.

Markings indicate two things: that men so marked can marry the women from groups who adopt similar markings, and that boys of such groups are often initiated in the same age-sets together.

sides engaged in looting in Duk Fadiat. No civilians were killed or injured in Duk Fadiat then, and no huts were burned. The Garang forces retreated to Pok Tap in Dinka territory, south of the Duk Ridge. There the SPLA-Nasir under Commander Elijah Hon Top attacked and overran Pok Tap on September 15.

The SPLA-Nasir then proceeded to Duk Faiwil, a village of about 500 Bor Dinka, four hours south of Duk Fadiat, according to a chief of that village. Prior to the Nasir revolt, there had been no fighting in Duk Faiwil. The SPLA-Nasir forces arrived at 5 A.M. and looted all the cattle, goats, sheep, tobacco, and grain. The village chief told HRW/Africa that all of his 103 cattle and 150 goats were looted. A second chief lost an entire herd of 2,000 cattle.

The father, mother, and three children of the first chief were killed. "No people were captured; they just killed whomever they saw," he said. He escaped by fleeing to the toic.

The youngest wife and three children--ages seven, four, and an infant--of the second chief were killed in the attack. "I saw so many bodies lying down, dead, as I fled. My people are all killed," he said. The attackers had burned his stored-up sorghum inside his hut. "I remain with nothing," he said. He described the devastation caused by the attackers:

> The attackers did not leave anything standing. They destroyed what they could not carry with them. They destroyed the hand pump and wells. They did not leave anything useful to human life. If they could not carry the grain, they burned it or dumped it in the water to make the water rotten, useless.

The attackers were in two groups: soldiers wearing khaki and military boots came first, armed with Kalashnikovs, RPGs (rocket-propelled grenade launchers), and mortars. Another group, who wore sheets and were armed with sticks and spears, came behind the soldiers.

Despite the confusion of facial scars, the villagers knew who was on which side because "it was known which side the different chiefs were on, and their followers automatically were on the same side." Indeed, after this looting in Duk Fadiat, the local Ghor Dinka civilians and chiefs, including the court president and chief, left Duk Fadiat and fled north to Ayod, a Nuer outpost, where their Nuer relatives were.

They all came on foot, without vehicles, because the area was flooded and impassable.

The first chief returned to the village after the raid but when he saw that everything had been destroyed, he returned to the toic, where survivors were forced to eat water lilies, a traditional famine food.

The second chief said he and many other Dinka stayed in the toic for three months while the Nuer occupied Bor and Kongor. Hunger and mosquitos were constant problems. Two of the second chief's wives survived, but his seven children, who survived the attack, died of hunger, either in the toic or after they moved back to Duk Faiwil.

As they pushed south, the SPLA-Nasir forces also attacked Wernyol, a Dinka village south of Pok Tap and north of Kongor, in September 1991. The SPLA-Nasir forces killed an unknown number of civilians in the raid, including the six uncles, one cousin, and one niece of a twenty-year-old Dinka woman who spoke with HRW/Africa. The raiders took women and female children captive, including five of her cousins. She was not sure whether they took them as wives or slaves. Riek's forces would "rape them and take the ones that they liked. They took only female children. If they could, they killed the boys," she said. Typical of the other villagers, she and her husband lost all their animals to the raiders: they had seventy head of cattle, fifteen goats, and ten chickens. All of their stored grain was looted. The attackers burned some of the tukls. She and her surviving relatives ran to the toic and returned to Wernyol in December 1991. She was there when it was reattacked in 1992.

The Garang troops pulled back south to Kongor, a Dinka center, by October 9, 1991, followed by the Nasir forces who occupied it without resistance from SPLA-Torit but at considerable cost in civilian life. The Kongor area is a grain-producing area, the home of the Twic Dinka, who historically migrated annually during the dry season north to the toic of the Nuer to water their cattle.[9] Kongor was the main commercial center of Kongor district, although the more permanent settlements were the dispersed villages and districts that surrounded Kongor.

A chief of Kongor was in one of these outlying villages during the attack. When it was over, he entered Kongor and found its entire center burned down. His people told him that the Nuer had attacked. He found

---

[9]Historically, occasional raids occurred between tribes but they were settled by negotiations. The Dinka and Nuer in this area had economic and familial ties.

many bodies of children, women, and men who had been shot. Two sons, one nineteen and one seventeen years old, tried to move his cows to the toic to hide them. The Nuer caught the sons and killed them; they also took his 200 cattle. They also killed his fifteen-year-old daughter who was with his sons in the cattle camp. On the way out of Kongor that morning, the chief caught sight of the Nuer as they were stealing cows, and he hid from them. "They were mostly wearing uniforms, but some had on sheets," he said.

The chief and others fled to the toic, where they did not build any houses but "collected grass on the water and slept on it." He described the hardships of life in the toic:

> There were so many difficulties with the rain and mosquitos. We had no proper food. We sometimes ate fish and sometimes did not have anything to eat. If you want to count by name all the people who died of hunger in the toic, it will take until evening.

After a few days in Kongor, the Nasir forces abandoned Kongor and returned north to their home territory with the cattle they had looted along the way.

SPLA-Torit Attack on Adok, Upper Nile

In the meantime, the SPLA-Torit under Commander William Nyuon Bany tried to open another front in western Upper Nile, around Bentiu.[10] The SPLA-Torit forces occupied the area for one week, attacking Adok, Riek's home town. The SPLA-Torit apparently commandeered an ICRC barge in Bentiu, filled it with 400 soldiers, and proceeded to Adok where the small SPLA-Nasir force was easily defeated. There was a clash in Ler, also in western Upper Nile, where the hospital was ransacked. It is not clear if the ransacking was done by Anya-Nya II reinforcements called in to assist SPLA-Nasir, or by SPLA-Torit. SPLA-Torit forces then returned to Bor, raiding cattle from Adok.

SPLA-Nasir Second Raids into Kongor/Bor Area in 1991

Commander Riek at the time expressed annoyance at the attack on his hometown and announced that his troops then in Badiet (a Dinka

---

[10]*See* Western Equatoria and Bahr El Ghazal map, facing Chapter III.

area north of Bor) would take Bor,[11] the heartland of Garang's support.[12] Garang may have been readying his forces for a counterattack into Nuer territory at the time; his troops moved north. The two factions clashed in Duk Fadiat again, in November 1991. By that time the Duk Fadiat residents were all in hiding. Commander Elijah Hon Top told HRW/Africa that he took his SPLA-Nasir troops south at that time only as far as Duk Fadiat and that Commander Gordon Kong Banypin[13] of Nasir, the zonal commander, took over from him there and conducted the rest of the campaign.[14] In this raid, the attackers reached Kongor and then continued farther south, to capture Bor on November 23 and then Jemeiza.[15]

HRW/Africa interviewed several witnesses to attacks on various villages during this second thrust into Dinka territory. One, a chief of Jonglei, a village approximately twenty-four miles or six hours south of Kongor, said that the villagers did not hear the attack on Kongor or see the smoke. The attack was conducted by uniformed armed men and by men in sheets wielding axes and spears. When the attackers entered at about 5 A.M., this Jonglei chief said he quickly hid in a pool of water and high grass (the area was flooded). He stayed in chest-high water out of sight until 10 P.M. when he thought it was safe to flee. He said that at 10 A.M., he "was a witness to the Nuer dividing up people into groups or lines of fifty, by age." He was about seventy-five feet from the place

---

[11]Riek stated this intention in an interview conducted in mid-November 1991 with a U.N. staffperson.

[12]Garang's hometown is Aborom, south of Kongor.

[13]Gordon Kong Banypin is not to be confused with Commander Gordon Kong Cuol, also of SPLA-Nasir, who led his Nuer government-backed Anya-Nya II militia into the SPLA in 1987. In 1993, according to SPLA-Nasir Commander Elijah Hon Top, Gordon Kong Cuol was secretary of International Affairs of the SPLA-Nasir/United in Nairobi. Commander Gordon Kong Banypiny of Nasir was stationed at Abwong on the Sobat River in 1993 but had been ill.

[14]Commander Gordon Kong Banypin joined the SPLA from the government-sponsored Anya-Nya II in 1986.

[15]It is unclear what role the SPLA-Nasir troops in Badiet played in this campaign.

where this was happening, an open area of which he had an unobstructed view. The attackers could not see him. After dividing up the village by age, the Nuer started killing the residents in groups: small children, women, and men. They separated out "the more beautiful" young women and girls and took them away; they were killed if they refused to go.[16] About an hour after the raiders finished killing, he saw them take the cooking fire and set the roofs of the huts ablaze.

He sneaked away that night and only reentered the village after the Nuer had taken the cows and left. He counted the bodies of some forty children, 160 women, and 400 men that had been left lying on the ground. He and other Dinka civilians moved to the toic and lived on leaves and water lilies.

Another attack occurred on Paliau village to the south of Kongor center. As described by a fifty-five-year-old Dinka survivor from Paliau, the attackers came from the north during the flood time and began killing and looting: "It was Riek's soldiers plus Nuer militia and Nuer villagers. They came in the morning and took all the cattle, shot all the men that they could, and took whatever women they could capture."

The troops took some of the sorghum that was growing and burned the rest. The entire attack by the Nasir forces lasted twelve days. The troops shot and killed this survivor's brother when he was trying to take back some of his cattle. They kidnapped his daughter, then fifteen years old. He has not seen her since, and has no knowledge of her fate. He lost his entire herd of sixty head of cattle and eight goats. "Riek's forces" disassembled his house and used the wood for cooking, and looted his possessions, including utensils and grain.

Many residents ran under bushes to hide, then went to the toic when they got sick and too hungry. A few months later, after Riek's forces had left, they came back to Paliau. During the raids, there was no defense from Garang's forces. The Riek forces reportedly laid down land mines in Maar, another village in Kongor district, which killed one woman and injured others.

Still the Nasir forces continued south, toward Bor. A twenty-eight-year-old Dinka said that his family was in Jalle, a village in Bor district

---

[16]The chief understood one word they were speaking, which was in Arabic: "Adrup!," which he understood to mean "Fire!" (Literally, "adrup" means "hit.") An officer in uniform would give this order, and the others would raise their guns and fire at a group.

thirty miles north of Bor, at the time the Nuer came in November 1991. His grandfather, guarding his cattle, was killed and the cows taken. Another nineteen family members were killed at the same time and place, of whom nine were children, the youngest age five. This young man was with his cows south of Bor when the Nuer raided Bor center. He moved them six hours farther south, traveling with five other men and their cattle; they acted quickly to save their herds when word reached them of the looters.

On his way back to his home in Bor, after the Nuer left, he saw many people lying dead on the ground. "There were no cattle and all the houses were burned, including mine in Bor."

No accurate count was ever made of those who were killed in all the raided villages; Amnesty International estimates it was at least 2,000.[17]

Fighting Resumes After First Cease-Fire in 1991

Through the mediation of the churches, representatives of the two SPLA factions met in Nairobi on November 23 and agreed to a cease-fire, effective November 27, 1991, at 6 A.M.[18] It lasted only a few days. Garang's SPLA-Torit recaptured Bor on or about November 29, 1991. In December, 1991, Garang's forces re-occupied Kongor and Pok Tap, moving farther north but still in Dinka territory.

The two factions issued a joint press statement on December 17, 1991, reconfirming the cease-fire. It was soon broken. SPLA-Torit Commander Bior Ajang Duot admitted that he started a counterattack into Nuer territory from Mongalla on December 30, 1991, pursuing the Riek forces to Kuac Deng in the border territory.

SPLA-Nasir Accountability for the Bor Massacre

International law, set forth in greater detail in the appendix, is quite clear that summary executions and targeting of civilians are

---

[17]Amnesty International, "Sudan: A continuing human rights crisis," AI Index: AFR 54/03/92 (London: Amnesty International, April 15, 1992), p. 17.

[18]Press Release, Agreement signed by Commander James Wani Igga [SPLA-Torit] and Commander Lam Akol Ajawin [SPLA-Nasir], Nairobi, Kenya, November 26, 1991.

prohibited, as are kidnapping women and children, pillaging, looting, and destruction of civilian property.

The atrocities that occurred in the course of the SPLA-Nasir raids are the responsibility of the SPLA-Nasir faction. The 1991 raids initially were conducted by SPLA-Nasir and its followers for the military objective of capturing Bor Dinka territory, Garang's homeland, to turn the military and political tide in favor of the SPLA-Nasir forces. That faction has taken no serious steps to investigate and discipline the individuals and commanders responsible.

The SPLA-Nasir Forces Involved

Those who participated in the Bor Massacre comprised three separate groups:

1. SPLA military forces which responded to Riek, Lam Akol, and Gordon Kong's call to depose Garang, principally the unit based in Ayod[19] under the command of Vincent Kuang. Commander Elijah Hon Top and Thomas Duoth, a local Gaawar Nuer commander, were there also. A relief worker in the area at the time told HRW/Africa that Commander Elijah Hon Top set off with his troops for Kongor in October-November 1991, while Thomas Duoth and Vincent Kuang remained in Ayod, contrary to what Commander Elijah maintains;

2. Members of Anya-Nya II, a government-sponsored Nuer militia that switched its allegiance to Riek when he broke from Garang. It is not known which units participated in the raids, but those who sided with the Nasir faction included Brig. Paulino Matiep Nhial;

3. Nuer civilians loosely known as the "White Army" who took up arms, or sometimes spears, to participate in the military campaign, mostly for purposes of looting and revenge.

Members of the SPLA-Nasir tried to deny responsibility for the Bor Massacre because of the participation of Anya-Nya II and civilian

---

[19]The old SPLA garrison in Ayod, which defected to Riek, was not numerous; many troops had been transferred to the battlefront at the southern "capital" of Juba in Equatoria, whose capture was the focus of the SPLA's concerted military efforts.

Nuer raiding groups they could not control. However, as the testimonies demonstrate, the SPLA-Nasir forces participated in the raids and killing of civilians. Furthermore, the civilian participants were not sufficiently well armed to penetrate deep into Dinka territory unless they were operating in tandem with the SPLA-Nasir and Anya-Nya II.

The SPLA-Nasir is responsible for the conduct of the whole army because it encouraged these part-time combatants to participate in the raids. SPLA-Nasir and Anya-Nya II forces together apparently were not judged sufficiently strong to take the campaign to Kongor, and the White Army was encouraged to go along to participate, almost certainly with the lure of looting cattle. SPLA-Nasir is also responsible for the conduct of the Anya-Nya II militia units that joined the raids.

According to an informed observer, the first Kongor invasion was led by the Anya-Nya II group that so recently joined Riek's forces and civilians who had no relatives living in Kongor. The SPLA-Torit estimated that about 30,000 forces were used against them in Bor, of which Riek's troops were 10,000, Anya-Nya II's were 5,000, and the 15,000 remaining were Nuer civilian "White Army." Riek maintains that Anya-Nya II did not even have 200 men at the time. Probably neither figure is correct.

Anya-Nya II

When it was still a government militia, Anya-Nya II had suffered numerous defeats at the hands of the SPLA and was eager for an opportunity for revenge. The Anya-Nya II units that had just joined the SPLA in mid-1991[20] had not been incorporated into its military structure; they had no SPLA training, officers, or duties. (SPLA training until May 1991 was conducted at its training camps in Ethiopia.) Another Anya-Nya II unit did not desert the government until the Nasir faction split from Garang.[21] As late as October, 1992, some Anya-Nya II units were still drawing rations and pay from the government, although they

---

[20]Vincent Kuang, an old Any-Nya II commander before he joined the SPLA, had been sent by Garang in about April 1991 to persuade the Anya-Nya II at New Fangak and Doleib Hill in Upper Nile to join the SPLA. By June 1991 it was being reported that these Anya-Nya II units had joined the SPLA.

[21]This included Brig. Paulino Matiep Nhial of Mayom, who drew his support from the Bul Nuer of the Bentiu area, Upper Nile. Johnson and Prunier, "Formation and Expansion," p. 152.

had mixed in with the Nasir faction forces by that time; some had been transferred to Nasir and replaced by regular SPLA.

"White Army"

The "White Army" or "Decbor" is a term now used for what was at the time a very informal arrangement among Nuer men in Upper Nile,[22] named "white" named because of its weapons, the white metal of their spears or *pangas*,[23] a cheap and readily available weapon. It was an informal part-time military force drawn by local leaders from civilians in their home areas for the purpose of conducting traditional cattle raids or of settling scores for cattle raids. The White Army members live in their own homes and have their own commanders. They are not considered by the SPLA-Nasir to be a militia because they are untrained and have no semi-automatic weapons.

Many Nuer believed it was time to settle scores with the Dinka, which they equated with the SPLA-Torit. Nuer civilians from Upper Nile had been targeted in SPLA reprisals against Anya-Nya II operational areas.[24] These Nuer claimed they had been heavily taxed by the SPLA and were subjected to SPLA abuses, such as looting cattle, confiscating food, taking young women to be wives of soldiers,[25] and forced

---

[22]In 1993, under Wut Nyang, the White Army took on a more permanent organization and many of his followers wore white sheets or covered themselves in white ash. They played a role in the attack on government-held Malakal in October 1992.

[23]Normally the razor-sharp spears are used to cut the throat of cattle. The blade is shaped somewhat like a foot-long flat iron leaf at the end of a long wooden pole.

[24]The SPLA reprisals were brought on by Anya-Nya II's attacks in the mid-1980s on Dinka recruits passing through to Ethiopia for military training, and on other Dinka civilians fleeing Arab militia raiding and famine in Bahr El Ghazal. They had to pass through Nuer territory to reach Ethiopia. Johnson and Prunier, "Foundation and Expansion," pp. 127-28. But the Nuer attacks of the mid-1980s were also the product of Dinka/SPLA attacks on Nuer earlier, and on and on.

[25]Soldiers taking advantage of combat to abduct women to marry, without paying the usual dowry, is a common complaint.

recruitment. Some of the grievances, however, particularly the references to heavy taxation, may well be *post hoc* justification for the Bor Massacre.

Some believed that Garang's forces diverted to Kongor and the Dinka those U.N. supplies destined for Ayod. Dinka civilians brought these relief supplies back up to trade for Nuer cattle. "We in the White Army went with Riek to retake the cattle that had been traded for supplies that should have gone to the Nuer anyway, or that were taken as an unfair tax," in the words of a Nuer chief. Of 500 people who lived in his village of Pagau, 300 went to Kongor/Bor with Riek in September 1991. The same numbers came from Kuac Deng, Pading, and Pathai villages, "all with the intention of retaking our cattle." He believed that the raids then sparked retaliatory raids in 1992 and 1993 by Garang on these same Nuer villages.

According to a later study,[26] the Nuers' suspicion in August and September 1991 that Garang and the SPLA were hoarding U.N. relief supplies in Bor for the Dinka was not accurate. The U.N. had information about the need in this Nuer area, but a plan of action to bring supplies from the south to this area was vetoed by higher authorities in the U.N./WFP, because the Sudan government refused permission. The SPLA did not veto the plan.

In the early days of the split, in order to secure popular support against Garang, the Nasir faction deliberately propagated the false allegation that Garang diverted relief supplies to Bor. The propaganda fed on the existing perception that the Nuer districts were being shortchanged by the U.N. and others in development resources, which in early 1991 were concentrated in Kongor and Bor. The U.N.'s refusal to stand up to the Sudan government thus contributed in part to the later tragedy, but was not responsible for it.

Ayod residents reported later that one reason why their men joined the SPLA-Nasir faction in raiding the Dinka in Kongor and Bor was that the Nuer cattle were dying. The plan backfired: Not only did it provoke reprisal raids in early 1992, but the raided Dinka cattle brought diseases to the Nuer cattle, and both died by the thousands. Some of the Nuer raiders did not keep the looted cattle because of the fear that the Dinka would come to reclaim them, so they rushed to sell them in Malakal, Kosti, and Khartoum. According to one report, Anya-Nya II

---

[26]Scott-Villiers, "Repatriation of Sudanese Refugees," pp. 206-07.

forces that participated in the raids retreated to Malakal with over a
thousand head of livestock, sharply driving the price down.

Steps Taken by SPLA-Nasir to Investigate and Punish Their Own Forces Who Violated the Rules of War

HRW/Africa concludes that there was no serious investigation
undertaken or punishment meted out by SPLA-Nasir to forces under its
control, including Anya-Nya II and the White Army, in connection with
the Bor Massacre. This lack of responsibility continues despite repeated
inquiries and requests for such accountability, and the fact that more than
two years have elapsed since the events in question.

Military commanders have a duty under the rules of war to assure
that those under their command respect the rules of war, do not target
civilians, and respect civilian property. If a soldier deviates from respect
for these rules, then it is the duty of the command to investigate and
mete out appropriately severe punishment. Regardless of the difficulty of
identifying each individual soldier responsible when many participate in
a massacre, it is possible to identify the chain of command. Commanders
are responsible for the conduct of their troops and should themselves be
investigated and punished if they ordered troops to commit violations of
the rules of war. They are responsible even if they passively permitted or
tolerated abuses by their troops. They are also responsible for any cover-
ups after the fact.

The lack of will and/or the ability to deal with charges of violating
the rules of war is demonstrated by the contradictory responses of SPLA-
Nasir commanders to HRW/Africa's questions about accountability for the
abuses.

Commander Riek told HRW/Africa in July 1993 that he himself
"investigated" the allegations of killings of civilians in Bor in 1991.[27]
His investigation consisted of going to Bor and Kongor and talking "to
everyone." Upon further questioning, however, it became clear that his
investigation consisted only of attending political meetings where
questions about the Bor Massacre were raised by local Dinka chiefs.

Commander Riek claimed that there were no civilians in Bor
when it was attacked: "My troops attacked by night. They used heavy
artillery. All civilians were evacuated. People came back, about 500, the
day after we captured Bor. They came back for food, the commander told

---

[27]Interview with Commander Riek Machar, Upper Nile, Sudan, July 5, 1993.

me." As described above, however, the massacres occurred in many villages in addition to Bor.

Commander Riek stressed that it was difficult to know whom to punish because the situation was too confused. "Bor was a big fight. You cannot know who did what," he said. This excuse might explain one isolated battle, but the Bor Massacre was not a one-day incident. Sustained campaigns cannot be brushed off as "confusion."

In 1992, Commander Riek offered a different version of accountability for the massacre. He told the U.N. that he had dismissed Commander Vincent Kuang as the man responsible for Bor.[28] According to a relief worker who saw Commander Vincent before the raid on Bor, he was depressed, and after Bor he was in a severe depression even though he was not actually in Bor itself. He was the most senior officer in charge and appeared distressed about what happened there. In 1993, Riek did not mention to HRW/Africa that Commander Vincent had any responsibility or had received any punishment.

Yet another version of accountability was offered by SPLA-Nasir Commander Elijah Hon Top of Ayod.[29] In late 1991, Commander Elijah was in a position to assume responsibility because he participated as a commander in the raids and may be one of the ones ultimately responsible. He tried initially to excuse the SPLA-Nasir's failure to assign blame as a function of extraordinary circumstances. Upon being pressed, however, Commander Elijah claimed that several officers were court-martialed in early 1993 and eventually came up with their names: Capt. Lom Luat Chol and Capt. David Thon Dang, who were "demoted for fighting at Kongor and Pok Tap and for carrying out abuses." Commander Elijah said the two were in custody in Ayod jail until they were tried in a court martial in early 1993. Their punishment was being demoted to lieutenant, a rank they still hold. They were demoted during a general parade.

If his version of events is true, the punishment is wholly inadequate for the nature and extent of the abuses committed, including

---

[28]At the time in 1991 Commander Vincent Kuang was in charge of Ayod and Commander Elijah Hon Top and Thomas Duoth, a local Gaawar Nuer commander, were there also.

[29]Interview with Commander Elijah Hon Top, Upper Nile, Sudan, July 11, 1993.

thousands of civilian deaths, kidnapping women and children, widespread cattle raiding, and house burning. Commander Elijah then claimed that he was the one who pursued the proceedings and formed the court martial, on orders from Riek, to whom the decision was sent and who confirmed the decision. However, Commander Riek, in an interview with HRW/Africa earlier the same month, did not mention any of these names, events or punishments.

As to the defense that the civilians were outside of his control, Riek later admitted that the White Army "can be controlled if the other side respects cease-fire or demilitarized zone agreements." Commander Elijah also claimed that the White Army regularly went off on their own to raid cattle. He conceded, however, that they cannot operate alone but need regular soldiers to facilitate their raids far from home.

As to the Dinka women and children abducted during the raids, Commander Riek claimed that civilians returning from Bor had women with them whom he released and sent back. A historian, however, told HRW/Africa that during the first civil war it was easier to have cattle than women returned through tribal negotiations, and added that it would have been difficult for Riek to enforce any order to return the women and children taken. Indeed, several Dinka witnesses mentioned names of female family members who were abducted and never seen again.

When the idea was raised of compensation for the cattle that were raided, a traditional means of solving this type of dispute, one SPLA-Nasir/United leader, Simon Mori, succinctly rejected such a solution: "Raiding is what takes place in peacetime. This is booty."

SPLA-Torit Accountability for the Counterattack

As already discussed, the SPLA-Torit leadership did not meet with HRW/Africa, despite repeated requests for an interview. They have not even attempted to offer any excuses or insights into their continuing abuses of the rules of war.

Publicly, the forces of the SPLA-Torit have offered no excuse for their conduct; they claim that the abuses never took place. The responsibility of the SPLA-Torit to account for the conduct of their troops is the same as described above: to investigate reports of violations of the rules of war and punish their troops accordingly. Nothing of the kind has been done, as far as we have learned.

SPLA-Torit accountability for other violations of the rules of war will be discussed further below.

SPLA-Nasir Attacks in Bahr El Ghazal in 1992

Western Bahr El Ghazal[30] was formerly the most densely populated area of southern Sudan, with a population of the flood plain area of Aweil and Gogrial estimated at 1.5 million in 1986.[31] Flooding was responsible for a poor harvest in 1991 and destroyed many crops in 1992. Permission to fly into the area to deliver relief supplies was suspended by the government in early 1990 and was only reinstated in December 1992.

The relative calm in the area was disrupted in early 1992 when the SPLA-Nasir forces along with Nuer civilians carried out numerous incursions into the Dinka areas of eastern Bahr El Ghazal. Most of the attacks in the Yirol, Rumbek, Tonj, and Gogrial areas of Bahr El Ghazal were either against areas with little or no SPLA-Torit presence, or were carried out soon after government raids in April 1992.[32]

Amnesty International reported that on January 22, 1992, SPLA-Nasir forces attacked the villages of Pagarau and Adermuoth near Yirol in eastern Bahr El Ghazal, arbitrarily killing ninety-two civilians, among them patients at a leprosy hospital. Some twenty women and children were reported to have been abducted and villages burned down. Amnesty International also reported an attack by SPLA-Nasir on a large Dinka cattle camp, Wun Riit, near Shambe, which resulted in forty civilian deaths.[33]

Shortly thereafter, the fighting in this area between the SPLA factions was contained. In an interview with HRW/Africa, Commander Riek said that the tribes settled their differences through negotiations and that women and children abducted by the Nuer had been returned, although some say such a directive is very difficult to enforce. This April

---

[30]*See* Western Equatoria and Bahr El Ghazal map, facing Chapter III.

[31]OLS (Southern Sector), "1992/93 Situation Assessment," Nairobi, Kenya, February 1993, p. 20. Others note that the 1983 census for Aweil area council was 691,309 and for Gogrial area council 322,734, totaling 1,214,043. This census was disrupted, however, and its figures are often rejected by southerners.

[32]*See* Chapter III above.

[33]Amnesty International, "Ravages of war," p. 23.

1992 local peace agreement with the SPLA-Torit lasted until an attack by the Garang forces in June 1993, according to SPLA-Nasir.

SPLA-Torit Counterattack on Nasir Territory in Early 1992

In early 1992, the SPLA-Torit continued the counterattack, while the SPLA-Nasir attacked and then withdrew from some Dinka areas of western Bahr El Ghazal.

The government took advantage of the opening that the faction fighting provided and made its most significant military gains in years, starting in March 1992 by launching a four-pronged attack on SPLA territory and recapturing most of the main population centers held by the SPLA, including Bor, on April 4, 1992. (*See* Chapter III.)

Wunerud, a Nuer village in the Ayod district "one morning's walk" from the Ayod outpost, was raided by "the Dinka," some in uniform, some in civilian clothes, in January 1992, according to a thirty-eight-year-old male Nuer resident. Prior to the raid, Dinkas had lived in the Ayod district and its villages and had enjoyed good relations and intermarried with the Nuer. The Dinka in the village were not spared in the attack. The witness said that the attackers came at 8 A.M., some with rifles, some with spears "like us." The Nuer had only fishing spears and sticks with which to defend themselves. The witness's fifteen head of cattle were all taken. He said that some of the villagers were killed when they ran after the attackers to try to reclaim their cattle. "There was too much starvation. We could not endure it," he said. The attackers were responsible for taking all cattle of the village and for "killing and injuring many Nuer."

After the raid, there was no food left because the area had recently been flooded. The villagers received no food assistance, and many children died from illness and starvation. In December, 1992, the witness's family (he had ten children, ages fifteen to infant) and three other families walked fifteen days to Nasir for food, eating leaves on the way.

SPLA-Torit continued the counterattack with raids in Pagau and nearby villages to the east of Ayod. There was no military presence of the SPLA-Nasir in Pagau at the time of the SPLA-Torit raid. There were some twenty people in Pagau who were part of the White Army, a number "too small to fight Garang's forces," according to a forty-five-year-old Nuer chief from Pagau who believed that Garang's forces came to attack villages and "take back their cattle."[34] This witness told HRW/Africa that by February 1992, Garang's forces had reached Pagau village where many of the Nuer cattle from the region had been taken for water. This man lost fifty-one cattle, fifteen sheep, and twenty-two goats to the raiders. Thirty-three people were burned to death during the raid, including two of his children. In addition, ninety-seven people were shot and killed, either in the village or while running out of the village, he estimated.

During this period in 1992, Commander George Asor of SPLA-Torit emerged from his base in Atar to the north, near Malakal, and entered the Nuer area of Jol, near Waidien and north of Ayod, where he looted cattle and killed civilians. Then he withdrew north to Atar again.[35]

Witnesses told HRW/Africa that the SPLA-Torit continued its counterattack into Nuer territory in March. A fifty-year-old Nuer man from Fadiak (two hours' walk south of Yuai) was present during four attacks by SPLA-Torit forces in the three villages of Fadiak, Pathai, and Kuac Deng. He told HRW/Africa that in February 1992, "Dinka soldiers" came and burned Fadiak completely and engaged in widespread random shooting. This witness lost all of his livestock except for three cows. In March 1992, Garang's forces attacked Kuac Deng near Ayod, where the witness and his family had fled after the Fadiak attack. There, as in Fadiak, many civilians were shot and killed, including the witness's stepbrother. Again, grain, livestock, and other property were looted from

---

[34]This witness was sick, he told HRW/Africa, so he did not go to Kongor with SPLA-Nasir and the White Army as many of his relatives did. In the attack on Kongor, these combatants "killed Dinka cattle and goats and ate them."

[35]Commander George Asor was also reported by Nuer in the area to have attacked from his SPLA-Torit base in Atar into the Pagil administrative district five days north of Ayod, looting, killing and capturing Nuers there, in September 1991.

On February 24, 1994, Commander George attracted attention when he detained five U.N. staff engaging in relief assessment and vaccinations in Abek village near his Atar SPLA-Torit base; they had arrived in the area in a U.N. barge. He accused them of "spying for the government" but treated them well. They were not released until March 6, 1994.

the villagers, and most of the houses were burned to the ground. His family fled to Pathai, east of Kuac Deng.

Fighting in Upper Nile in mid-1992

On June 7, 1992, SPLA-Torit succeeded in penetrating into the southern capital of Juba before being driven out by the government. The SPLA-Torit again attacked Juba on July 6, 1992, holding onto some areas of the city for a few days before withdrawing.

In Nairobi on June 19, 1992, the two factions agreed to take immediate steps to revive the reunification talks as reflected in their joint statement of December 17, 1991.[36] During this period of mid-1992, the two factions conducted raids back and forth on villages along the Duk Ridge. HRW/Africa was unable to ascertain the exact chronology of these attacks.

In June or July, 1992, Garang's forces again attacked north into Nuer territory around Ayod, including the village of Pathai, which this time they burned to the ground, according to a witness. The attack once again involved systematic looting of the personal property of the villagers and indiscriminate shooting. This was the third SPLA-Torit attack on Pathai in 1992.

The next and fourth attack on Pathai by SPLA-Torit in 1992 took place in July. The witness told HRW/Africa that "soldiers of Garang" attacked in the morning. The witness's brother, stepbrother, and sons of two brothers were shot and killed.

SPLA-Nasir attacked the Dinka village of Pok Tap, about five miles south of Duk Fadiat, in June or July 1992. The SPLA-Nasir entered the Pok Tap area at dawn, surrounded it, and started shooting. They killed the head chief, Panom Atem Goc, along with Chief Lual Akoc Lual and Chief Awuol Malual, and all their families. Another chief of that town told HRW/Africa that he and his wife escaped back to the toic, but that the Nuer cut and destroyed his new crops. The witness came back when the attackers left and helped bury the three chiefs and their wives. He saw how they had been shot: Panom was shot in the temple and Lual in the stomach; Lual died two days later. In all, in the Pok Tap area,

---

[36]Agreement on Reconciliation of the Divided SPLM/SPLA, Nairobi, Kenya, June 19, 1992, signed by Commander William Nyuon Bany (for SPLA-Torit) and Commander Lam Akol Ajawin (for SPLA-Nasir).

seventy-eight civilians were killed. All the huts in Pok Tap and the surrounding area were burned.

The ethnic enmity that was building up with the factional fighting is reflected in the chief's comment that "The Nuers do not like the Dinkas to live, to survive. They were looking for people to kill in 1992; there were no more cows, sheep or goats left by that time."

A twenty-year-old Dinka woman from Wernyol, south of Pok Tap and north of Kongor, was present during the second attack on her village, which she believed occurred in June or July 1992. In the indiscriminate shooting, the SPLA-Nasir raiders killed eleven of her relatives, seven of whom were women. Her family's sorghum and pumpkin crops were cut down and destroyed, and more houses were burned. She fled to the toic with her family and never again returned to Wernyol.

Two chiefs of Wernyol village displaced by the 1991 fighting walked back to their village during the wet season of 1992 in order to plant with U.N.-donated seeds. Each had built two or three tukls, depending on the number of his wives. They were in Wernyol during the SPLA-Nasir attack in June or July 1992. The Nuer destroyed their new crops and new tukls, and the two witnesses, along with other survivors, fled to the toic again, but there was no food. "Many children died of hunger. The number killed by hunger is three times the number alive now," they said. Ten children, the wife, and a brother of one of the chiefs died of hunger while in the toic or on the way back to the village. About twenty-five family members of the other chief died of hunger on the same journey. They included two wives, a brother, his brother's three children, and several of his own children.

The SPLA-Nasir forces apparently went as far south as Paliau, south of Kongor town, in June or July 1992. According to a fifty-five-year-old resident, the SPLA-Nasir forces killed the oldest man in the area, Bior Aguer, who was over one hundred years old.[37] "They killed many who could not run," he added. This witness's six children and wife died of hunger after they fled into the toic to hide. He said they had not been able to go to Kongor "because Riek's forces were there." He described the

---

[37]An historian notes that this man was in his late twenties or early thirties in 1931, making him slightly less than 100 years old in 1993. He was clearly the oldest man in the area.

SPLA-Nasir attack bluntly: "They kill who they wanted to kill, and take what they wanted to take," including women and children.

ABUSES IN EQUATORIA DURING 1992

SPLA-Torit Abuses During and After its Two Attacks on Juba from June-August 1992

In the summer of 1992 SPLA-Torit made two military incursions into the southern capital of Juba, and nearly captured the city. The SPLA-Torit allegedly committed summary executions during the June 7 incursion, and indiscriminate shelling during and after the July 6 incursion. The shelling of the airport after the battle for Juba was over violated the rules of war because, under the circumstances at the time, the airport was the sole point of entry for relief food to reach over 100,000 recently displaced in that garrison town.

HRW/Africa attempts to investigate reports of summary executions by the SPLA were stymied in part by the government's denial of permission for us to visit government-controlled areas where these abuses allegedly occurred. Thereafter the government cut off all dialogue with HRW/Africa. We were therefore unable to confirm or deny the summary execution allegations, including allegations that the SPLA-Torit entered Juba through Lalogo and summarily executed sixty-nine soldiers from Battalion 116 by killing them in their beds. Soldiers are legitimate military targets, and further examination of the circumstances is required before it can be concluded that their deaths were violations of the rules of war.

Shelling of Juba Airport

There have been frequent allegations that the SPLA-Torit has shelled the town of Juba, in violation of the rules of war. We examine those allegations with reference to mid-1992.[38]

------

[38]It is evident that some were injured in the June 1992 fighting in Juba, but it is not clear who was responsible for the injuries or how they were inflicted, whether in cross-fire, by SPLA shelling, or by direct government attacks. Some 198 war wounded from this June fighting in Juba were taken over the border by land to the ICRC hospital in Lokichokio, Kenya. In Juba, local ICRC staff and the Sudanese Red Crescent assisted the victims and transported hundreds of

The worst SPLA-Torit shelling of Juba occurred from July 6-15, 1992, affecting both civilian and military areas. The targets apparently were the military headquarters and the airport, but the shells often went astray. On July 13 an SPLA shell hit the United Nations Development Program (UNDP) compound, damaging it but injuring no one.

The SPLA advised foreigners and civilians to leave Juba "for their own safety" during this July assault on Juba. "SPLA is dead serious of this warning. Those who cannot leave Juba are advised to remain in their houses wherever there is shooting and to take cover. The SPLA has strict orders to avoid civilian areas and to protect and to take to safety civilians who may be in distress," an SPLA communiqué said.[39]

Even after the battle for Juba subsided in mid-July, the SPLA-Torit continued to shell the airport and the town. As of August 5, there had been no U.N. relief airlifts into Juba since July 18[40] inpart because of the SPLA-Torit shelling of the airport. Relief agencies estimated that available food stocks would last only through August 7.[41]

On August 11, the consortium of nongovernmental organizations supporting CART (Combined Agencies Relief Team)[42] asserted:

> 300,000 people trapped in the besieged town of Juba
> have run out of food and face imminent starvation. The
> airlift bringing food into the town has been suspended.

---

wounded to hospital. *ICRC Annual Report 1992*, p. 51.

[39]"Renewed Assault on Juba," *Sudan Update*, vol. 3, no. 21 (London: July 13, 1992), p.1, quoting SPLM/A bulletin issued in London on July 7, 1992.

[40]OLS (Southern Sector), Bi-Monthly Situation Report No. 22, July 21-August 5, 1992, p. 2.

[41]*Ibid.*

[42]CART was established by international and national NGOs based in Juba and as of 1986 shouldered the main responsibility for receiving and allocating a shared pool of relief supplies for Juba.

Aid agencies now say if the airlift is not resumed immediately people will die.[43]

These public warnings were repeated by Amb. Darko Silovic of the U.N. department of humanitarian affairs a few days later. "Today in Juba there is no food left. If immediate assistance is not provided, large-scale deaths will certainly follow."[44]

In the case of Juba in mid-1992, preventing any planes from landing was the culmination of a long process of debilitation of the civilian population. It came on top of a several-years-long siege of Juba by the SPLA-Torit, which for many years had totally prevented land access (vehicles were subject to attacks and land mines) and access through the White Nile (which passed through SPLA-Torit territory to reach Juba). Airlifts became a very significant source of food to the population of almost 300,000.

Food supplementation was necessary in part because the population of Juba had doubled since the start of the war, swelled by the arrivals of the war-displaced. Furthermore, the majority of the displaced newcomers consisted probably of persons who did not support the SPLA and who had fled their homes as a result of SPLA military advances and, in some cases, SPLA abuses.

The actions of the government also contributed to the dire straits on which CART sounded the alarm. For military and political reasons, the government had forcibly displaced whole neighborhoods and suburbs of Juba in the aftermath of the SPLA-Torit July attack, driving the civilians into the crowded and unhygienic center of the town and burning their homes and crops. Many of those so affected were displaced persons from outside Juba. (See Chapter III.)

The shelling of the airport must be judged in the circumstances in which it occurred, that is, of extraordinary pressure on the food supply and the precarious survival of the civilian population. Under these particular circumstances, which were known to the SPLA-Torit since they

---

[43]Oxfam, Christian Aid, CAFOD, Norwegian Church Aid, Appeal of August 11, 1992, cited in "Starvation Imminent," *Sudan Update*, vol. 3, no. 24 (London: August 20, 1992), p.1.

[44]Julian Ozanne, "UN relief attacked by south Sudan rebels," *The Financial Times (London)*, August 18, 1992.

were a matter of public protest by relief agencies, shelling attacks upon the airport which led to its closure would have the foreseeable effect of causing excessive civilian casualties.

After Amb. Darko Silovic of the U.N. department of humanitarian affairs told reporters on August 17 that a resumed U.N. airlift would begin to move 1,075 tons of food, medicine, and shelter materials to the city, the initiative was attacked by the SPLA as "provocative."[45]

U.N. flights carrying food relief resumed on August 20 after a four-week suspension. Twice-daily trips were scheduled.[46] The WFP airlift to Juba was interrupted on August 23 when a shell fell less than 100 metres from a U.N. airplane unloading relief supplies in Juba. It resumed two days later, although without clearance from the SPLA-Torit.[47]

In late August 1992 the Southern Sudan Peace Forum called for the creation of "safe havens" for civilians. It summed up the dilemma for Juban civilians: the army herded people into crowded open spaces where they became sitting ducks for the SPLA. "In the first place, Garang and his SPLA men chased most of the villagers into Juba through their policy of 'live out of your gun.' Thus their advice for the civilians to get out has always been seen as a mockery by the defenseless inhabitants and displaced people."[48] The SPLA knew the perimeter was heavily mined and guarded by armed fanatics who shot on sight. "Yet," as the letter read, "the helpless people are being treated as if it is within their choice

---

[45]Julian Ozanne, "U.N. relief attacked by south Sudan rebels," *The Financial Times* (London), August 18, 1992.

[46]"U.N. Begins Sudan Airlift Despite Rebel Threats," Reuter, Nairobi, Kenya, August 20, 1992.

[47]OLS (Southern Sector) Bi-Monthly Situation Report No. 24, August 23 - September 4, 1992, p. 1.

[48]Letter, The Southern Sudan Peace Forum to U.N. Secretary-General (Nairobi, Kenya: Peace Forum, August 20, 1992), p. 2. "Live out of your gun" in this context means using the gun to extort a living. As with many tactics during this long war, this one has been more true during certain years and in certain regions than in others. Thus, "living out of your gun" was very much the policy in Eastern Equatoria in 1984-88, and since 1992.

to leave or stay in such a precarious situation."[49] The group advocated that the parties agree to a cease-fire, that Juba be designated a safe haven, and that U.N. security forces deliver food and other necessities to Juba to "ensure their fair distribution. It is an open secret that both combatants have earlier confiscated food meant for the displaced and defenseless civilians."[50]

CART also called on the parties to establish safe corridors out of Juba so that civilians could evacuate to a non-war zone of their choice.[51]

The SPLA-Torit also called on the Sudan regime to allow the evacuation of the city, with questionable *bona fides* since its military and political strategy often called for civilians to abandon the garrison towns.

The relief flights to Juba continued with interruptions and always under threat. In mid September 1992, *The New York Times* reported that the situation remained precarious:

> The relief planes stay on the ground just long enough to unload, but often come under shelling on the airstrip and are forced to take off before doing so. Emergency food flights to Juba resumed on Monday after a weeklong suspension to repair the runway, which was damaged by rebel artillery . . . . [52]

While this report's analysis of the legality of the SPLA-Torit shelling of the airport is limited to the July-August 1992 period, it is worth mentioning that even after the flights recommenced in September, the situation remained precarious. In the fall of 1992, U.N. Under Secretary for Humanitarian Affairs Amb. Jan Eliasson visited Juba and reported 70 percent malnutrition among children located around Juba

---

[49]*Ibid.*

[50]*Ibid.*, p. 4.

[51]"Starvation Imminent," *Sudan Update*, vol. 3, no. 24 (London, August 20, 1992), p. 1.

[52]Jane Perlez, "A Hidden Disaster Looms in Sudan, Aid Officials Say," *The New York Times*, September 16, 1992.

Hospital.[53] At the beginning of October 1992, U.S.AID reported that the 240,000 to 300,000 civilians[54] trapped in Juba faced starvation unless safe corridors for their evacuation were opened and a regular food pipeline was immediately established. UNIMIX (enriched biscuits) stocks were completely exhausted, and people were forced prematurely to harvest sorghum crops to survive. Because those remaining in Juba were forced to live on one-quarter of the land area of the town to escape the fighting, the "concentration of people in such a small area has caused the virtual collapse of sanitation systems in Juba."[55]

The SPLA-Torit offered various defenses for its acts. After the BBC and Voice of America reported in August that the SPLA-Torit had fired two missiles (which missed) at U.N. relief aircraft over Juba, SPLA Radio announced that "the U.N. Operation Lifeline Sudan officials who said that their aircraft came under fire at Juba airport should be made to understand that they had no agreement with the SPLA."[56] The SPLA-Torit said that it was not aiming at aircraft used for supplying relief, but warned that there was combat going on in Juba. It said that the U.N. aircraft "landed at a time when the government troops were attacking the SPLA in their positions. . . . It is the U.N. which insists on coming to a place of fierce fighting like this. Well, it is up to them."[57] It said that

> there was no way anyone could stop one, two, or even 50 shells or missiles from falling near aircraft of the U.N.'s

---

[53]Burr, *Genocide*, p. 54.

[54]As always, these numbers are open to question, especially since the government prevents accurate counts. The government claimed there were 500,000 in Juba in mid-1991; the U.N. accepted half that number. There have been no reliable reports of large influxes of civilians into Juba since then, and there are reports of people managing to leave.

[55]USAID/OFDA Situation Report No. 55 (Sudan) (Washington, D.C.: U.S. AID, October 7, 1992), p. 6.

[56]SPLA Radio in *Foreign Broadcast Information Service* (hereafter FBIS), August 26, 1992.

[57]*Ibid.*

> Operation Lifeline Sudan or an aircraft standing at Juba
> airport . . . . The relief aircraft of Operation Lifeline
> which landed in Juba still land at their own risk because
> fighting is still going on up to this moment.[58]

The SPLA commander in charge of operations on the Juba front,
Oiei Deng Ajak, admitted that for military reasons he was trying to close
the airport by long-distance shelling from ten kilometers away. He also
said his forces were under strict instructions from Garang not to shoot
down any relief planes. He threatened that at a later time he might try
to shoot down any planes entering Juba because the government was
using civilian aircraft to supply its troops with guns.[59] The SPLA-Torit's
suspicion of "relief" flights used by the government for military
purposes[60] perhaps made the SPLA-Torit less than careful of their
targeting. The SPLA has shot down civilian aircraft, most spectacularly one
taking off from Malakal in Upper Nile in 1986, killing sixty.[61]

The SPLA-Torit was also resentful of what it perceived as the
U.N.'s lack of even-handedness in delivery of relief supplies. The Sudan
government on many occasions had refused permission for U.N. relief
efforts in SPLA-Torit areas, and the U.N. had acquiesced in this, while
continuing to provide relief to government-held areas. The SPLA-Torit
interruption of OLS relief supplies going into Juba and other towns
under siege may have been part of a strategy to pressure the U.N. for
equal treatment.

These justifications must be examined in light of the prohibition
on indiscriminate attacks and the rule of proportionality. Ordinarily, an

---

[58] *Ibid.*

[59] Carstensen, "Southern Sudan - Report on a Forgotten Crisis," p. 3.

[60] SPLA-Torit's suspicion of U.N. aircraft was heightened by the incident of
a month before when the government used aircraft with U.N. insignia to deliver
arms to Juba.

[61] Africa Watch, *Denying the Honor of Living*, p. 116.

airport used to bring in military supplies is a legitimate military target.[62] The SPLA-Torit admitted that it was trying to close the airport by shelling. Shelling might deter aircraft from landing and also damage the runway.

An attack, even on a legitimate military target, may be prohibited as indiscriminate under certain circumstances. That is when the attack "may be expected to cause incidental loss of civilian life, injury to civilians, damage to civilian objects, or a combination thereof, which would be excessive in relation to the concrete and direct military advantage anticipated."[63] This is the principle of proportionality.

In this case, the Juba airport may not be attacked when there would be excessive damage to civilian objects in relation to the anticipated "concrete and direct" military advantage. In the case of Juba in late July and early August 1992, the airport served as the only way in which the relief food on which hundreds of thousands of people were dependent could be delivered. Putting the airport out of commission had a definitely adverse effect on the survival of the civilian population. The real possibility of imminent starvation because of a cutoff of relief supplies, which would be the direct result of an attack on the only access route to Juba, constitutes excessive damage.

As to what military advantage might outweigh this suffering, it must be concrete and direct. "Direct" means "'without intervening condition of agency.' . . . A remote advantage to be gained at some unknown time in the future would not be a proper consideration to weigh against civilian losses."[64] Creating conditions "conducive to surrender by means of attacks which incidentally harm the civilian

---

[62]Military objectives are limited to those objects which by their nature, location, purpose or use make an effective contribution to military action, and whose total or partial destruction, capture or neutralization, in the circumstances ruling at the time, offers a definite military advantage. Protocol I, article 52 (2).

[63]Protocol I, article 51 (5) (b). This codifies the principle of proportionality. See Appendix A.

[64]M. Bothe, K. Partsch, & W. Solf, *New Rules for Victims of Armed Conflicts: Commentary on the Two 1977 Protocols Additional to the Geneva Conventions of 1949* (The Hague: Martinus Nijhoff, 1982), p. 365.

population"[65] is too remote and insufficiently military to qualify as a "concrete and direct" military advantage. "A military advantage can only consist in ground gained and in annilihation or weakening the enemy armed forces."[66]

If there is no ongoing combat in Juba, the SPLA-Torit's "concrete and direct military advantage" in the destruction or neutralization of the airport and all planes landing there is not readily apparent.

The SPLA-Torit would have liked to prevent the Juba garrison from resupplying and bringing in troops by air. Those troops might possibly launch an attack on SPLA-Torit positions, which were on the frontline in Kit many kilometers south of the airstrip. With supplies, the garrison could continue to resist the siege. While this would make the airport a legitimate military target, it does not seem sufficiently "concrete and direct." The possibility that the government would launch an attack from Juba during this period of the rainy season and right after a debilitating SPLA-Torit attack on Juba was not remote and not concrete.

The situation at the time of these attacks on the airport had reverted to the siege which had been in effect for years. While a successful siege would weaken the enemy armed forces, it would also starve civilians. The possibility that the Juba garrison would fall by siege in August 1992 was insufficiently "direct," defined as "without intervening condition of agency,"[67] to justify the excessive cost, in injury and death, to hundreds of thousands of displaced civilians.

If the motivation for the attack was not a strictly military one, but was a mixed political/military motive, such as to impede food deliveries to Juba in order to pressure the U.N. to operate in a more even-handed manner, such an attack would be additionally prohibited. Attacks on relief food for civilians are attacks on civilian objects, not on military objects, and are strictly forbidden.

Finally, the SPLA-Torit's duty to avoid attacks which excessively injure the civilian population is not discharged by its endorsement of evacuation of the town. Such an opportunity for the civilian population

---

[65]International Committee of the Red Cross, *Commentary on the Additional Protocols of 1977* (Geneva: Martinus Nijhoff, 1987), p. 685.

[66]ICRC, *Commentary on the Additional Protocols*, p. 685.

[67]*See* Appendix A.

never occurred, in part because the government did not agree and in part because the town was ringed by government and SPLA mines. Nor would evacuation of such a large and weakened population to another destination on foot during the rainy season be practical. The SPLA-Torit's obligations must be judged according to the actual circumstances of the attack, not the hypothetical circumstances that the SPLA-Torit would prefer. Juba had a desperately needy and trapped population of several hundred thousand at the time of the attacks on its only line of relief supply, the airport.

Therefore, under the specific circumstances of late July and August 1992, the military advantage anticipated from the attacks on the airport does not appear to be sufficiently "concrete and direct" to justify the foreseeable excessive injury to civilians. This shelling of the Juba airport violates the rules of war.

Siege of Garrison Towns by the SPLA-Torit and the Prohibition on Starvation of Civilians as a Method of Combat

The SPLA-Torit on some occasions has attempted to starve civilians as a method of combat, in violation of the rules of war. The attacks on the Juba airport described above may qualify as using starvation of the civilian population as a method of combat.

Customary international law is clear in prohibiting the intentional starvation of civilians as a method of combat. Protocol II, article 14,[68] is declarative of this customary law. It places legal limits on the military tactic of targeting the civilian population by causing it hunger. This prohibition is a rule from which no derogation may be made. No exception was made for imperative military necessity, for instance.

What is crucial is the intention of using starvation as a method or weapon to attack the civilian population.

---

[68]Protocol II, Article 14 -- Protection of objects indispensable to the survival of the civilian population

> Starvation of civilians as a method of combat is prohibited. It is prohibited to attack, destroy, remove or render useless, for that purpose, objects indispensable to the survival of the civilian population, such as foodstuffs, agricultural areas for the production of foodstuffs, crops, livestock, drinking water installations and supplies and irrigation works.

Starvation of combatants, however, remains a permitted method of combat, as in siege warfare or blockades. A siege "consists of encircling an enemy location, cutting off those inside from any communication in order to bring about their surrender."[69] This is theoretically aimed at preventing military matériel from reaching the combatants.

Except for the case where food supplies are specifically intended as provisions for combatants, however, it is prohibited to destroy or attack objects indispensable for civilian survival, even if the adversary may benefit from them.[70] Therefore, even if the army might be diverting civilian relief food, commercializing it or illegally benefiting from it, which has happened in southern Sudan and which is also a violation of the rules of war, relief destined for civilians may not be blocked, confiscated, prevented or destroyed.

Furthermore, under the duty to distinguish civilians from combatants, besieging forces may not close their eyes to the effect upon civilians of a food blockade or siege. It is well recognized that, "in case of shortages occasioned by armed conflict, the highest priority of available sustenance materials is assigned to combatants".[71]

Sieges are a form of starvation by omission. Commentary by the International Committee for the Red Cross notes that:

> Starvation can also result from an omission. To deliberately decide not to take measures to supply the population with objects indispensable for its survival in a way would become a method of combat by default, and would be prohibited under this rule.[72]

The SPLA's intention to starve civilians as a method of combat has been discussed elsewhere. In the period between 1984 and 1988, "The SPLA policy on food relief . . . was straightforward. They were determined to prevent food relief from reaching government-held towns,

---

[69]ICRC, *Commentary on the Additional Protocols*, p. 1457.

[70]*See* Appendix A.

[71]Bothe, *New Rules for Victims of Armed Conflicts*, p. 680.

[72]ICRC, *Commentary on the 1977 Protocols*, p. 1458.

in order to starve the population and force them to surrender or leave."[73] The SPLA surrounded Juba and started to attack the city's airport by mortars and artillery by the end of 1985.[74] The SPLA attacked the various Equatorian tribal militias that were armed by the government such as the Mundari militia in Terekeka and Jemeiza and also retaliated against the civilian Mundari population,[75] in September 1985 driving some 60,000 Mundari out of Terekeka to the safety of Juba.[76] The Mundari militia the next year attacked Dinkas inside Juba, killing scores of civilians.[77]

The SPLA ringed Juba with land mines. During 1987-88, road convoys to Juba were at best intermittent; the SPLA mined the roads and ambushed anything that moved on them.[78] The SPLA also patrolled the outskirts of Juba and captured those who managed to escape the army's

---

[73]Africa Watch, *Denying the Honor of Living*, p. 115. Among the cited actions the SPLA took was refusing permission for a convoy of 60 relief trucks for Juba from Kenya (February 1986); shooting at a UNICEF plane in Wau (March 1986); attacking a food convoy near Nimule, killing nine drivers (June 1986); rejecting the appeal of 10 relief agencies for a food truce to allow relief to reach Juba (June 1986); forcing closure of Juba airport from July to December 1986 by attacks; shooting down a civilian airplane taking off from Malakal, killing 60 (August 1986; as a result, no more airlifts to Wau until December 1988); stating that it will continue to shoot down civilian aircraft (August 1986); threats to shoot down a UN airplane (September 1986). *Ibid.*, p. 116.

[74]Burr, *Genocide*, p. 17.

[75]De Waal, "Starving out the South," p. 161.

[76]Johnson and Prunier, "Foundation and Expansion," p. 130.

[77]Burr, *Genocide*, p. 21.

[78]Africa Watch, *Denying the Honor of Living*, p. 117. In September 1988 an attack killed 23 drivers and their assistants and cut off Juba from overland access for three months. *Ibid.*

clutches, frequently forcibly inducting the young men among them into the SPLA-Torit army.[79]

The displaced population in Juba grew in the early months of 1989 alone by over 50,000 people, because of SPLA destruction and looting of villages in the area.[80] The population of Juba came to be totally dependent on airlifts for most food supplies due to insecurity of overland routes. Until recently, no agreement could be achieved with the parties to the conflict to respect relief convoys moving overland or by river.

One authority notes that from 1986:

> until the start of Operation Lifeline [mid-1989], the siege of Juba by the SPLA contributed to famine conditions, particularly among the up-to-180,000 displaced people in the town. The severity of these conditions increased and decreased with the tightness of the siege and the numbers of displaced people. Perhaps the worst period occurred between June and December 1988, during which time only one overland convoy reached the town, and the airport was open only intermittently.[81]

The SPLA was not the only party responsible. The actions of profiteering merchants and government military officers allied with them also influenced the severity of the situation.[82]

The senior medical officer at the government hospital in Juba claimed in March 1989 that up to two-thirds of Juba's displaced suffered from malnutrition. Even prisoners in Juba jail had died of hunger, and

---

[79]The SPLA has also helped civilians escape from Juba. For instance, in 1990 those who left Juba crossing the White Nile to the east bank said that they did so with SPLA assistance. The SPLA-Torit has not been consistent in this.

[80]de Waal, "Starving out the South," p. 167.

[81]De Waal, "Starving out the South," p. 160.

[82]*Ibid.*, p. 166.

others were dying of disease brought on or complicated by lack of food.[83] In February 1989 ten children were reported to die every day in Juba's two hospitals from famine and disease, and undoubtedly more died at home, too weak to get to the hospitals. This lasted the rest of the year.[84]

In November 1988, in a change of policy, the SPLA called on civilians to leave Juba.[85] The SPLA siege was maintained for all but airlifts, the SPLA permitting ICRC airlifts to reach Juba in December 1988. In March 1989 the SPLA also agreed to Operation Lifeline Sudan, the U.N. relief program, whereby relief food was to reach SPLA-controlled areas as well as government garrison towns.

In January 1990, however, the SPLA threatened to shoot down any planes flying to Juba,[86] but relented after pressure the next month.[87] At the same time, the government cut off relief flights from November 1989 to February 1990.[88]

In 1990, relief agencies operating in Juba registered nearly 190,000 people inside the city in need of food aid; most subsisted on half rations. "Starving people attempting to leave to forage for food in the countryside [were] turned back by the army."[89]

After the SPLA-Torit lost its two battles for Juba in June and July 1992, it continued the siege, including shelling the airport which had served as the only place through which relief supplies could arrive. The shelling abated after an international outcry on behalf of the starving

---

[83]Burr, *Genocide*, p. 39-40.

[84]*Ibid.*, p. 40.

[85]Africa Watch, *Denying the Honor of Living*, p. 77.

[86]In January 1990 the SPLA attacked the airport and headquarters of the army's Southern Command, killing nearly a score of civilians.

[87]Africa Watch, *Denying the Honor of Living*, p. 118.

[88]Burr, *Genocide*, p. 47.

[89]CART, "CART Budget for the Period 1st March 1989 to 28th February 1990," Juba, Sudan, February 1990, quoted in Burr, *Genocide*, p. 47, n. 199.

civilians of Juba, and by early 1993, a WFP relief airlift from Entebbe to Juba was reaching 236,000 beneficiaries.[90]

Since Juba is the largest city in the south and several NGO and U.N. relief agencies have persisted over the years in trying to assist the vast displaced population in Juba, there is perhaps more information and institutional memory in Juba on the roles of all parties in contributing to the extreme hardship suffered by civilians than elsewhere in Sudan. In other government garrison towns under siege, the history is less accessible, especially since the government is hostile to relief efforts not under its control and to human rights organizations that might otherwise document abuses through visits to those towns.[91]

For instance, Torit was under siege by the SPLA from 1986 until it fell in 1989. During the SPLA siege of Torit, the Catholic Church among others had actively advocated the cause of the civilians, and insisted that food be brought in for their relief. The town suffered terribly during the siege; one person affiliated with the Catholic Church told HRW/Africa that they buried 130 people in 1988 who died from hunger while waiting for the relief convoy to arrive. When the convoy finally arrived from Juba, it came with army escort. The SPLA opposed the convoy and accused the government of bringing this convoy into Torit not for civilian use but to feed the garrison. According to the same Catholic Church source, the brigadier of the local government army base refused to take any of that relief. Nor did this brigadier contribute to the famine conditions, by preventing civilians from leaving Torit, as did the army commander in charge of Juba. The Torit army commander permitted Torit residents to come and go from the surrounding villages to look for food. This helped save some people from starvation.

When Torit was taken by the SPLA in 1989, Bishop Paride Taban and three priests of the Catholic Church's Diocese of Torit were arrested

---

[90]USAID/OFDA Situation Report on Sudan, No. 2 (Washington, D.C.: U.S. AID, February 13, 1993), p. 4. A nutritional survey of Juba concluded that the malnutrition rate among children was 12.4 percent, an improvement over the 1992 rate. *Ibid*.

[91]Time-consuming efforts to document (including from relief agency documents) the dynamics of hunger and relief in several locations in south Sudan have paid off, particularly in the writings of de Waal, including but not limited to his study "Starving out the South."

by the SPLA. They were accused of prolonging Torit's resistance to the SPLA siege because they ran a school and dispensary and provided food for the poor. They were accused of feeding the army, which they denied.

The bishop and three priests spent three months in SPLA custody, along with over 100 civilians who flooded into their compound as the SPLA was entering Torit, fearing SPLA retaliation. All these captives were held in Kidepo, just across the border from a large Ugandan national park and river. The priests could sit outside the huts but they could not walk around the village, which was the location for a school run for "unaccompanied minors" by an SPLA foundation,[92] and for SPLA prisoners, including 200 Sudan army soldiers and two officers captured during the fall of Torit. The clergy were released after three months and the civilians were released at about the same time.

The arrest of the clergy for assisting the civilian population of Torit demonstrates the SPLA intention to deprive the civilian population of necessary relief supplies and to punish even those who acted out of humanitarian impulses to relieve the suffering of southerners.[93] The SPLA intended in Torit to use civilian starvation as a method of combat which, combined with other siege tactics, would achieve the military goal of capturing Torit. It is impermissible to so target civilians.

These actions of the SPLA-Torit in Torit and in Juba demonstrate an intention to use starvation of civilians as a method of combat, in violation of the rules of war. It is simply not permissible to target civilians and make them bear the brunt of the war.

Abuses Committed during William Nyuon's Defection from SPLA-Torit and Associated Fighting in Equatoria in late 1992

In fighting between the SPLA-Torit and another breakaway faction in Equatoria in late 1992, a number of serious abuses were committed for which there has been no accounting. In particular the

---

[92]*See* below in this Chapter.

[93]While relations between the SPLA and the Catholic Church have gone through various phases, sometimes bad and more frequently good, those individuals who were arrested by the SPLA were and are regarded with much greater hostility and suspicion by the Khartoum government, which believes that they are effectively SPLA members. Both the government and the SPLA have difficulty with the activities of an institution which is not under their control.

killing of three expatriate relief workers and a Norwegian journalist
during the Nyuon defection remains unexplained by either the SPLA-
Torit or the breakaway Commander William Nyuon Bany faction; neither
has taken serious steps to investigate the events. Nor has the U.N. made
its investigation public. The killers remain at large, enjoying impunity. ✇

There is more information about the killing of these three
expatriate relief workers and one journalist than about most killings in
Sudan, although the information remains incomplete. Attention paid to
foreign deaths does not in any way discount the seriousness of abuses
against Sudanese that have escaped scrutiny. Killings of journalists,
however, make the press less likely to cover the war and the
humanitarian emergency in Sudan. Killings of relief workers may affect
the willingness and ability of U.N. and relief organizations to help
Sudanese victims of the war. In these circumstances, it is even more
disturbing that an official U.N. judgment of responsibility in the case has
never been arrived at or made public by the U.N. No excuse has been
offered for the U.N.'s continuing official muteness on this highly unusual
and well-publicized event.

The Killing of Three Expatriate Workers and a Journalist

William Nyuon and troops sympathetic to him defected from
SPLA-Torit to join the Nasir faction on September 27, 1992, a Saturday.
They departed from the SPLA-Torit headquarters in Pageri, heading
northeast on the road to Magwe.

At about 5 P.M., the first or advance truck of defecting soldiers,
carrying between eighty-five and a hundred men, was ambushed at the
junction to Ame, north of Opari. Some of the defecting soldiers in that
truck said they noticed a small white car passing their truck on the left or
west side, heading south, at the time the ambush commenced from both
sides of the road. The white car was "within the ambush zone."[94] The
truck and the white car were hit by the ambush, and both came to a stop
in the intersection, about five to seven meters apart.

Inside the white car were four expatriates: Myint Maung, resident
project officer for UNICEF (Burmese), Francis Ngure, UNICEF driver
(Kenyan), Vilma Gomez, working with the NGO InterAid (Philippina),

---

[94]Statement from Sgt. James Kueth Jam, taken in Nasir, June 9, 1993, taken
by Jarl Honoré, "Interviews with William Nyuon and Some of His Men about the
Killings at Ame Junction 27.9.92," Nairobi, Kenya, June 30, 1993, p. 7.

and Tron Helge Hummelvoll, a freelance journalist (Norwegian).[95] The three relief workers were last seen alive by their colleagues on the morning of September 27, Saturday, when they left the OLS camp at Loa to visit Palataka, where bombings had been reported the day before.[96] The Norwegian journalist had a few days earlier left Torit and was likely picked up at the Magwe junction by the three relief workers as they were returning to Loa on Saturday night. He had earlier attempted to radio the Norwegian People's Aid, which has an office in the area, for a truck to pick him up, but apparently his message was not received until after his death.

A separate party of William Nyuon's followers who were in Opari heard the shooting and came to the junction and saw the truck and car, but they left without looking inside the car.[97]

A clearing-squad party sent to the ambush area later by Nyuon's troops between 11 P.M. and midnight found the two vehicles, and inside the white car found a man, a "foreigner," alive in the front seat, hanging over the steering wheel, sobbing or sneezing. In the rear seat were two people. (The witness did not mention a fourth passenger, although the woman passenger Gomez was alive at the time.) Dr. Hoguor with the clearing-squad party examined the two in the back seat and pronounced them dead. The party quickly moved on.[98]

Autopsies showed that Maung and Hummelvoll each died of multiple gunshot wounds, probably on September 27, the date of the ambush.[99] It may be that the deaths of the two were unavoidable. They

---

[95]OLS (Southern Sector) Bi-Monthly Situation Report No. 26, September 23 - October 6, 1992, p. 2.

[96]*Ibid.*

[97]Statement from Grant, Honoré, "Interviews with William Nyuon," p. 8.

[98]Statement from Capt. Michael Kuol, Honoré, "Interviews with William Nyuon," p. 10. Dr. Hoguor was not available for interview because he was apprehended by SPLA-Torit in October 1992 and executed, according to Capt. Michael Kud. *Ibid.*

[99]OLS (Southern Sector) Bi-Monthly Situation Report No. 26, September 23 to October 6, 1992, p. 2.

may have been the victims of crossfire; if civilians are in an area of military combat, they assume the risk of injury or death. The ambush was a surprise, as all ambushes are intended to be. Its principal target was a truckful of enemy soldiers, which is a legitimate military target. It would have been the better course of action, for the attackers to have held their fire once they caught sight of a white non-military car in the ambush range, to verify that the car was a legitimate military target and to take reasonable precautions to avoid civilian casualties.

It is not entirely certain, however, that the two were killed in the ambush. As allegedly reported in a UNICEF internal document, an autopsy indicated that they were shot in the back, as if running away.[100]

The white car was found blocking the road and "riddled with bullets," according to those who came on the scene later that night.[101] Others who saw the car later, however, doubted from the condition of the car that anyone had been killed while inside it. There was a lack of blood inside the car, and the angles of the bullets that sprayed the car suggested that the car was shot up without anyone inside it, perhaps in an attempt to create the impression that those inside were killed in crossfire.

On Monday, September 29, the forces of SPLA-Torit delivered the bodies of Maung and Hummelvoll to Nimule to be picked up by the U.N. A staff member of the Aswa Hospital told HRW/Africa that he washed the already dead bodies in the Aswa Hospital on Saturday night, the night of the ambush.

The two foreigners surviving the ambush were missing for several days. Their bodies were delivered to the U.N. on Wednesday, October

---

[100]Reuter saw the early UNICEF report to U.N. headquarters which concluded that two were shot in the back, probably while trying to escape. Andrew Hill, "U.N. Document accuses SPLA of 'Callous' Killings," Reuter, Nairobi, Kenya, October 4, 1992. The BBC was said to have reported, "Post-mortem examinations carried out in Nairobi show that Maung and Hummelvoll were hit several times from the back. One had sixteen wounds, the other six, and the angle of the bullets suggests that they were running away from their captors." *BBC Focus on Africa*, October 1992, cited in "Vital Questions Unanswered," *Sudan Update*, vol. 4, no. 3 (London: October 19, 1992), p.1.

[101]Statement from Grant, Honoré, "Interviews with William Nyuon, p.8.

1, by the SPLA-Torit forces.[102] The two, Mr. Ngure and Ms. Gomez, each died of a single gunshot wound to the head, probably on Tuesday, September 30.[103] The same medical worker who washed the first two bodies at the Aswa Hospital told HRW/Africa that the dead bodies of the two "missing" foreigners were brought to the hospital on Monday evening, which would be September 29, where they were washed.[104] He observed a fresh dressing on a wound on the woman's arm. He believed that she had been treated in the Ame clinic. The wound on the woman's arm was older than the wound on her head.

Those who saw the bodies on the day of their delivery to the U.N., and who knew the victims, said that both the Kenyan driver and the Philippina relief worker had their heads freshly shaved. They both were shot in the head, execution style. They too observed that the woman had an arm wound that had been freshly bandaged.

The conclusion compelled by these facts is that the two were captured and later executed.[105] This makes their deaths a violation of the most elementary rules of war prohibiting summary execution of captured persons.

Apparently the SPLA-Torit had second thoughts about turning over the bodies, because they reportedly tried at the last minute to retrieve them, telling the U.N. workers who came to pick them up that they were "not the right bodies." Since the dead had already been recognized, the bodies were not turned back over to the SPLA-Torit.

---

[102]A statement put out by Elijah Malok of SPLA-Torit shortly after the incident claimed that these bodies were found on a bush road forty-three miles north of the Ugandan border, next to their vehicle. Didrikke Schanche, "Two More Relief Workers Killed in Southern Sudan," Associated Press, Nairobi, Kenya, October 1, 1992.

[103]OLS (Southern Sector) Bi-Monthly Situation Report No. 26, September 23 - October 6, 1992, p. 2.

[104]The autopsy date of death, September 30, is inconsistent with this report of seeing the dead bodies. The autopsy date is an estimate.

[105]The BBC reported, "The examinations carried out on Wilma Gomez and Francis Ngure show that they died later - possibly three days later. Gomez had been shot in the neck, and Ngure in the temple, as if cold-bloodedly killed." *BBC Focus on Africa*, cited in "Vital Questions Unanswered," *Sudan Update*, p.1.

A UNICEF report to the U.N. headquarters allegedly claimed that autopsies of the three aid workers and the journalist refuted the rebel claims they died in crossfire, and concluded that the SPLA tried to mislead the U.N. about the deaths.[106] "'Throughout this sad episode, the SPLA response can be best summarized as callous, obstructive and deliberately committed to misinforming us,'" Reuter quoted the UNICEF report.[107]

Each SPLA faction blamed the other. John Garang said the victims were abducted by the breakaway William Nyuon faction, to cover its tracks. He said that the victims' bodies were found by SPLA-Torit troops.[108] Another SPLA-Torit spokesman, Elijah Malok, said that Nyuon killed Maung and Hummelvoll when they refused to hand over the vehicle, and took Gomez and Ngure with him as he fled the Garang-held region, killing them when the car ran out of gas.[109]

At first, the SPLA-Nasir claimed that the victims had been killed by a Garang ambush.[110] An SPLA-Nasir source later claimed that SPLA-Torit Commander Obote Mamur, a Lotuko, captured the U.N. personnel and killed them on higher orders. During a military confrontation between the troops of Commander William and those of SPLA-Torit in Magwe a few weeks later, Commander William Nyuon's troops claimed to have captured a briefcase belonging to SPLA-Torit Commander Salva Kiir. In the briefcase, they allege, was a radio message regarding the two foreigners who had been captured after the ambush, indicating they were killed as a result of higher orders in the SPLA-Torit.

---

[106]Several journalists obtained a copy of the report. The U.N. refused to release it publicly. Andrew Hill, "U.N. Document Accuses SPLA of 'Callous' Killings," Reuter, Nairobi, Kenya, October 4, 1992. Didrikke Schanche, "U.N. Urges Investigation Into Killings of Aid Workers, Journalist," Associated Press, Nairobi, Kenya, October 8, 1992.

[107]Ibid.

[108]Andrew Hill, "U.N. Document Accuses SPLA of 'Callous' Killings."

[109]Didrikke Schanche, "Two More Relief Workers Killed in Southern Sudan." Many saw the car at the ambush site, however.

[110]Ibid.

HRW/Africa requested a copy of the alleged radio message from SPLA-Nasir but never received it; nor has it been produced to the U.N. Special Rapporteur on Sudan as requested.

In December, 1992, Garang reportedly conceded that his own forces "might" have been responsible.[111] It appears that the two were executed while in custody, probably while in SPLA-Torit custody, although the alternative, that they were killed by the forces of Commander William Nyuon, has not been entirely discarded because no satisfactory public investigation has been concluded.

An immediate result of the killings was the OLS suspension of all its programs in this southern Torit area pending the outcome of U.N. and SPLA-Torit investigations. The U.N. commenced negotiations with the SPLA-Torit for new ground rules that would assure the safety of their workers, which took some time to work out.

In the meantime, the deaths and suspension of OLS activities in the area had an extremely detrimental effect on the displaced civilians. Ms. Gomez had been responsible for a feeding program, which came to a stop with her death. While Norwegian People's Aid did not pull out of the area and a few NGOs and foreigners soon returned with or without safety understandings with the SPLA-Torit forces who controlled the area, their numbers were not adequate to the situation.[112]

There were approximately 100,000 displaced persons in the "Triple A" camps of Ame, Aswa, and Atepi, which were accessible by SPLA-Torit-controlled road from Uganda. In November 1992, Catholic Relief Services decided to begin to bring in relief food by this route.[113] Unfortunately for the displaced, however, the food was not sufficient, and malnutrition worsened. In March 1993, a survey by the U.S. Centers for

---

[111]Scott Peterson, *Daily Telegraph* (London), December 3, 1992, quoted in "Garang Concession on U.N. Killings," *Sudan Update*, vol. 4, no. 6 (London: December 12, 1992), p. 2.

[112]International aid agencies operating in south Sudan are not required to belong to OLS, and some, such as Norwegian People's Aid and Lutheran World Federation, have chosen to remain outside the OLS umbrella. Agencies belonging to OLS are required to adhere to its safety and other guidelines.

[113]OFDA Quarterly Report (Sudan), Nov. 1992-March 1993 (Washington, D.C.: U.S. AID, March 1993), p. 1.

Disease Control conducted in Ame indicated severe child malnutrition and substantial excess mortality, even for the Horn of Africa; one half of child deaths in the forty days preceding the study were attributed to starvation.[114] The OLS returned to work in the area on April 22, 1993, after an agreement with SPLA-Torit regarding respect for relief personnel.[115]

Other Abuses in Equatoria during the Fighting between SPLA-Torit and William Nyuon's Faction

SPLA-Torit forces targeted villages or centers which Commander Nyuon's forces either passed through or took refuge in, in late 1992, including Lopit, Lafon, and Magwe, and areas around Palataka and Ikotos, and burned some villages, killed civilians, and abused some women to punish those civilians believed to have sided with Commander William Nyuon, in violation of the rules of war. As a long-time resident of south Sudan commented, "When people are perceived to support the other side in the conflict, Garang feels they must be punished. This is why villages are burned."

For instance, two Acholi men from Magwe, which was under Garang's control in 1992, said that when William Nyuon defected, his forces passed through Magwe from Pageri, fighting SPLA-Torit forces along the way but not attacking any civilians. Three days after William Nyuon left, Garang's forces attacked the civilian areas Nyuon passed through. The witnesses saw seven civilians executed by the SPLA-Torit then: five young men had their throats cut in Meri, and a small girl and small boy were shot. Several women were sexually abused, including one of the witnesses' younger sisters. Clothes, food, and other items were

---

[114]Centers for Disease Control and Prevention, "Nutrition and Mortality Assessment-Southern Sudan, March 1993," *Morbidity and Mortality Weekly Report*, Vol. 24, No. 16 (Atlanta, Georgia: April 30, 1993), pp. 304-08. The Ame camp, settled first of the three camps in early January, 1992, by people fleeing the Bor Massacre, should have been in best condition because of the availability of farmland and good infrastructure.

[115]That agreement was breached on July 3, 1993, when thirty uniformed SPLA-Torit troops broke into the OLS compound in Nimule at midnight, beat up the guard, and searched the compound for "deserters," holding the terrified U.N. workers at gunpoint.

taken from houses. The houses in Magwe center were not burned because the SPLA forces took them over, but livestock was taken. The goats, chicken, and sheep were taken from the Acholi in the area, who normally do not have cattle, and grain was stolen. The many granaries in Magwe were looted of sesame, sorghum, beans, and millet.

Garang's forces followed William Nyuon to an area nine kilometers away from Magwe, burning houses and killing people. Before burning the houses, the soldiers dismantled the roofs and used the wood for cooking. Garang's troops brought many captives to Magwe center and held them there. The women were released, but some of the men were killed, suspected of supporting William Nyuon. Beginning in November, 1992, Garang's forces began looting items from the Magwe market and attacking women going to the market.

William Nyuon returned to the area in November, 1992, attacking Magwe center one morning and recapturing it. He held it for a week. According to the two witnesses, he did not abuse the civilians. He then returned to the Torit area to fight the Garang forces on the road to Ikotos. Garang re-occupied Magwe after three days. To hide, civilians went to the bush or to Uganda. Garang's forces under Commander Salva Kiir repeatedly thereafter attacked areas around Magwe in raids reported to consist of looting, raping and killing.

Other reports indicate that in January 1993, at Ikotos, William Nyuon forces defeated SPLA-Torit forces, who retaliated by looting the local Acholis of the just-harvested grain and the property of the Catholic Church (Diocese of Torit) in Palataka, including a tractor and Landcruiser.

In pursuit of the William Nyuon forces, the SPLA-Torit then attacked from Obbo village, six miles from Palataka, according to an Acholi resident who was present. They burned grass around Obbo because people were hiding there. Then they burned houses, took four sheep and two chickens, raped many women, cut three people's throats, and shot one person. Some were captured and taken to Palataka. The SPLA-Torit soldiers allegedly charged the families money to release the captives from prison.

The attacks on Obbo continued through at least July 1993. The witness commented that "a unit of soldiers comes almost every day looking to loot." In February 1993, a Garang soldier beat the witness's brother's pregnant wife. She was kicked in the stomach, and later died.

Ethnically-Based Fears of Persecution

As was the case after the Nasir group broke away from the SPLA, the William Nyuon split from the SPLA-Torit aggravated ethnic tensions and led to some targeted killing of people on account of their ethnic origin. Most of the reports received indicate that such attacks took place in SPLA-controlled territory in Eastern Equatoria against Nuers.

In July, 1992, the SPLA-Torit captured some Nuer civilians and held them until the Nuer staff of the Aswa Hospital (in SPLA-Torit territory of Eastern Equatoria, near the Triple A displaced persons camps) intervened and the matter was settled by a higher-up SPLA officer.

Separately but on the same night of William Nyuon's defection, some 1,500 Nuer civilians displaced from Upper Nile living in Atepi displaced persons camp (one of the Triple A camps) abruptly departed. They feared retaliation for Nyuon's defection; he is a Nuer and they had heard about Dinka retaliation against the Nuer after Nuer commander Riek Machar defected the previous year. Many of the Nuer in the Atepi group had suffered harassment and beatings on account of being Nuer. Although there were still Nuer officers in the SPLA-Torit, no ranking Nuer officers were believed to be in the area of the Triple A camps.

In Aswa, the house of the Nuer director of the Aswa Hospital, Dr. Timothy Tutlam, was surrounded on or about November 18, 1992, by armed SPLA-Torit soldiers. Dr. Tutlam, who had received threats from some SPLA-Torit Dinka officers, managed to escape with his life to Uganda, with the help of some SPLA-Nasir combatants he had treated in the Aswa Hospital. The group was detained by Ugandan authorities and kept in isolation from December 2, 1992, to January 4, 1993, until they were delivered to the UNHCR as refugees, following negotiations between the Ugandan government and the UNHCR.

VILLAGE BURNINGS IN EQUATORIA IN EARLY 1993

SPLA in Lafon

Lafon is a Pari settlement in eastern Equatoria consisting of seven villages located around a hill in the middle of a fertile flat plain. The area provides a case study of how the SPLA-Torit gained and then, because of human rights abuses, lost support among Equatorians. The 1993 abuses include looting and burning down the entire seven-village complex and killing and injuring an unknown number of civilians.

Lafon's population in late 1992 was estimated by the OLS at 75,000 plus some 3,000 displaced.[116] The cattle were kept on the hill at night to protect them from Toposa raiders.[117] The Lafon area is considered militarily strategic by both factions of the SPLA because it is the last source of food for those going north and northwest over the desert to Upper Nile and the contested area of Kongor. The Lafon area is fertile and usually produces a good supply of food.

An army garrison was located from 1985-86 in the Lafon Catholic school, vacant since the expulsion of foreign missionaries by the government in 1964.

The SPLA first came to the area in 1985. The villagers responded to the SPLA's message and provided what one called the first battalion of soldiers recruited by the SPLA from Equatoria; many village sons went to Ethiopia for military training at the SPLA bases there. Food in Lafon was shared with the SPLA soldiers, as well. The local Paris who had been trained in Ethiopia returned a year later as SPLA troops and attacked the government army garrison in Lafon in April 1986. The army abandoned Lafon and to date have not returned.[118]

In 1988, the SPLA set up a headquarters in Lafon. The headquarters of the SPLA was transferred to Torit in 1989 after its capture and villagers were required to porter SPLA supplies to Torit, a three-day walk. Villagers complained that they then felt abandoned by the SPLA, despite their considerable contribution in men and food to the capture of Torit. They believed that they were short-changed by the SRRA, the SPLA's relief arm, in medical and other supplies, and they complained that the top administrative and military positions in Torit were filled by Dinka, who are not native to the area.

In Lafon, the Pari, who were traditionally armed with guns bought or bartered from some of the many Ugandan refugees fleeing strife in that country, were "very organized and confrontational"

---

[116]The OLS reported that these included 500 to 1,000 Nuer who fled from Garang-controlled areas. OLS, "Situation Assessment 1992/93," p. 30.

[117]*Ibid.*, p. 29.

[118]*See* Johnson and Prunier, "Foundation and Expansion," pp. 133-34.

according to one observer. The area was never allied with government forces and initially did not take sides when the Nasir group attempted to oust Garang in August, 1991. Some Equatorian commanders, including some Pari, joined the Nasir faction in late 1991.

In 1992, the first crop failed, and the area was badly in need of food relief. Reports from Torit indicated that 18,000 displaced persons from Lafon and Lopit reached Torit in search of grain in June 1992, before it fell to the government. Many of these displaced moved to the Triple A camps.

In October, 1992, a month after Commander William Nyuon defected from the SPLA-Torit, he and his decimated band arrived in Lafon. The local leaders[119] refused to take sides among the SPLA factions, instead urging reconciliation. William Nyuon stayed two weeks in Lafon. Meanwhile, several hundred troops of the Nasir faction moved down from Upper Nile to bolster Nyuon's troops. Together they moved south to engage the SPLA-Torit troops in the Ifoto area. After various clashes, some of which they lost, the SPLA-Nasir and Nyuon troops withdrew again in the direction of Lafon, with SPLA-Torit troops in pursuit.

Attack on Lopit Villages by SPLA-Torit in December 1992

The Garang troops reached Lafon's southern neighbor, Lopit, burning two and looting five villages there on December 25, 1992, and killing three women and four men.[120]

Shortly before the Christmas Day attack on the Lopit village of Ngaboli, two SPLA-Torit officers approached the village and asked a chief to give them goats for their forces. The chief gave them five goats, but the officers insisted they needed all the goats. He refused. The two officers also asked for manpower to fight Riek. The leader refused, saying that the village had no problem with Riek so they did not want to fight him. The soldiers asked about William Nyuon. The chief replied that he had seen some men passing in the distance but he did not know the

---

[119]Authority among the Pari is exercised by the "Majomiji" or ruling age graders.

[120]Ngaboli and Longiro (total population 2,000) were looted and every house burned, and Hurumo, Khaba and Akhamiling (total population 3,000) were looted but not burned, according to a chief.

whereabouts of William Nyuon. That same morning the leader was told by two village women that they had just been raped by the Garang soldiers, so he asked the emissaries, "What is wrong with you men of Garang? Why are you raping women?" The officers had sharp words with the chief and left.

Shortly thereafter, at about 8 A.M., the soldiers opened fire on the village and the people scattered, according to several men of the village. The soldiers looted all the property and food in five villages, removing it in five lorries, then set fire to the houses in two villages. As a result, the villagers had to eat wild fruit from the bush; four people died from hunger and sickness.

This SPLA-Torit force then moved north in the direction of Lafon, joining another Garang force in the Lopit Mountains less than twenty miles from Lafon.[121]

Attack on Lafon in January 1993

From this mountain area, on January 4, 1993, SPLA-Torit shelled Lafon with long-range artillery. Even those present do not agree whether William Nyuon and his troops were still in Lafon at that time, but it is clear that they had been staying there just prior to the attack, some sleeping under a tree near the unrepaired Catholic compound.

The SPLA-Torit, under the command of Isaac Obutu Mamur and Pieng Deng Kuol, and William-Nasir forces clashed between Lopit and Lafon, and the SPLA-Torit prevailed. Commander William Nyuon was advised by the Pari leadership to leave the area to avoid further harm to the civilians, and he withdrew west in the direction of Lirya, a government-controlled town.

The villagers meanwhile had fled the Garang attack to their fields, several hours away. Local Pari task forces and officers, created by the SPLA years before to protect Lafon, fled as civilians with their families to the bush. They put up no resistance and did not take sides.

---

[121]One version of the events of December 1992 in Lafon, told by some villagers, is that Garang's forces came December 15, seeking the support of the area in the form of recruits, which the leaders declined to give them. The troops demanded bulls and grain, and took "twelve stables" of cattle, one stable being from 500 to 4,000 head of cattle. Other accounts do not mention a Garang presence in Lafon in the two months before it was shelled on January 4, 1993.

A chief told HRW/Africa that thirty-one villagers were killed during this January 4, 1993, attack on the Wiatwe village, one of the seven Lafon villages around the hill. People were still sleeping when the surprise attack was launched. Two women neighbors in the same village said that after the attack their tukls were looted of all their grain and personal items, including cooking utensils, then burned. All of the livestock both families possessed was taken.

A fifty-year-old woman from another Lafon village said that two of her sons, nine-year-old Otar and eighteen-year-old Okidi, were killed when gunshots were fired during this January attack. After the rest of the family fled, the soldiers looted thirty-nine cows, goats, and sheep from her family; burned the house; stole the groundnuts, sesame, and cowpeas; and burned the granaries of the village. "They took everything. Now we have to go to a feeding program to survive," she said.

It is difficult to know how many civilians were killed during the shelling of Lafon, but the local RASS,[122] the relief wing of SPLA-Nasir, put the number at 114. Some houses nearest the Norwegian Church Aid (NCA) compound were damaged in the shelling.[123] The SPLA-Torit forces entered an empty Lafon and occupied the NCA compound.

The villagers did not return to Lafon, fearing a counterattack by William Nyuon. During the first month that they lived in the bush, many villagers died of diseases, including malaria. The SPLA-Torit commander in Lafon, Piang Deng, used threats to force the Pari civilians to return.

SPLA-Torit Burning and Looting of Lafon in February 1993

A chief said that on February 8 the SPLA-Torit and the Pari leadership celebrated a new agreement at a ceremony. Bulls were brought to the SPLA, which promised peace, food, and no further problems. Based on the promises, many began to return to the areas.

Two days later, however, the peace was shattered. On or about February 9, 1993, Commander William Nyuon apparently tried to approach the NCA compound that was serving as an SPLA-Torit base. From over the hill, he shelled the SPLA-Torit positions at the compound

---

[122]The Relief Association of Southern Sudan.

[123]As a result of military insecurity in the area, in 1985 NCA, which had built a large brick complex and operated a development program in Lafon, pulled out.

before being repulsed by Garang forces. Most civilians fled again from the crossfire.[124]

After the Nyuon forces left, the SPLA-Torit commander took revenge on the Lafon population, looting their deserted homes and burning down all the houses in the seven villages. Nothing remained standing except for the NCA buildings, some brick stores deserted by Arab traders almost a decade earlier, and the crumbling brick Catholic compound. Reportedly thirty-seven people were burned to death in their houses, wells and water sources (with the exception of two hand pumps) were poisoned and six women were raped. No captives or prisoners were taken.

RASS officials in Nairobi estimated the dead during this attack at ninety-eight civilians, including the burn victims.[125] Among the items looted were valued costumes of ostrich feathers and leather skins used in Pari traditional dancing.

At some point, SPLA-Torit sent a Pari commander and Pari soldiers to meet with the leadership, but it was too late--the village had turned against that faction because of the extensive destruction and looting of Lafon. The villagers built huts in the fields and stayed there. When the SPLA-Torit troops based in Lafon raided a Pari cattle camp, the Pari put up armed resistance.

In April, the SPLA-Torit forces pulled out of Lafon, heading in the direction of Kongor, which other SPLA-Torit forces had just recaptured. The SPLA-Nasir troops entered Lafon shortly thereafter, staying only a few days. At last report the Pari of Lafon remained estranged from SPLA-Torit.

The Didinga of Chukudum

The Didinga are a small Equatorian tribe living on the Sudan side of the Ugandan border, separated by high mountains from the Sudanese

---

[124]The accounts of February 9, 1993, in Lafon are not consistent. Some villagers say that SPLA-Torit attacked the village, without mentioning the presence of Commander William Nyuon. We conclude that the most likely truth is that Nyuon tried to attack the SPLA-Torit base.

[125]The numbers are not consistent. RASS officials in Lafon say that 179 people were killed in the January attack, and in the February attack fifty-nine were shot to death and eighty-three were burned inside their huts.

towns of Torit and Kapoeta. In the 1983 census the Didinga numbered 68,000.[126] In 1993, several hundred Didinga families fled their homes because of SPLA-Torit abuses, including summary executions, looting, and the burning of three villages. A refugee said they had fled "because we were chased by Arab bombs and by the people with us, the SPLA. They fight the common man instead of the enemy."

In Eastern Equatoria, many small tribes nursed grievances against the SPLA-Torit, which they saw as Dinka-dominated and heavy-handed in its relations with the civilian population. Villagers noted that in 1993 the SPLA commander in Chukudum was Salvator Achuel and in Lotukei was Salva Matong, both Dinka.[127]

Food Confiscation

When the SPLA first came to the fertile farming area, the Didinga willingly gave food to the SPLA. "Civilians here contributed food and treated them nicely. We contributed goats and cows in the beginning," a refugee told HRW/Africa. "Suddenly, things changed. They wanted one tin of flour per day per family. It was like a timetable."

Refugees complained that they were harassed by the SPLA when they were trying to plant and that even children were forced to porter food to the SPLA bases. A refugee told HRW/Africa about the relentlessness of the soldiers:

> There was no time they failed to come. Some of the soldiers did not follow orders and took two tins instead of one. They would usually bring a container or basin and order each family, 'Fill this with grain.' They came constantly, they never stopped. People could not refuse them. If people told them they had nothing, the soldiers would enter the house just to see if it was really empty.

---

[126]The 1983 census for the largest Didinga town, Chukudum, was 58,550, without a tribal breakdown.

[127]Although government troops had been absent from the Didinga area after it was occupied by the SPLA in 1985, the area hosted SPLA military bases in the two largest Didinga towns, Chukudum and Lotukei. These bases were the targets of government aerial bombardment at least three times in early 1993, with civilian casualties. See Chapter III.

In 1986, a village man was killed by the soldiers when he protested. After this killing, the man's family and others moved to the mountains, where they could watch the approach of SPLA patrols and have time to hide their grain and cows. Little by little, more people fled SPLA harassment and moved to the mountains from the villages. Many would sleep in the hills and return to their fields to cultivate. The SPLA would go to the hills where the people had relocated, track them down and ask for food.

Forced Recruitment

At first, many young men went to join the SPLA voluntarily, but in 1992, the SPLA came and recruited the young men by force. "They did not even ask the chief. They just surrounded the village and took all the young men they could find," a refugee said. As a result, many men hid from the SPLA patrols. When the men refused to go, the SPLA took cows and goats from their families. The recruited men were not deployed to fight in the area, but very far away.

A Didinga man said that the SPLA tried to recruit him in Lotukei because he is a skilled worker. He told them he could not leave his wife and children.

Village Burnings and Summary Executions

The SPLA-Torit surrounded the cattle camp of the village of Lamoja near Lotukei in July 1992 during the day, and started shooting. There was no resistance. Two men and a boy guarding their cattle were shot dead. One man was wounded and is now lame. The SPLA-Torit soldiers then stole the cattle.

Lothiathei, a village near the road to Lotukei, was known locally as a place where people were held in detention by the SPLA-Torit. It was also the home of a Didinga subchief who was working with the SPLA, and it was a source of food for the SPLA.

An SPLA-Torit soldier formerly based there volunteered that he fought "against the Didinga civilians" in Lotukei in July 1992. He said the civilians had harassed and killed some SPLA-Torit troops that month. He confirmed that in Lothiathei the SPLA-Torit looted and burned Didinga houses, killed some Didinga men, and captured four of them, three of whom escaped and the last of whom was released.[128]

In March, 1993, the SPLA-Torit attacked the village, injuring civilians and looting and burning civilian property. One resident was awakened by shooting. The villagers, who were unarmed (they had never been formed into a militia by the SPLA-Torit) ran for their lives. Five were injured. The soldiers entered the village and burned sixteen of the huts and the grain storehouses.[129] Some of the grain was looted and some was burned. About 715 goats were also looted. "People are now very hungry," one refugee said.

The situation grew more tense when, also in April, 1993, four men were arrested and summarily executed by the SPLA-Torit in Chukudum. Two of the victims had gone to Chukudum to shop and were arrested there during the day. Witnesses saw the SPLA-Torit tie them up and take them away. "You know you're dead when they do that," said one.

The following day, the relatives and others searched for the missing and found their bodies "beyond the airstrip" of Chukudum, in the direction where the SPLA-Torit took them. A witness who saw the bodies said both were tied with their elbows behind them and one had his head cut off. The second had his throat cut. The witness did not know their names but he recognized them as men from the village of Moneta.

At the end of the month, a man named Lokekono left Kikilei to cut wood for his house. On his way to Chukudum he was arrested by SPLA-Torit soldiers, in front of witnesses. He was killed and his body left on the road to Lotukei, where his relatives and others found it the next morning. A member of this group said that the victim had suffocated to death on cotton that had been placed in his mouth to muffle his cries.

The fourth victim, a man named Popo, left Lorema to visit a friend in Chukudum on April 29, 1993. He was arrested in Chukudum and brought to Lotukei, forty kilometers away. He was charged falsely, "with no evidence," according to a woman relative. The chiefs, alerted to his arrest, went to the SPLA-Torit commander and complained. The

---

[128]He volunteered this information in the course of an interview on another topic and prior to HRW/Africa interviews with the Didinga.

[129]During this village burning, the home of the subchief who was collaborating with the SPLA-Torit was not spared.

SPLA-Torit commander wanted to know why they were helping the man. The same night, the soldiers of SPLA-Torit tied him behind a truck in Chukudum and dragged him along the road to Lotukei. His dead body was left near Lotukei, where his relatives found it the next morning and buried it.

Buthi, in the outskirts of Chukudum, was burned on or about April 10, 1993. Witnesses, who saw the burning from a distance at night, were too afraid to approach. They were later told that two women and four men had been killed by the SPLA-Torit when it attacked the village.

Another village burning was in Kikilei, twelve miles east of Chukudum, in May, 1993, and three women killed. The SPLA-Torit suspected villagers of "being linked to the Arabs," according to one.

The soldiers surrounded the village at 4 A.M. and started shooting mortars and rifles; the surprised residents fled. Two women were shot dead and one was injured inside a hut that was burned; she died later of her injuries. A total of seventy-five houses with their contents were burned. Only a very few houses were left standing. "Thousands" of cows were stolen. A man in a village twenty kilometers away saw the smoke from the burning village and heard the shooting starting at 4 A.M. The SPLA-Torit said that they had "taken action against some specific individuals" in the village because they were suspected of laying land mines in the road for the SPLA-Torit.

The villagers reacted fiercely, especially to the deaths of the women. When an Oxfam/USA team carrying meningitis vaccine and drugs to Chukudum came up the road in an unmarked car a few days later, the villagers ambushed the car, mistaking it for an SPLA-Torit vehicle. The driver was shot in the foot. The three other occupants were uninjured but spent the day hiding in the bush until the misunderstanding was sorted out.[130] The car was completely vandalized and looted, including the radio which was later returned. The villagers were deeply chagrined to find they had mistakenly attacked the vehicle of an agency that had assisted the area for years.

---

[130]Telephone interview, Rob Buchanan, Oxfam/USA, June 11, 1993.

FACTION FIGHTING IN 1993 IN THE UPPER NILE

The government did not launch its customary dry season offensive in early 1993, perhaps watching the U.S./U.N. troop movement into Somalia in late 1992. The government undertook a diplomatic offensive at the same time, probably another factor in deciding not to pursue a large military offensive.

Unfortunately the civilians of Upper Nile had no respite from the war. Faction fighting of 1991-92 displaced hundreds of thousands and killed, through hunger and disease, countless thousands more in the Upper Nile areas of Waat, Ayod, and Kongor, earning that zone the name of the "Hunger Triangle." While many other areas of southern Sudan also deserved that label in the past ten years of war, events in this Hunger Triangle which encompasses the fought-over Duk Ridge were better documented because the government ceased its usual obstruction of relief, allowing the OLS and NGOs to step in. Southern Sudanese continued to die at each other's hands in stepped-up faction fighting in early 1993, but during this period there were outside witnesses.

What the outsiders saw when they arrived was the most dire situation of hunger in the world. WFP Executive Director Catherine Bertini was among those who sounded the alarm.

> The needs for emergency assistance in southern Sudan should have the highest priority because nowhere else in the world are people in such dire straits. . . . The situation in some parts of Sudan is absolutely bleak with starvation rampant in the south.[131]

The WFP was not receiving enough money from the international community to "stop starvation on a massive scale," she said, despite the fact that the agency at last had access to the victims.

The OLS summarized the situation of especially vulnerable groups at the end of 1992 and the beginning of 1993.[132] Many of those groups had been subjected to indiscriminate attacks and had

---

[131]WFP News Release, "WFP appeals for more food and funds for Southern Sudan," Nairobi, Kenya, April 6, 1993.

[132]OLS, "Situation Assessment 1992/93," p. 6.

suffered hundreds of dead and wounded as well as extensive property looting and damage during the faction fighting and the 1992 government attacks. This stepped-up fighting, conducted in violation of the rules of war, seriously interfered with the civilians' self-help efforts and international attempts to help them bridge the hunger gap.

The groups that the OLS designated especially vulnerable in late 1992, and who suffered even more because of human rights abuses in 1993, included:

- the people of Bor, Kongor, Waat, and Ayod, totalling 165,000. In 1993, Kongor was attacked twice (once by each faction) and Ayod burned to the ground once by SPLA-Torit. The village of Yuai (population 15,000) in the same area was attacked and burned down twice by SPLA-Torit;

- the 25,000 people in Panaru district, western Upper Nile, stricken with a Kala Azar epidemic. In 1993, planes bringing medicine to them were looted, and those Dinka attempting to walk five days to a medical center for help were attacked by SPLA-Nasir;

- a total of 7,150 unaccompanied minors entirely dependent on outside assistance and in camps at Nasir, Moli, Borongolei, and Palataka. The minors at Moli and Borongolei were "evacuated" by SPLA-Torit for their "safety" in early 1993, but it is believed that they were inducted into the SPLA-Torit as soldiers; the minors in Palataka continued to scrape by in an area of increasing combat between SPLA-Torit and William Nyuon troops until they were evacuated in early 1994;

- about 700,000 persons living in east bank Equatoria[133] and those living along the boundary of the Nasir/Torit faction split, where the faction fighting continued to flare;

- some 220,000 displaced persons at the Triple A camps (Ame, Aswa, Atepi) and at other displaced camps in Yondu, Aguran, Mundri, and Yambio. A government offensive in July-August 1993 resulted in the displacement of Yondu; Mundri was bombed several times by the government; and by mid-1994 the Triple A camps were deserted because of the 1994 government offensive.

---

[133]This number includes about 250,000 people in Juba.

• vulnerable groups in Bahr El Ghazal and western Upper Nile, numbering about 380,000 persons. They were subjected in 1993 to government scorched earth attacks from garrison towns such as Yirol and Rumbek, and by 1994 the population had rapidly deteriorated.[134]

The New Sudan Council of Churches issued a letter of appeal to the SPLA leaders on February 4, 1993, highlighting the desperate situation of the civilian population, which was brought about, in large part, by the faction fighting and faction abuses against the civilian population. It asked that no SPLA soldier do any "violence against any civilians. Commanders should move their soldiers out of populated areas toward the front lines and maintain the soldiers under strict discipline."[135]

The SPLA leadership ignored the appeal, and the factional violence worsened. On March 27, 1993, the SPLA-Torit attacked a gathering of all dissident leaders in Kongor and then pushed north into Nuer territory, burning and looting and killing civilians.

In May 1993, the SPLA-Torit and the government unilaterally declared cease-fires in preparation for their peace talks in Abuja, Nigeria. On May 28, 1993, the factions agreed to a cease-fire and military pull-back forty-five kilometers from the airstrips at Kongor, Waat, Yuai, and Ayod. This lasted no more than a few weeks, however. In late July, as the government-SPLA-Torit cease-fire was broken by a government attack around Yei in Equatoria, the SPLA-Nasir/United attacked Kongor but did not hold it.

Although both factions continued to deny that the fighting was tribal in nature, combatants and civilians on both sides increasingly viewed and expressed it as such. For example, a journalist saw the following message on a blackboard in the Hunger Triangle: "1993 is the year for the Dinka and Nuer to fight to elimination."[136]

---

[134] Medecins Sans Frontier press release, "Medical Aid Group Says the Stage is Set for a New Humanitarian Disaster in Sudan," New York, May 24, 1994.

[135] The Church Leaders of Southern Sudan, "Letter of Appeal to the SPLA Leaders," Nairobi, Kenya, February 4, 1993.

[136] *Newsweek* (New York), July 19, 1993, p. 12.

One mitigating factor, however, in a "Dinka versus all other southern tribes" breakdown fostered by the Sudan government was the emergence in early 1993 of several SPLA Dinka leaders from long-term imprisonment by SPLA-Torit. (*See* below in this Chapter) Having no love lost for Garang's leadership, these Dinka leaders aligned themselves with SPLA-United,[137] as it was called after the March 27, 1993, meeting of SPLA-Nasir and other dissidents in Kongor. They carried the message to Dinka and non-Dinka areas alike that the struggle within the SPLA was not tribal but one of the principles (independence of the south versus union with the north) and/or personalities (John Garang).

Pariang 1993, Kala Azar Epidemic Worsened by Nuer and Government Raids

It is impossible to single out any area of south Sudan as the most pathetic, but certainly western Upper Nile illustrates how human rights abuses can make a bad situation--in this case, an epidemic--so much worse for civilian victims.

In western Upper Nile, the largely Dinka population was stricken by an epidemic of Kala Azar disease (visceral Leishmaniasis) some years ago. The disease is caused by a parasite and transmitted to humans by sandflies whose habitat is the forest (red acacia seyal trees). Kala Azar was a growing problem in this region in the early 1980s, even before the war.

The fighting contributed considerably to the spread of the disease. The population of Pariang, in Panaru district, western Upper Nile,[138] estimated in early 1993 at 25,000,[139] fled to the forest for two reasons: food and security. Their cattle were almost all raided by the Arab militia supported by elements in the government or by Nuer raiders. Other cattle died of disease.

Losing their cattle wealth was compounded in some areas by a very poor harvest, forcing people into the forest to search for wild fruits to eat. The forest was also a place to hide from several serious threats: recurring attacks by the Arab militia and Nuer raiders; continuous

---

[137]To avoid confusion, we refer in this report to the group formed after March 27, 1993 as SPLA-Nasir/United.

[138]*See* Western Equatoria and Bahr El Ghazal map, facing Chapter III.

[139]OLS "Situation Assessment 1992/93," p. 6.

fighting between SPLA-Torit and the government in the northern part of Panaru and in the southern Nuba mountains in 1992; government troops making incursions in 1992 from the main north-south road[140] eastward toward the airstrip at Nyarweng village; and continuous low-level fighting between the two SPLA factions along the Bahr el Ghazal river south of Nyarweng.[141]

There are no medical facilities in the area at all. The nearest treatment center for Kala Azar is in Duar, a five-day walk south of the Panaru county airstrip at Nyarweng, in a predominately Nuer area. The Dinka from Panaru county have been unable to travel to the Duar medical center because Nuer have engaged in looting of Dinka along the route. Some Dinka attempting the journey have been shot.

As a result, according to a doctor, perhaps as much as 70 percent of the population has died of Kala Azar in the four years from 1989-93. Several hundred children in the area have been orphaned by the disease.[142] The assessment team concluded that the medical situation in Panaru County was critical, and that Kala Azar would wipe out nearly the entire population in the next several years if there were no intervention.[143]

In August 1993, a U.N. assessment team visited the Pariang area of Panaru district, estimated population then 30,000. There was still no Kala Azar treatment available due to looting of medical supplies by Nuer,

---

[140]Government convoys between Kadugli (in the Nuba mountains of South Kordofan) to the north and Bentiu (in Upper Nile) to the south traveled this road, which runs along the western side of Panaru district.

[141]OLS, "Situation Assessment 1992/93," p. 16.

[142]WFP, "Joint WFP/UNICEF Assessment Report," Pariang, January 16-18, 1993, Nairobi, Kenya, p. 1-2.

[143]*Ibid.*, p. 5.

they were told.[144] As of February 1994, permission was denied for planes to land in Pariang.[145]

On January 21, 1994, a Kola Azar project in Niemne was evacuated after an attack in which three were killed. Nevertheless, due to agency action, it appeared that the epidemic was abating and the number of patients in the three threatment centers decreased from 4,000 in 1992 to 1,500 in 1993.[146]

Kuac Deng Attacked by SPLA-Torit Twice in Early 1993

Kuac Deng, the seat of a court and a six-hour walk south of Ayod, is well into the Nuer-Dinka front line and therefore in the center of the "Hunger Triangle." It is east of the Jonglei Canal and the Duk Ridge. Its mainly Nuer population moved north to Ayod, Bie, and Canal court centers in 1992. It was estimated that the population of Kuac Deng was once 14,000, but by the time of a food assessment in late 1992, most residents had been displaced.[147]

As always, some civilians trickled back to what had been their homes. One of the Kuac Deng chiefs was among them, and he was there when Kuac Deng was attacked three times by SPLA-Torit forces in 1993: January, February, and April. He said that during the January 1993 attack, Garang's forces opened fire with machine guns, bazookas, and howitzers. The chief described the ferocity of the attack as follows: "They burned every tukl in the village, and killed women and children. My

---

[144]U.N. Situation Report, July 29 - August 25, 1993, Khartoum, Sudan (New York: United Nations, 1993), p. 3. In October 1993 the World Health Organization launched an appeal for Kala Azar in eastern and southern Sudan, and asked for $4.4 million to treat the 30,000 cases in the area. U.S.AID/OFDA Situation Report for Sudan, No. 8 (Washington, D.C.: U.S. AID, January 14, 1994), p. 3. Other health problems reported were AIDS (12.5 percent of southern Sudanese are reported to be HIV positive) and a polio epidemic in Duar. *Ibid.*

[145]OLS (Southern Sector) Situation Report No. 53, February 1-15, 1994, p. 5.

[146] Medecins Sans Frontier Research Centre, "Sudan: Report on Humanitarian Situation in Southern Sudan," New York, March 15, 1994, p. 7.

[147]OLS, "Situation Assessment 1992/93," p. 27.

brother was killed in his tukl with his four children." The troops killed some men after capture and interrogation and others when they were running away. Some of the villagers set off for Malakal, but one of Garang's commanders intercepted and killed them all, the chief claimed. The soldiers took at least sixty women and children from Kuac Deng, including the chief's daughter and his brother's wife. The chief said that Garang's forces stole everything, including the chief's uniform and his 250 livestock. In all, the village lost nearly 6,000 head of cattle. The troops also spoiled the water reserve of the village by putting a dead body in it. They burned the grain and seeds.

People who escaped from the January 1993 attack returned to the village and lived in camps "near the water places" with their remaining cattle. A month later, an SPLA-Torit advance unit captured some boys and forced them to lead the troops to the camps. The troops shot into the crowd and took all the cattle. They also attacked the village of Deet and its cattle camp and looted all the property. According to the chief, soldiers rounded up whomever they could, put grass on top of them, and burned them alive. They killed forty women and children like this.

Panyakur and Kongor, Occupied by SPLA-Nasir in Late 1992

As 1993 opened, Riek's forces occupied districts at least as far south as Kongor in the Dinka territory of Upper Nile. The troops moved into the Upper Nile vacuum,[148] fanning out from Kongor to other Dinka areas such as Jonglei and Paliau, south of Kongor, and Duk Faiwil, to the north. At the time that the OLS airlifts began in early 1993, SPLA-Nasir/Unity controlled all three points on the "Hunger Triangle" (Kongor, Ayod, and Waat) as well as Akobo to the east.

After the brutal raids by SPLA-Nasir, Anya-Nya II, and the Nuer White Army of late 1991, many Dinka civilians who had returned home fled again when they heard the Nuer forces were returning. They suspected that the Nuer were returning in order to expel them from their lands. A chief from Jonglei village told HRW/Africa that he believed that "Riek told them [the Nuer forces] to go to the land of the Dinka, [which is] to be your land; I do not want any Dinka to be on this side of the river

---

[148]The government had taken the towns of Bor and Yirol in 1992. The SPLA-Torit was occupied in Equatoria with the fighting following the defection of Commander William Nyuon after September 1992, and the main SPLA-Torit forces were still engaged in the siege of Juba.

[the east bank of the White Nile]." The chief took a small canoe, crossed the White Nile, and hid on the west bank when he heard in February 1993 that the Nuer were coming back.[149]

Not all civilians could or would leave, but those who were still living in the area were in very bad condition. The U.N. was aware of the high death rate there and told the SPLA factions that if protection could be organized for the relief workers, U.N. relief operations would begin.[150]

A relief assessment team visiting Kongor in December 1992, for the first time in over a year, found a complete lack of foodstocks. Massive flooding from April to October 1991 had prevented planting and subsequent harvests. The tribal conflict with massive loss of life and looting of cattle in late 1991 had forced people to flee. There was no trade in the area whatsoever nor had there been any since before the floods in 1991. People were not fishing in the toic because it was too difficult in the absence of cattle or mosquito nets; malaria is very common in the toic. (Cattle dung is burned at night to keep off the mosquitos.)

Jean Luc Siblot, the WFP emergency coordinator who visited the Kongor area, said, "In my six years of work all over Southern Sudan, I have never seen people survive for so long on what amounts to almost nothing."[151] The relief team concluded that Kongor was a disaster area:

> Perhaps one third of the original population remains, some 30,000. The rest have either fled south or have died. An average of four people in every household of

---

[149]In December 1992, "Riek himself came" to Paliau south of Kongor, another man said. He and his relatives fled to the toic before the Nasir forces arrived.

[150]As of late 1992, there was still no resolution of the killing of the four expatriates in Equatoria in September 1992, nor were any new ground rules worked out with the SPLA-Torit faction.

[151]WFP, News Release, "Assessment Mission to Southern Sudan Reveals Hunger Within Ghost-Town Like Atmospheres," Nairobi, Kenya, December 18, 1992. The area around the airstrip at Panyakur, ten kilometers southeast of Kongor, was assessed.

seven died in 1992--there are no infants left. There are
no cows, there is no grain; the people are living on fruit.
Malnourishment is evident not just in the children, but
in adults of all ages.[152]

The area suffered also because of the deliberate blockage of relief by the
government. "Insecurity and lack of flight permission meant no
humanitarian assistance reached Kongor in 1992," the OLS noted.[153]

In late February 1993, a UNICEF field officer was stationed in
Kongor. Programs were expanded in March after 65 percent of the
children in Kongor were found by UNICEF to be severely malnourished.
The survey also found many adults were weak and frail; they began to
receive therapeutic feeding at a feeding center run by the Irish NGO,
Concern. New arrivals, mainly from Pok Tap to the north, were also
weak.[154] The Centers for Disease Control visited Kongor in March
1993, and concluded that the "prevalence rates of severe
undernutrition...are among the highest ever documented."[155]

---

[152]OLS, "Assessment Report/Kongor," Nairobi, Kenya, December 22, 1992,
p. 2.

[153]OLS "Situation Assessment 1992/93," p. 10.

[154]OLS (Southern Sector) Bi-Monthly Situation Report No. 35, February 21 -
March 24, 1993, p. 4.

[155]CDC, "Nutrition and Mortality Assessment, Southern Sudan," p. 306. The
CDC surveyed three sites in southern Sudan. Unlike the surveys in Ame and
Ayod, the survey in Kongor was not done on a house to house basis but only
from a sample of children who gathered at the U.N. compound in response to
messages from local relief officials and therefore might not have been
representative of all children in the area, as the CDC pointed out. *Ibid.*, p. 305.

Duk Faiwil Attacked by SPLA-Nasir in February/March 1993

A Duk Faiwil chief was present in February 1993 when "the Nuer" returned. "Even Riek came with them," he said. The chief fled to the toic,[156] and when he returned two months later he found that the houses, rebuilt after the last raid, had been burned and some people had died inside them; a total of fifteen civilians were killed. No cattle had been in the village since prior raids. The SPLA-Nasir forces stayed only three days and burned the houses as they left.

SPLA-Nasir Occupation of Panyakur/Kongor in Early 1993

The SPLA-Nasir troops that passed through Duk Faiwil in February continued south into Dinka territory to Panyakur and Kongor, where they stayed for about two months. During that time, Dinka civilians in Panyakur and Kongor complained, the SPLA-Nasir forces committed abuses, including killings, kidnapping of women, beatings, and theft of food.

The U.N. began to deliver food at a time when SPLA-Nasir was in control of the Kongor area. Their hunger overcoming their mistrust and fear of the "Nuer" forces, many Dinka nevertheless walked from the toic, a two- or three-day journey, to the airstrip in Panyakur for the food distribution.

A chief in Kongor district tried to keep track of civilian deaths during the SPLA-Nasir occupation of Panyakur and Kongor in early 1993. "When Riek came and stayed for two months in Panyakur, he killed so many people," he claimed.[157] Some of the victims were killed during the attack, some captured later and then killed. He found the

---

[156]Right before the SPLA-Nasir forces arrived, about 200 people, mostly women and children, were living in Duk Faiwil. The civilians fled into the toic, crossed the White Nile or dispersed in various directions to hide before Riek came. When Rieks forces were routed from Kongor, they pulled back north to Nuer territory in late March. Then the civilians returned to Duk Faiwil.

[157]He listed twenty names: Boul Daw, Malwal Anyang, Gurec Kuot, Majak Mayen, Lual Duot, Deng Adow, Majak Kuol, Kuany Ngot, Nyan Deng (a pregnant woman), Adaw Pager (with a new infant), Kual Ater (with two small children), Apajok Mayom (older woman), Achol Akodum, Mayang Ngan Kual (older), Daw Lual, Nuandeng Kual (girl), Pajok Mayam (a woman in her twenties), Adut Deng, Adit Akui, Ngandeng Anyang, Awak Deng.

bodies of some. The relatives of others reported the deaths to him as chief.

The Riek forces reportedly captured many women and girls. They were taken away and none had returned as of the time of the interview, several months later. The captured women included three young unmarried girls.

A man from Duk Faiwil, Ruot Atem, was beaten by the SPLA-Nasir forces and died three days later. He was beaten when these forces came her²at night and asked him why he had not "reported" the presence of his daughter, then took her away. A friend of Ruot's commented on the message imparted in such beatings: "This is why others fear to talk if their daughters are taken in their presence. They say nothing."

Kongor Captured by SPLA-Torit on March 27, 1993

On March 27, 1993, the SPLA-Torit led by Commander Bior Ajang Duot under the overall command of Kuol Manyang Juk[158] attacked Kongor and succeeded in driving out the SPLA-Nasir forces. Reportedly between sixty and eighty-one people, the majority of them civilians, were killed during the fighting.[159] A U.N. relief worker was brutalized and nearly killed by SPLA-Torit troops.

The SPLA-Nasir called a political meeting in Kongor for March 27, which many SPLA dissidents, up to 5,000, attended. The purpose of the meeting was to unify all factions in a new movement to be called "SPLA-United." The leadership of the SPLA-Torit took umbrage at the choice of Kongor for this political meeting, since it is a Dinka area close to John Garang's birthplace, and took advantage of the publicized gathering of their enemies to attack.

Four relatives of Arok Thon Arok, a Dinka SPLA long-term political prisoner who escaped in late 1992 and was in Kongor for the

---

[158]"Death in the Sudd," *Africa Confidential*, Vol. 34, No. 7 (London: April 2, 1993), p. 2.

[159]Mark Huband, "While the People Starve," *Africa Report* (May/June 1993), p. 36, quotes an eyewitness that eighty-one were killed; another source said that the SPLA-Torit attacking troops killed fifteen SPLA-Nasir forces and forty-five civilians. "Death in the Sudd," *Africa Confidential*, p. 2.

meeting, were taken into a house used by Riek and deliberately shot.[160] Joseph Oduho, an older, respected Lotuko political leader of the SPLA who had been arrested by Garang in 1986 and imprisoned for over five years, also died in the attack.[161]

The WFP coordinator in Kongor, Jean Francois Darcq, a French national, was brutalized by SPLA-Torit. Darcq, who was in the U.N. compound when the center was attacked, took refuge in the storeroom behind a wall of maize sacks. He emerged during a lull in the fighting and identified himself to the forces of SPLA-Torit, then in control of the center. They accused the WFP of supplying the SPLA-Nasir faction with arms and food and forced Darcq to open U.N. food stores. They ordered him to strip naked and marched him at gunpoint through the bush for an hour. According to Darcq's report:

> My guard ordered me out and ordered me to come towards the south as well, still at gunpoint. I was very tired, my bare feet giving me great pain. I fell down several times. The guard was still rushing me -- I could not run any more. I could hardly walk. The guard was ahead of me. He stopped, aimed at me and fired a number of times (I believe eight). While he was firing I hopped left and right in a zig zag pattern shouting No No in French. I fell down again -- hard -- with my face to the ground. I then turned my head and could see the guard moving away. I was thinking, "I'm still alive!"[162]

He took refuge in the bush where he was later rescued by the SPLA-Nasir forces and evacuated by the U.N. on March 28.[163]

After the event, Garang retracted the accusation that the WFP was knowingly supplying SPLA-Nasir with food. Garang apologized to the

---

[160]Amnesty International, "Ravages of war," p. 24.

[161]"Death in the Sudd," *Africa Confidential*, p.2.

[162]WFP, News Release, "WFP Executive Director Condemns Attack on Staff in Southern Sudan," Nairobi, Kenya, April 2, 1993.

[163]*Ibid.*

U.N. for the mistreatment of Darcq and the violation of the agreement with the U.N. guaranteeing safe access for relief staff to southern Sudan locations, including Kongor.[164]

Accountability of SPLA-Torit for Deaths and Injuries in Kongor Attack

HRW/Africa concludes that the SPLA-Torit has inadequately investigated and has avoided taking responsibility for the deaths that occurred in the attack on Kongor, in violation of the rules of war and of its duties to maintain the discipline of its troops and to enforce adherence to the rules of war.

We had the opportunity to ask SPLA-Torit Commander Bior Ajang Duot, commander of the attack on Kongor, about the abuses committed during the attack and the steps the SPLA-Torit had taken to punish those responsible.[165] Commander Bior claimed that Oduho was killed in cross-fire, and that, since all the commanders knew him, no one would deliberately kill him. However, from the descriptions of the events that day, it appears that the elderly Oduho, too tired to run, was left behind under a tree by the retreating Nasir troops, and it is a fair inference that when the SPLA-Torit troops came upon him, there was no combat taking place in that area.

Commander Bior even admitted that there was only one real military exchange that day. "Riek and the NGOs fled north together from Panyakur in Toyota trucks. There was heavy firing from Riek, so our ambushers, who were on the road, did not lift their heads up, and the Riek forces escaped the ambush. Riek's forces fled at the beginning of the attack. They did not put up any resistance."

The death of Joseph Oduho in all likelihood was the result of a killing *hors de combat* of an unarmed person, a violation of the rules of war.[166] The same could be said for the deaths of those relatives of Arok Thon Arok who were burned to death inside a house, and probably for most of the civilians killed that day.

---

[164]*See* Huband, "While the People Starve," p. 39.

[165]Interview of Commander Bior Ajang Duot, Upper Nile, Sudan, July 9, 1993.

[166]*See* Appendix A.

Regarding the brutal treatment of the U.N. relief worker, Commander Bior offered first one excuse, then another. First, he said "Some soldiers are not conscientious. They assumed that everyone was an enemy." Then he offered another excuse: "The intent was to rob him. The one who mistreated Jean François was not caught." Then he claimed not to know which side was responsible for the mistreatment: "We do not know if he was mistreated by Riek or Garang forces." Despite his supposed ignorance, he then said, "They shot at him but not to kill him. He was caught and then shot at. They did not want to kill him but to terrorize him." Finally, he said, "This was an isolated incident."

Having virtually conceded responsibility, he said, "Someone was assigned by commander Kol Manyang to investigate [the incident]. All attempts to find out what happened failed. The field commanders were asked which unit [it could have been]. They said that others were responsible for the ambush."

This confusion of responses only confirms our conclusion that the SPLA-Torit was responsible for this violation of the rules of war, and that they did not seriously investigate or punish anyone for it, even after extensive public demands for an accounting.

Effects of Fighting in Kongor

The fighting resulted in more lives lost indirectly than in actual shooting or burning. The OLS estimated that 200-300 severely malnourished children died as a direct result of the March 27 attack on Kongor because the intensive feeding programs were disrupted. In a written statement, Acting U.S. AID Administrator James Michel strongly criticized the attack:

> Launching offensive military operations in this environment of human suffering indicates a callous disregard for human life . . . . Military actions by any faction or group in this area of extreme need deserve the world's utter condemnation and contempt . . . and calls [sic] into question the motives and basic humanity of the participants.[167]

One of the first outside visitors to Kongor after the fighting subsided, on April 16, 1993, observed a visible population of 4-5,000 and

---

[167]*Hubard*, "While the People Starve," p. 39, quoting Michel.

an estimated 30,000 people in the area, with new arrivals from Dinka
areas of Bor, Shambe, and the Duks.[168] A headcount on May 3, 1993,
showed there were 7,000 people in Kongor, despite a warning of an
impending counterattack by SPLA-Nasir.[169]

After the fighting subsided, the relief operations resumed, some
by the OLS and some by Lutheran World Federation operating outside
the OLS. A chief from Jonglei who was in Kongor in July 1993 said, "This
is why you see me healthy. I have been here one month eating normally.
Few remain now in Jonglei. They are eating leaves only." He came to
secure and bring back rations for the village, which had not received U.N.
food.

SPLA-Nasir Abducts Women in Duk Faiwil in April 1993

During their passage through Duk Faiwil for a day in late March
1993 on the way north, Riek's forces killed a woman and captured several
children and thirty-seven young women from among the remaining
inhabitants, who were subsisting on leaves. The captives were taken back
to the Nuer area. The huts in Duk Faiwil were burned.

The son of the woman who was killed said that she was shot while
searching for leaves to eat. He found her body in the bush. Another
resident of Duk Faiwil said that the twenty-year-old wife of his uncle was
one of those taken, along with her baby. Four other children of this
uncle, by another wife, also were taken, three girls and a boy, all under
nine years old. Three children, ages one, two and four, named by the
chief, were also taken; none of them had returned months later. The
chief's group returned to Duk right after SPLA-Nasir's departure to find
their huts burned.

Kuac Deng Attacked by SPLA-Torit in April 1993

The third 1993 SPLA-Torit attack on Kuac Deng came on April
1, in the wake of their capture of Kongor. Residents claim that the SPLA-
Torit killed five civilians.

---

[168]OLS (Southern Sector) Bi-Monthly Situation Report No. 36, March 24 -
April 23, 1993, p. 3.

[169]OLS (Southern Sector) Bi-Monthly Situation Report No. 37, April 24 -
May 31, 1993, p. 4.

After the February SPLA-Torit attack, the residents of Kuac Deng scattered; some went to the toic and some to Waat for relief food. The group in the toic was surviving with difficulty on wild fruits and fishing, so many returned to Kuac Deng and were there when two battles took place on April 1 between SPLA-Torit and SPLA-Nasir/United forces.

Most of the civilians ran away, but a fifteen-year-old boy was captured by SPLA-Torit forces at the water reservoir and held at gunpoint along with ten other boys. He said they managed to escape during the counterattack by SPLA-Nasir/United troops. The chief reported that five people who did not escape were shot and killed at the water reservoir by the SPLA-Torit.

Ayod Attacked by SPLA-Torit on April 2, 1993

In April 1993, SPLA-Torit forces razed and burned to the ground Ayod and Yuai, two population centers in northern Upper Nile where SPLA-Nasir/United had stationed troops. Possibly hundreds of Nuer civilians were killed in indiscriminate shooting and deliberate killings by the SPLA-Torit. Many were elderly, weak, sick or for other reasons could not run fast enough; they were among those who burned to death inside huts the soldiers knowingly set on fire. Surrounding areas were also attacked and looted.

The SPLA-Torit was in pursuit of Riek Machar himself; they pursued him from Kongor on March 27 to Kuac Deng and then to Ayod. SPLA-Torit Commander Bior, in charge of that incursion into Nuer territory, said that Garang's forces believed that if they could capture Riek, the SPLA-Nasir would collapse and they could win over the Nuer population. Their treatment of the Nuer living in the area, however, belies any strategy of winning them over. Those who could not escape the sudden attacks often were killed.

In Ayod, the SPLA-Torit attacked a weak population, in part because it was supporting an SPLA-Nasir garrison; in December 1992, a visitor noted that the SPLA-Nasir troops in Ayod were "living entirely off the population who are manifestly unable to provide,"[170] an abuse of the civilian population. The malnutrition rate of children under five was

---

[170]The garrison had reportedly been eating "nothing but meat," for months, referring to slaughter of the partial civilian herds that remained. The people said that "since fighting began cattle have had to breed with sick stock and the major portion of livestock have died."

40 percent by late January, 1993. The situation in Ayod was "critical, with daily arrivals of more displaced in search of food. Families in the area have little or no food, except for Lalob (a wild fruit), which contains little carbohydrates and no proteins."[171] Of the 12,000 in Ayod, 10,000 had come from surrounding areas.

The situation worsened in March, when a head count estimated "20,200 people, the worst affected of whom are Dinka and Nuer refugees from the south. Deaths continue at a rate of between ten and thirteen people per day, mainly amongst the elderly."[172]

The Centers for Disease Control and U.S. AID assessed mortality in Ayod in March 1993. The CDC concluded that "the prevalence rates of severe undernutrition in Ayod were among the highest ever documented, and that the average daily crude mortality rate during February-March 1993 was similar to that in Baidoa, Somalia, during November-December 1992."[173] The CDC attributed the recent increase in the crude mortality rate in part to the suspension of food airlifts during an eighteen-day period in February.[174] That the death rate could increase so much due to a short gap in food deliveries underlines how precariously life hung in the balance.

Only a few weeks after the CDC assessment, on April 2, 1993, the SPLA-Torit forces attacked Ayod, causing another suspension in food deliveries and greatly compounding the disaster by outright killing, burning and looting as well as by disrupting the flow of relief food. The SPLA-Torit occupied Ayod for eight or nine days, then withdrew.

Many of the killings, committed as the troops entered Ayod, appeared to have been motivated by tribal hatred; some Dinka who had fled to Ayod to join Nuer relatives were excoriated by the SPLA-Torit forces because they had aligned themselves with the Nuer. A twenty-five-year-old Dinka woman, displaced from Duk Fadiat in 1991, said Garang's

---

[171]OLS (Southern Sector) Bi-Monthly Situation Report No. 33, February 1993, p. 4.

[172]OLS (Southern Sector) Bi-Monthly Situation Report No. 35, February 21-March 24, 1993, pp. 2-3.

[173]CDC, "Nutrition and Mortality Assessment, Southern Sudan," pp. 306-07.

[174]*Ibid*. The airlift was suspended for mechanical reasons.

forces burned her house, with four sick female relatives inside who were unable to run away and burned to death.[175] The soldiers knew that the women victims were Dinka; they shouted at them that they had "sided with the Nuer." Four children, two boys and two girls, were taken captive. She saw women being raped and afterwards killed. She fled to Wau village.

A thirty-year-old Dinka man, displaced from Duk Fadiat in early 1992, said the Garang soldiers trapped his uncle and the husband of his sister inside their Ayod hut and burned them to death. They also burned his house, clothes, cooking utensils, and other personal possessions. As this witness was running away, he saw Garang's soldiers push approximately twenty Dinka inside one tukl and set fire to it while shouting at the people inside that they were "Nuer now," and they would have to die.[176]

A church official in Ayod witnessed soldiers looting people inside the Presbyterian church and then setting it on fire. An estimated thirty-eight people died in the blaze. It was also reported that the Catholic church was burned with people inside.

A Nuer woman from Bentiu lost her thirty-eight-year-old husband, who was "sick with malaria and could not run" when the fighters reached them; she fled with their six children. Garang's soldiers lit her house on fire, and her husband was consumed by the flames. "Many others died this way," she said.

She fled with her children to Wau village, which was attacked shortly thereafter by Garang's forces. Her husband's brother was among those shot and killed in Wau. The cattle this woman and her children had managed to bring with them from Bentiu and Ayod were seized in Wau by the soldiers, who looted all the cattle in Wau. Her family fled again, this time to Rakyen village, where they were safe but destitute.

SPLA-Torit remained in Ayod for nine days and withdrew. Rory Nugent, a journalist traveling with SPLA-Nasir/United, entered Ayod after SPLA-Torit departed. He wrote the following account of the devastation:

---

[175]Also burned inside the house were her family's food stocks and clothes.

[176]Commander Thomas Duoth of SPLA-Nasir and others were claiming that the border Dinka were "really Nuer" as early as October-December, 1991. Perhaps SPLA-Torit accepted this claim.

Ayod no longer exists. Every home has been burned. Circles and rectangles of charred earth are all that remain. There is no thatched church there any more.

The feeding centre run by the Irish group Concern turned into a crematorium when troops loyal to rebel leader John Garang stormed the area. A total of 122 skulls were found in heaps of ashes and bones when troops backing the rival Christian faction of Riek Machar regained control.[177]

The U.N. stopped flights on April 2 and only resumed them a few weeks later. Outside relief workers returning to Ayod saw that Ayod has been razed and everything looted and burned to the ground, including the U.N. compound. About twenty-five bodies were found near the airstrip, and some inside the burnt tukls. They found only 200 civilians and 200 SPLA-Nasir/United soldiers in Ayod. They estimated there were another 10,000 people at a distance of one or two hours' walk. Anti-personnel mines had been planted around the remains of the U.N. compound.

An OLS headcount on May 30 revealed that civilians had returned to Ayod; there were an estimated 4,500 people there, compared to 20,000 before the fighting, and 25,000 still in the surrounding county.[178]

Yuai, Created by SPLA-Nasir, Attacked by SPLA-Torit on April 16, 1993

The SPLA-Torit bears the responsibility for indiscriminately attacking Yuai and then deliberately killing civilians found still inside the village, all in violation of the rules of war. The SPLA-Nasir/United, however, bears some responsibility for the deaths, since it directed displaced persons to move there, knowing it was a frontline area, and

---

[177]Rory Nugent, "Feeding center destroyed in Sudan massacre," *The Observer* London), May 16, 1993, p. 15.

[178]OLS (Southern Sector) Bi-Monthly Situation Report No. 37, April 24 - May 31, 1993, p. 4.

then placed its headquarters there, thus exposing the civilians to the likelihood of attack.[179] This does not in any fashion excuse, however, the SPLA-Torit's brutal attack on the civilians of Yuai.

SPLA-Torit forces swept on from Ayod to attack Yuai on April 16, 1993, continuing their pursuit of Commander Riek. An observer noted that a rocket hit the U.N. compound in Yuai five minutes before Riek was to be interviewed there.

Right before the attack, Yuai's population was estimated at 15,000; over 7,000 people had just arrived, mainly from the south.[180] They were drawn to Yuai by the availability of relief food.

From a height, journalist Rory Nugent watched the attack on Yuai:

> I hurriedly climbed aboard a truck at Yuai as a series of rocket-propelled grenades exploded inside a U.N. feeding centre. . . .
>
> For the next 28 hours, I watched the entire surviving population of Yuai, more than 22,000 people, walk by me in single file.[181]

He saw the SPLA-Torit troops in action inside Yuai:

> Most of the enemy troops head directly for the U.N. complex. A series of mortar rounds and grenades land squarely inside the feeding center and clinic, which, being built of straw, go up in flames within seconds. We're downwind, and it's not long before the fetor of burning flesh and hair engulfs us. Earlier in the day, I visited the compound. . . . More than 100 people were laid out in the medical compound, and another 1600 were living in the feeding center. Horror-struck, I stare

---

[179]*See* below in this Chapter.

[180]OLS (Southern Sector) Bi-Monthly Situation Report No. 35, February 21-March 24, 1993, p. 4.

[181]Rory Nugent, "Feeding centre destroyed," p. 15.

at the aid station now as war transforms it into a crematorium.[182]

A thirty-two-year-old Dinka woman was carrying water from a well when Garang's forces attacked. She ran after seeing soldiers in vehicles and on foot shooting. They killed "many people" including her husband's sister and uncle, with guns. Her tukl was burned along with the rest of the town. All of her clothes, cooking utensils, and a little meat were all burned inside her tukl.

A fifty-year-old Nuer man said that during the attack Garang's forces began shooting randomly, killing four female relatives: his twenty-eight-year-old daughter, shot in the stomach when she was tukl carrying her infant daughter, who was also killed, another daughter of the witness, and the daughter of his brother. "The sick and old of Yuai were brought into the center of town and slaughtered; many had their heads cut off with pangas," he said. His disabled sister was beheaded. The witness said that the villagers later found the bones of 110 people who were burned alive inside their tukls. All the livestock was looted.

His family (he had five wives and twenty children) and other families had been preparing to plant. He had received seeds from UNICEF and grain from the U.N. was stored inside his tukls. The seeds were looted and loaded on lorries. Some Yuai people were captured and forced to porter supplies to Pathai, between Waat and Yuai. He had heard that after carrying goods to Pathai, the porters were killed; they never returned.

A fifteen-year-old Nuer said Garang's forces surrounded Yuai the night before and attacked in the early morning. The boy heard the sound of gunfire and ran outside his tukl. A soldier shot and killed his father from behind. His twenty-five-year-old brother was shot and killed also. The witness and his friend lost 105 cattle, a few sheep, and fishing nets. The soldiers took all these possessions.

Rory Nugent, the journalist traveling with SPLA-Nasir/United, entered Yuai after the SPLA-Torit withdrew and wrote the following account of the attack:

---

[182]Rory Nugent, "Sudan: Rebels of the Apocalypse," *Men's Journal*, September 1993, p. 12.

> At Yuai . . . where the two rebel factions did most of
> their fighting, I gave up my inspection after viewing
> dozens of bodies uncovered from their shallow graves.
> The old, the weak and the young, all those unable to
> flee, were butchered.[183]

Three German journalists also reported that Yuai had been
overrun on April 16 and the U.N. compound destroyed in the first round
of fire, and subsequently torched. A U.N. overflight on April 20 near Yuai
confirmed it was burned out and that about 25,000 people were heading
east.[184]

For safety reasons, the U.N. closed its operations in Ayod, Yuai,
and Waat for more than two weeks. Nugent commented on the
humanitarian aspects of this series of attacks:

> It was a dire period for more than 70,000 people left to
> fend for themselves by eating leaves and roots. No one
> had shelter, few wore clothes, and the wet season was
> about to begin.
>
> It was impossible to move without stumbling on corpses
> and skeletons. I can only guess at the number of people
> who died in this 17-day period, but one in seven strikes
> me as a conservative estimate.[185]

Unfortunately, such attacks had become the rule in south Sudan. These
particular ones were exceptional only because so many foreigners saw the
aftermath.

Pagau and Pathai Attacked by SPLA-Torit from April-May 1993

In April, 1993, the forces of Garang retreating from the Yuai
attack passed through Pagau, indiscriminately and deliberately attacking

---

[183]Rory Nugent, "Feeding centre destroyed," p. 15.

[184]OLS (Southern Sector) Bi-Monthly Situation Report No. 36, March 24-
April 23, 1993, p. 3.

[185]Rory Nugent, "Feeding centre destroyed," p. 15.

the civilian population and looting their possessions. Nugent, the journalist traveling with the SPLA-Nasir/United forces, took pictures after the departure of SPLA-Torit:

> Walking from Waat to Ayod, I took pictures of what was left of massacre victims, most of them women split in half by a machete, their legs spread apart and sticks from the baskets they used to carry on their heads shoved up their vaginas.
>
> In the village of Pathai, not a building was left standing. Foxholes dug by the troops had been filled with bodies and covered with dirt by Riek's men on cleaning up after Garang's troops had fled. There were scores of these mounds....
>
> Fifteen miles from Pathai, in the village of Paguea, the bodies of 32 women were laid out in line, each shot in the head at close range. In nearby Parvai, I photographed 19 bodies that had been bludgeoned to death.
>
> As we kept walking, more and more bodies littered the way. Famine victims were usually found singly under a tree; war casualties were grouped together, their bones picked clean and then bleached by an unblinking equatorial sun.[186]

A Nuer man, whose cattle survived the SPLA-Torit attack of February 1992, because they were grazing in another area, lost the livestock in Pagau where the Garang soldiers finally looted it in the April 1993, attack. It seemed to this witness that the attackers' sole intention was to raid cattle.

After retreating with the cattle, according to another resident of Pagau, Garang's forces returned to Pagau on May 1, 1993. They came in vehicles, and reportedly captured many women and raped and killed

---

[186]*Ibid.*

them. Many children in the village were killed. Garang's soldiers burned the village down again; they also burned the crops.

Mogogh Area Attacked by SPLA-Torit in April 1993

Commander George Asar of the SPLA-Torit left his Atar base and passed from north to south to reinforce Garang in Ayod in April 1993. On the way to Ayod, passing through Mogogh, the forces reportedly shot civilians, looted cattle, and abducted women.

When the Garang forces left Ayod in April 1993, some of Commander George Asar's forces returned north to the Atar base, passing through Timerial and Manial, burning these villages again and killing more people, according to civilians.

The SPLA-Torit forces reached Timerial early in the morning. Villagers were not yet fully resettled in Timerial; many were still in the toic. However, the elderly had returned early to prepare the farms for cultivation. The attackers stayed only a few hours, took the cattle from Timerial, and proceeded through the forest. The Timerial residents returned immediately after the raid and found bodies of the elderly in the fields where they were farming and others inside houses. They found the grain looted and the contents of the huts burned.

Gar and Surrounding Villages Attacked by SPLA-Torit in April 1993

SPLA-Torit burned and looted villages north of Ayod in April and also killed many civilians. An elderly chief of Gar, a village about twenty kilometers north of Ayod, said that the villagers fled after seeing other villages burning.[187] The chief saw the attackers, who rode in trucks and were wearing dark-colored uniforms. They were "Dinka from Bahr El Ghazal," he said. Twelve of his family were killed along with many others from other families. He escaped and spent ten hours away from the village. Upon his return, he found that some of his family members had been killed with bullets, and others with pangas (spears). Five of his dead relatives were civilian men; three were children aged ten years to infancy; and the other four were women. Two of the children were killed with bullets and one with a panga.

The attackers spent four days in other villages roaming around and killing people. They destroyed the borehole at Wau village from

---

[187]The villages that were burning were Bol, Tem, Gung, Jiak Guar, Wai, Maluang, and Juglei.

which Gar village previously drew its water. No buildings in Gar were left standing. The SPLA-Torit soldiers burned the small quantities of grain and seeds that had been stored.

Twenty cattle were taken from the witness, which he had received when his daughter married subsequent to a 1991 raid in which he lost his prior herd. He again had nothing left. "That is why we go to the U.N.," he said.

Accountability for SPLA-Torit Attacks on Ayod and Yuai in April 1993

Evasion is the method used by both the SPLA-Torit and SPLA-Nasir/United when confronted with serious human rights abuses by their own troops. The SPLA-Torit has not investigated or punished any of the extremely abusive behavior of its troops set forth above, including deliberate killings of hundreds of civilians, destruction of their homes, and widespread looting, even though evidence of it was, for once, witnessed and reported by foreigners soon after the events.

SPLA-Torit Commander Bior denied killing civilians. He claimed that there was a forty-five-minute fight in the evening in Ayod, after which his forces entered Ayod and stayed for nine days. When asked how Ayod was burned to the ground, he claimed that Commander Riek "was using tracer bullets at night to attack us. The houses caught fire. The Riek forces came up to the airport, to the trenches." It is implausible that every hut in the village where 12,000 had lived would be burned to the ground as a result of tracer bullets. The huts were too widely dispersed for a fire to have spread in such a manner. Furthermore, the SPLA-Torit admits it remained in Ayod nine days after the attack. It is not likely it would have remained in a destroyed outpost. It appears that the SPLA-Torit set fire to the huts and left Ayod when they heard that SPLA-Nasir/United Commander Riek could be found in nearby Yuai.

Commander Bior said that Ayod is strategic to the SPLA-Torit from a military point of view because the Khartoum regime forces pass through Ayod to conduct dry season offenses, as in 1992. That Ayod's garrison might at certain times be a legitimate military target does not confer license to kill civilians and loot and burn their property after capturing the garrison.

Cease-fire Agreement on May 28, 1993

The U.S. ambassador to Sudan in Khartoum, Donald Petterson, made his second visit to south Sudan in April, 1993. He later called a press conference in Nairobi, and said,

"Washington will continue to condemn the military operations in the Kongor, Ayod, Yuai, and Waat area, which manifest a contemptuous disregard for the relief programme and a callous disregard for lives of starving people."[188]
He said that a promise from Garang not to initiate further military action beyond Kongor had turned out to be "meaningless." As a result, the ambassador added, the severely malnourished women and children he saw on his previous trip to Kongor weeks earlier were "gone and most likely dead."[189]

Under this pressure, the two SPLA factions agreed to withdraw all their military personnel from an area delineated by a forty-five-mile radius from the airstrips at Ayod, Kongor, Waat and Yuai, by June 5, 1993. They also agreed not to hinder the humanitarian relief efforts in the area, and to guarantee the continued safety of the relief workers and their property there. This agreement was signed in the presence of Amb. Petterson.[190] It was broken only a few weeks later, apparently by the SPLA-Torit.

It seems that neither side withdrew their military personnel from the area as promised. Commander Riek said that the subject of the militias did not come up in the negotiations on the demilitarized zone and that they did not consider that the agreement covered the militia forces. "The militia is for the defense of the population. They live in their own homes with arms. They are subject to discipline," he said. Militias are not police; SPLA-Nasir/United has a small police force deployed in the Waat, Ayod, and U.N. areas, he added, commenting that he was rather

---

[188]UNICEF, "Emergency Programme Status, Sudan, April 1993," (New York: UNICEF 1993), p. 2.

[189]*Ibid*.

[190]Agreement signed by Commander Simmon Mori Didumo for SPLA-Nasir and Commander John Kong Nyuon for SPLA-Torit in the presence of Donald Petterson, U.S. Ambassador to Sudan, on May 28, 1993.

surprised that the subject of the militias did not come up in the negotiations.

SPLA-Torit claimed that the SPLA-Nasir/United did not pull its troops back and was advancing south along the Duk Ridge when the SPLA-Torit troops attacked. The SPLA-Nasir/United claims that it moved down to meet SPLA-Torit when the latter advanced towards Ayod. The SPLA-Torit accused the other faction of always trying to "stab us in the back" when SPLA-Torit is engaged around Juba.

Pagau Attacked Again by SPLA-Torit in June 1993

On or about June 8, 1993, Garang's forces attacked Pagau yet again. This time they shot and killed a number of civilians, not only in Pagau but also in surrounding villages. For example, twenty-five people reportedly were killed in Pading village, twenty in Lek village, and ninety-five in Pagau village, for a total of 140 deaths. No livestock remained.

Second Attack on Yuai by SPLA-Torit on June 16, 1993

Garang's forces attacked Yuai again in June, causing many casualties among the civilians who had moved back when the U.N. resumed food deliveries to Yuai. A witness reported that the entire family of a friend was wiped out. The friend, his wife, two daughters, one son, and father were all asleep when soldiers entered their tukl, split their heads open with pangas, and then burned the tukl.

Another man's uncle was shot and killed. Most people ran to the bush, and many drowned in the river. "After the second attack, many people died of hunger," the man said. Many others were shot. The bones of forty-five people were found after this attack. Yuai was "burned to ashes."

A woman who had been burned out of her tukl in April returned to Yuai with her family in May. In the June attack she tried to run but was captured along with her two sons. She was forced to lie down on her stomach and was beaten repeatedly on the legs and back with sticks. She and her older son then were made porters; the boy carried looted cooking utensils for Garang's troops. Over thirty others were taken captive with them. In a village called Mut, they were asked, "Who wants to return to Yuai?" Those who raised their hands were executed. Five children and five women were beheaded there, including a woman and her three children known to this witness.

The group of captives and Garang's forces encountered Riek's forces in Keij village, northwest of Waat. Riek's forces attacked, but Garang's troops escaped with some cattle and captives. Three women were killed in the crossfire. The witness escaped with her children and four other women, and were rescued by Riek's forces.

Yuai was then deserted. A relief assessment team reported in September 1993, "The situation in Yuai remains unchanged since the village was burned down during fighting. Only about 100 people remain in town; most have moved to rural areas."[191]

Tip Village Attacked by SPLA-Torit in June 1993

Tip village, a two-hour walk north of Ayod, was not attacked until June 1993, after the second attack on Yuai. A Nuer man was in his tukl when Garang's forces surrounded Tip, taking eight men and women captive. Seven people were tortured, including a man who was shot in the leg, left on the ground, and died three days later.

Garang's forces burned the village, including the witness's house, and took all of the cattle. The residents were left only with the desire for revenge. "If there is fighting against Garang again, we will go if we get guns. I cannot go anywhere because I have lost everything," said one villager.

Kongor/Panyakur Attacked Again by SPLA-Nasir/United in July 1993

After a lull in the fighting, Kongor was attacked in late July 1993 by the SPLA-Nasir/United forces. This was the sixth time in two years that the town had come under attack. The population fled and has never returned. A U.N. assessment team in late August 1993 that noted that the population was "small, predominantly male and armed. Assessment teams view roughly 20 women and children."[192] Some 2,000 people reportedly appeared for food distributions and then returned to live outside of the town. Many, perhaps some 15,000, migrated to Paliau for a food distribution there in mid-August.[193]

---

[191]U.S. AID/OFDA Sudan Situation Report no. 6 (Washington, D.C.: U.S. AID, September 10, 1993), p. 6.

[192]U.N. Situation Report, Khartoum, July 29-August 25, 1993, p. 3.

[193]*Ibid.*

Because the rainy season was hampering food airlifts, relief
agencies were having trouble maintaining a continuous supply of
food,[194] but a large influx of displaced continued to move toward
Waat, the only area in Upper Nile receiving food on a regular basis. The
population in Waat tripled in the three months of June, July, and August,
1993, with 2,500 new arrivals during the first week of August, 1993. The
total population of Waat in August reached 53,600.[195]

SPLA FOOD POLICIES
ABUSIVE OF THE CIVILIAN POPULATION

Many southern Sudanese complained to HRW/Africa about the
SPLA taking food from them. The SPLA obtains food from a variety of
sources, including voluntary contributions from civilians. The SPLA also
obtains food through legitimate commerce. Some local garrisons produce
food, as one observer saw in Pok Tap.

HRW/Africa found, however, the following abuses by the SPLA
factions in connection with food supply:

1.   SPLA soldiers stealing food from civilians under their jurisdiction,
      either independently of any orders or with the tacit approval of
      a local commander;
2.   looting cattle and stealing grain from civilians under the
      jurisdiction of the other side, usually accompanied by violence--
      often considered "war booty," it is no more than pillage;
3.   forced unpaid farm labor on SPLA-organized farms;
4.   requisitioning or "taxing" of produce and/or animals from
      productive farmers by force, sometimes according to a quota
      system and sometimes arbitrarily;
5.   requisitioning or "taxing" food from individual emergency relief
      recipients, including women and children, often under
      compulsion;
6.   diverting relief supplies at their source;

---

[194]U.S. AID/OFDA Sudan Situation Report no. 5, May 26, 1993, p. 4.

[195]U.S. AID/OFDA Sudan Situation Report No. 6, September 10, 1993, p. 6.

7.   displacing the civilian population for reasons related to the conflict, that is, to locate civilians in dangerous but militarily significant areas in order to draw relief supplies there.

HRW/Africa was unable to determine the extent and duration of the food-related abuses, but the complaints from southern Sudanese civilians and the observations of food monitors suggest that the abuses persist. HRW/Africa was also unable to quantify the amounts of food involved, but from a human rights perspective, any forcible taking of food from civilians by a party to the conflict is illegitimate.

The government itself is guilty of food-related violations, including frequent arbitrary refusal to grant access by relief agencies to needy populations. The government is also guilty of diverting or permitting its army officers to engage in large-scale diversion of relief food.[196] The SPLA's violations by no means justify the government in denying access to relief food, which in south Sudan has kept alive hundreds of thousands of people, despite some diversion.

Background

The Maoist doctrine that has conferred a mythical status on guerrilla armies has obscured, to outsiders at least, some of the practices of predatory guerrilla armies.[197] The SPLA factions do not act as if they are bound by Mao's rule, "Do not steal from the people."[198] Indeed, the SPLA was brought into existence by political factors which were largely independent of the Cold War.

---

[196]Food manipulation by the government continues to follow the patterns described in the prior Africa Watch report, *Denying the Honor of Living*, and in de Waal, "Starving out the South."

[197]"Although some parties to conflict in Africa frequently use the rhetoric of national liberation, their practice on the ground often challenges the conventional (Maoist) wisdom that, in order to operate, a guerilla movement needs the support of local people. An extreme case is represented by RENAMO in Mozambique . . . ". Duffield, "The emergence of two-tier welfare in Africa," p. 143.

[198]Mao Tse-Tung, *On Guerrilla Warfare* (New York: Frederick A. Praeger, 1961), p. 92.

The second Sudanese civil war, unlike the first, began as a military revolt whereby a Sudanese army battalion defected to Ethiopia where, with some guerrilla groups, the SPLA was formed. Under Mengistu's supervision, it created base camps and received military training for a large army, which was supplied with arms, including artillery and vehicles, by Ethiopia's Soviet sponsors. For the most part, this SPLA did not grow up inside Sudan in small groups dependent on the help of local civilians.[199]

Feeding an army as large as the SPLA, which numbered at least several tens of thousands, presents tremendous difficulties. In southern Sudan's subsistence economy, food takes on particular importance.

One scholar noted the structural connection between war and famine:

> Internal war in Africa is fought through groups whose existence is largely based upon different forms of semi-subsistence. Modern conflict arises not as a process of regulation and adaptation but from the growing crises within governance and semi-subsistence. This instability has increased since the 1970s. Modern warfare, moreover, proceeds not by resolving tensions but by massively increasing imbalances and disparities between groups. It does so because the political economy of internal war dictates that systems of semi-subsistence are both targets and points of defence. . . . Conflict in Africa should not, therefore, be seen as a secondary or separate issue. It is an emergent trend which is increasingly influencing the growth of food insecurity.[200]

---

[199]"During the first war, Anya-Nya I forces would go to the chief and ask for food. SPLA forces, by contrast, split up into twos and threes and go around directly to village tukls demanding food to be cooked for them," said an Equatorian man. Although other observers note that civilians were looted by Any-Nya I in the first civil war, many Equatorian civilians today perceive a sharp difference in the practices of the two guerrilla armies.

[200]Duffield, "The emergence of two-tier welfare in Africa," p. 144.

In part, the SPLA's food problem was solved in Ethiopia while Mengistu was in power. He gave the SPLA, rather than relief agencies, the ultimate authority in the Sudanese refugee camps, and there was considerable overestimation of the numbers of refugees and diversion of food aid.[201] The Ethiopian camps, particularly Itang, became commercial centers for some areas of southern Sudan along the border and Sobat basin. They played a role in replacing the Arab traders who were the backbone of the south Sudan commercial economy but who pulled out of the smaller towns when the second civil war broke out.[202] Elsewhere in the south, commercial networks were also established near border areas (Kordofan, Uganda, Kenya, for instance).

This Itang network collapsed after the fall of Mengistu, the evaporation of the refugee camps, and the flight of the refugees back to Sudan. Getting food to the repatriatees, displaced in their own country, became a much more difficult task for the U.N. and NGOs. Each shipment had to be tortuously negotiated with the government, which apparently took as its principal military strategy blocking all relief supplies to civilians living in the vast SPLA areas of southern Sudan.

Stealing Food from Civilians

Stealing from civilians has been a persistent abuse committed by the SPLA factions. The abuse appears to occur more frequently in areas where there is a tribal difference between the troops and the civilian population, making it is a particular problem in Equatoria. A Kuku (Equatorian) man complained that the SPLA policy "had always been to acquire everything the soldier needs through his gun."

For instance, an SPLA-Torit recruit from southern Blue Nile province admitted that in 1992 he and his SPLA-Torit unit would loot food and livestock, especially in the Equatorian villages around Magwe, Parajok, and Nimule. On June 2, 1992, his unit, led by Capt. Manyang, reached Magwe. Maj. Paul Kop ordered troops to look for food in Magwe. They looted grain from people, including an old man who argued that he had nothing else left. The soldiers beat the old man and took three hens from him.

---

[201]Jean, *Life, Death and Aid*, p. 20.

[202]*See* Scott-Villiers, Repatriation of Sudanese Refugees," p. 204.

An Acholi man from Magwe said that people try to cultivate, but "Garang's forces constantly steal food and crops."[203] Another Equatorian reported that when the SPLA soldiers were traveling in groups, they would force villagers to cook for them, usually meat, and threaten the villagers if they refused. The Sudan People's Revolutionary Laws, SPLM/ SPLA Punitive Provisions 1983, ("Sudan Code") at section 34 (2), provides up to the death penalty for any SPLA soldier or related organization "who compels citizens to surrender food material, money, domestic animals, articles of dress, or articles for sleeping on, or in." Theft is also punished by up to a death sentence if the value of the property is more than one million Sudanese pounds, in SPLA Code, Section 40 (1). It is not clear that these provisions have been enforced.

Looting from Civilians Under Enemy Control

Both SPLA factions are guilty of looting or pillaging civilian property. As already set forth elsewhere in the report, looting or pillaging is a particularly severe problem for civilians living in areas of military conflict. The looting or pillaging occurs during or immediately after an armed engagement and is inflicted on civilians living in "enemy" territory, distinguishing the abuse from stealing food in territory that is controlled by the troops who do the stealing.

All too often, as is illustrated in this report, looting or pillaging occurs during a raid on a village or a cattle camp in which there is no military engagement and no legitimate military target. The looting often is not a collateral effect of military activities, but the main military objective.

The factions attempt to justify this as a form of "war booty" for those full- or part-time combatants who participate in the raid. Indeed, the SPLA Code, Section 25 (4), treats as SPLM revenue property "captured from the enemy or enemy's agents." The rules of war do not permit looting or pillaging.[204]

---

[203]This practice was stopped in one area near Kajo Kaji in 1992 when the chiefs threatened to go into exile if the local commander allowed it to go on.

[204]*See* Appendix A.

Forced Farm Labor

Under humanitarian law, the SPLA's practice of using force or the threat of force to compel civilians to serve as unpaid farm labor is illegal. The practice has a precedent in Sudanese history, but this fact does not excuse its continuation in modern times in the face of changed international law.

The SPLA tried to devise agricultural schemes that would permit its army a degree of self-sufficiency closer to the front lines. Such schemes are not abuses in and of themselves, but the use of forced, unpaid labor on such farms is.[205] For example, one man told HRW/Africa that it was the SPLA practice around Kajo Kaji to require civilians to work on the SPLA farms without pay. "If you didn't voluntarily participate, the SPLA would bring you by force and give you a large area to clear. You would have to work every day until you were finished. Goats and chickens would be taken also if you resisted."

The SPLA also used its own soldiers as farm workers. Although this does not seem to rise to the level of forced labor where the soldiers were volunteers to the SPLA, it nevertheless took on the appearance of forced labor because in at least one farm the police manned the gate, the farm was surrounded by high mountains, and there was only one road out, making escape difficult. An SPLA soldier from Bentiu told HRW/Africa that he ended up working on this "state farm" after joining the General Intelligence Section of the SPLA with an expectation of advanced training. He was sent to this farm near Torit in January 1990. In the farm there were 1,560 "students," young and old. They were all men, no women, from all ethnic groups, "even including Arabs." They spent only a few hours a day in class and the rest of the day working on an SPLA farm, where work started at 6 A.M. and continued to 12:45 P.M. They received limited food. "Prisoners got more food," he claimed.

After six months, the students stopped studying and started cultivating full time. Although assured by Commander Kol Manyang that the food would be exported and the profits returned to the students, these men never saw any of the profits from this enterprise. A clerk said they produced 298 sacks of onions and never received any benefit from it. "We

---

[205]Apparently there were some farms on which the original intention was to pay laborers, but the farms were not successful. One witness said the SPLA recruited people to work on SPLA farms in his region of Equatoria, but payments to laborers were irregular and laborers were abused.

were there naked. We had no uniforms, no clothes." The men were
released from the farm to fight around Juba in April 1992.

Ugandans Used for Farm Labor in Khor Shum (Pakok)

A group of about 500-600 Ugandan army officers and soldiers
fled across the border to Sudan in 1985 as refugees, after a coup in
Uganda. That border was controlled by the SPLA. According to them, the
SPLA gave them the choice of joining a Ugandan rebel force based in
SPLA territory, or being returned to Uganda, where they feared
persecution.[206] Almost all these Ugandans accepted joining the
Ugandan rebel force and were sent to SPLA bases in Ethiopia for
training, along with other Ugandan men of military age who later fled to
the SPLA-controlled areas of Sudan as refugees. They never saw action
in Uganda but were used by the SPLA as forced labor that benefitted the
SPLA.[207]

In February 1988 these Ugandan rebels were escorted by the
SPLA on foot from Ethiopia to the SPLA base in Khor Shum (renamed
Pakok when thousands of Sudanese repatriating refugees arrived in
1991), Upper Nile, Sudan, on the border with Ethiopia. The Ugandan
rebels built a camp where they stayed from February 1988 until
November 1992. All Ugandans, prisoners and non-prisoners alike, were
assigned by the SPLA to plant crops and build the huts for a nearby SPLA
base.

After Mengistu's overthrow, many of the Ugandans' crops were
destroyed when the first 40,000 Sudanese repatriated,[208] but they
managed to harvest some crops in 1991. A U.N. worker observed that

---

[206]Below in this chapter, we condemn as illegal the choice presented by the
SPLA to the Ugandan refugees.

[207]Some of these Ugandans were arrested by the SPLA and Ugandan rebel
officers and held in SPLA jails in Ethiopia and Sudan. (See below in this
Chapter.)

[208]By the end of 1991 in Pakok the U.N. registered just under 10,000
repatriatees, of whom 2,548 were unaccompanied minors.

some of the root crops were harvested and given to the repatriatees, but that most crops were taken away by the SPLA.[209]

The Ugandan area was off-limits to expatriates working in the relief effort, and the Ugandans were not allowed to approach the foreigners. The Ugandans were, however, required to build the airfield used for international food deliveries.

In 1992, the Ugandans planted a 300-acre SPLA-Torit farm near Khor Shum (Pakok) for SPLA military use. SPLA-Torit soldiers also participated in the planting, some soldiers standing guard while others planted sorghum, groundnuts, cassava, potatoes, maize, and peas. The Ugandans were forbidden to eat this "government" SPLA-Torit food, which was sent to the fronts.[210]

Taxation or Requisition of Food from Farmers

In the case of southern Sudan, the SPLA Code, section 25 (2), claims as revenue of SPLM "[l]ocal taxation, the rate and value of which shall have regard to the conditions of the people as approved by the Chairman." With few exceptions, the factions have not provided governmental services to civilians living in areas of rebel control.[211] The taxation, which is in the form of grain or animals, is invariably destined for the use of combatants. Under these circumstances, and especially considering the extremely deprived conditions in which most southern Sudanese live, HRW/Africa does not recognize the right of either faction to levy taxes on or requisition food from those considered to have no surplus or to be in need by objective criteria. When such

---

[209]That worker was unaware that the farmers were Ugandans.

[210]In mid-November 1992, the Ugandans were ordered to move because a government attack on nearby Boma was anticipated. They were evacuated by an SPLA-Torit task force of 300 soldiers.

[211]Both factions have formed relief associations to administer internationally donated funds, i.e., Sudan Relief and Rehabilitation Association (SRRA, formed by SPLA-Torit) and Relief Association of South Sudan (RASS, formed by SPLA-Nasir/United). When the SPLA controlled more urban centers, before loosing them to the government in 1992, it attempted greater administration, including a rudimentary justice system.

taxation or requisition is accompanied by force or threat of force, HRW/Africa considers those practices to be a violation of the rules of war.

Taxation in food occurred in colonial times when tribute was collected by chiefs in grain or cattle, and the SPLA used these earlier patterns of taxation as a model. A former U.N. official told HRW/Africa that he had seen SPLA tax lists for Ayod in Upper Nile in 1989-90 and 1990-91, levied by the court center, for both grain and cattle; the chiefs were responsible for collecting both.[212]

The system or method of taxation seems to vary in its specifics from area to area. Some if not all of the taxation system is at the discretion of the area's military commander. For instance, as area commander of Western Upper Nile, Riek introduced a tax in grain, ostensibly to protect the herds by making no demands for cattle.[213]

In many areas, civilians take for granted the need to pay taxes in produce or else to suffer some kind of punishment, usually confiscation of goods. For instance, in one area of Equatoria, every family head had to provide to the SPLA one tin of grain or cassava per month. If the family skipped a month, its required contribution would be doubled the next month. If it failed to contribute for two consecutive months, the SPLA would come and "loot everything they wanted from the household."

As an SPLA-Nasir/United spokesman said in attempted justification of taxation, "These people want the war fought against the northern government. They cannot have their cake and eat it too. They must know the implications of their politics. They say the north is oppressive, but you cannot fight the Arabs without sacrifices of lives. In spite of the clumsiness of the SPLA, the war has the support of the people. The alternative is submission to the Arabs." Nevertheless, HRW/Africa considers the asserted right of taxation of such a deprived population to be unconscionable.

---

[212]On these lists, levies in cattle were 100 head per court centre. The tax in grain varied from 240 to 435 sacks of grain, according to the size of the court center. One sack weighed 90 kilos. It worked out to be about forty-eight sacks (4,320 kilos) per subchief. At this time, very little relief food was reaching Ayod.

[213]A consistent complaint against all governments has been the levying of tribute or fines in cattle.

Requisition of Food from Emergency Relief Recipients

Taxation or requisitioning is even more objectionable when it is levied on the recipients of emergency food and other relief. A relief official described a situation in Nasir in which relief food was diverted by SPLA-Nasir soldiers going house to house, taking food, medicine, and fishing materials, despite the presence of twenty food monitors.

SPLA-Nasir/United officials say that their soldiers are men of the area who are married and go home at night to eat from the relief rations given to the family. As for food consumed on operations, they claimed that each soldier takes food from home and finds food along the way: "People on the way contribute bulls, goods, etc. For long operations, such as from Upper Nile to Equatoria or Bahr El Ghazal, they pass through villages. They send word ahead that they need food and people will contribute. In the past this food was taken by force, but that was counterproductive."

As in all parts of the world, even starving civilians asked for "contributions" by a large group of armed men know better than to refuse. It is abusive for the factions to seek food contributions from those whose principal source of food is emergency relief.

It is also an abuse of international good will for any party to divert food from the intended civilian beneficiaries of international relief. In 1994 the projected emergency relief needs for the Sudan are $279 million,[214] no small sum.[215] Most of that money is required for the southern population, where an estimated two million people are extremely vulnerable because of recent crop failures and the long-term breakdown of the economy and social services caused by ten years of war.[216]

---

[214]OLS (Southern Sector), "UNICEF and WFP Request Urgent Funding for War-Torn Southern Sudan," press release, Nairobi, Kenya, February 14, 1994.

[215]The U.S. government has supplied humanitarian assistance to Sudan, and mostly to southern Sudan, in the amounts of $60.2 million in fiscal 1992, $99.6 million in fiscal 1993, and $70.8 million so far in fiscal 1994 (October 1993 through May 1994, eight months). U.S. AID/Bureau for Humanitarian Response/OFDA, Situation Report No. 11: Sudan (Washington, D.C.: U.S.AID, May 24, 1994), p. 7. Some of this assistance is destined for Sudanese refugees.

[216]OLS (Southern Sector), "UNICEF and WFP Request Urgent Funding."

Diversion and Stealing of Relief Supplies

Diversion of international emergency food relief before it reaches its intended beneficiaries is another form of theft and an abuse of the civilian population.

One medical relief organization bluntly described the practice:

> The SPLA also plays a sinister game with relief food. For many years it has fed its troops from international aid. UN food simply disappeared into vast refugee camps in western Ethiopia, with no accountability. In the south iteself, some NGOs argued that if the SPLA soldiers were not fed, they would just plunder the local population.[217]

The SPLA created a relief arm, the SRRA, and when the SPLA-Nasir was formed it also created a relief arm, RASS. Their duties were to act as local authorities and liaise with the U.N. and NGOs to carry out the delivery of relief donations to needy civilians. Neither of these relief structures has any perceptible independence from the local military commander, although many competent individuals are associated with these efforts.

The OFDA concluded in 1993 about the government army and rebel factions:

> Although no hard figures are available, there continues to be concern about food leakages and diversions. During certain security incidents, some NGOs estimate that up to 80% of food has been stolen by the militaries. While the U.N. contests these figures, there are clearly cases of inadequate monitoring and diversions. This is particularly the case when U.N./NGO staff cannot remain in an area overnight.[218]

---

[217]Jean, *Life, Death and Aid*, p. 20.

[218]OFDA "Humanitarian Relief Operations in Sudan, Trip Report, July 1993 (Washington, D.C.: U.S. AID), p. 18.

There was much anecdotal evidence of diversion by the SPLA parties and even more such evidence of Sudan army diversion; it is impossible to quantify the numbers involved. A Blue Nile SPLA soldier, later jailed for allegedly sympathizing with Riek, said that in early 1992, before the displaced persons camp was established in Atepi, relief food was brought to Opari. The SPLA soldiers would come at night and take what they needed from the storehouse--food, medicine, and cooking oil-- back to Palataka or to the Juba front line. He claimed that in June 1992, when 2,000 sacks of sorghum were stored under the trees, the SPLA arrived the same night with orders to take the food to the front. When the foreign relief agency arrived for the distribution to civilians the next morning, they found only 150 sacks of sorghum. They were told that the SRRA "did the distribution the night before."

On January 17, 1993, a commander from SPLA-Nasir held up a U.N. convoy at Lake Jur and the following day seized three relief barges and their emergency relief cargo on Lake Jur.[219] This was by no means the only incident.

A relief worker in another area saw a list from the SPLA-Nasir to RASS itemizing its needs, which RASS was directed to supply from relief goods. Another relief worker who entered Bor in December 1991 found in one of the offices a radio message from SPLA-Torit Commander Kuol Manyang to the SRRA doctor in charge of the Bor hospital (dated just before the SPLA-Nasir attack on Bor), ordering him to provide 20 percent of his medicines for a new military training camp which had just been set up outside Torit.

Displacement of the Civilian Population for Reasons Related to the Conflict: Yuai

The SPLA factions have sought to direct or encourage the movement of displaced populations under their control to locations that are of military interest to them, in order to maintain U.N. food supplies-- which they can then "tax"--coming in to convenient locations near the front lines, thus saving days of portering by soldiers or press-ganged civilians. Such practices violate the important rule that civilians shall not

---

[219]"Barge Convoy Seizure," *Sudan Update*, vol. 4, no. 10, (London: February 28, 1993), p. 4.

be displaced for reasons connected with the conflict, as set forth in Protocol II, article 17.[220]

A French medical organization working in Sudan observed:

> After the SPLA split in August 1991, the contending factions have used relief suplies to attract civilians to the areas they control, and to keep them there, while denying relief to the other side.[221]

An egregious example of this violation is the SPLA-Nasir/United's manipulation of the civilian population and the international relief program to create a forward garrison in Yuai in 1993. The rebels accomplished their goal by ordering civilians living in Waat to move to Yuai, some forty kilometers southwest, creating a town of 15,000 where none existed before, right on the Nuer/Dinka border east of the Duk Ridge, in a region where faction fighting had raged up and down. This was a dangerous place for civilians. The SPLA-Nasir/United undertook to create this mass migration of civilians knowing that concerned relief officials, aware of the desperate plight of these displaced, would attempt to have food flown in to them, and that other civilians would arrive, drawn by the magnet of relief food.[222]

---

[220] Protocol II, article 17 (1):

> The displacement of the civilian population shall not be ordered for reasons related to the conflict unless the security of the civilians involved or imperative military reasons so demand. Should such displacements have to be carried out, all possible measures shall be taken in order that the civilian population may be received under satisfactory conditions of shelter, hygiene, health, safety and nutrition.

[221]Jean, *Life, Death and Aid*, p. 22.

[222]South Sudanese who do not have food will walk for days to a place where they can get food. People go where the food is, whether to trade in a market, to find work, to live with relatives and, now, to receive relief food at landing strips where the U.N. or nongovernmental organizations are said to be delivering it. The Nilotic population in particular is quite mobile historically because of the environment. They are used to moving with their cattle.

Said one displaced person who went to Yuai in January 1993 at the urging of the SPLA-Nasir commanders, "Now we are like flies. Wherever there is food that is where we go."

As early as October 1992, Commander Riek urged the U.N. to deliver food to Yuai, which he said was ideal for relocation from overcrowded Waat, because Yuai had fishing and a dry season river. By January 1993, people were organized by SPLA-Nasir/United and RASS to move south from Waat to Yuai, before any relief had been provided to Yuai. UNICEF reported that RASS was planning for many displaced in Waat, where the situation had actually improved, to move to Yuai. It was expected that some 16,000 people would leave Waat to go to Yuai, where the WFP plane was able to land.[223] At the time, SPLA-Nasir/United controlled all three points on the "Hunger Triangle" (Kongor, Ayod, and Waat) as well as Akobo to the east. Riek moved his headquarters to Yuai during the first quarter of 1993.[224]

The WFP started airlift operations to Yuai on January 26, 1993, for a local population of 3,564 that had sprung up, subsisting mainly on a diet of fruit and fish. The officials set up a base in preparation for the expected further inflow.[225]

The displaced, as ordered or attracted by word of food arriving in Yuai, poured in. A headcount on February 18, 1993, revealed a total of 7,048 people living in and around Yuai. In March, the population increased to about 15,000 on account of an influx mainly from the

---

[223]U.N. Special Coordinator, "Situation Report for Period 7 January - 10 February 1993" (Khartoum, Sudan: U.N., Office of the Special Coordinator of the U.N. Secretary General for Emergency and Relief Operations in the Sudan), p. 6.

[224]While the location of a military base near a population center is common enough and not in itself a violation of the rules of war, placing Nasir faction headquarters in this newly-created population center in a front line zone foreseeably exposed the civilians to the likelihood of an SPLA-Torit attack on the headquarters.

[225]OLS (Southern Sector) Bi-Monthly Situation Report No. 33, January 22 - February 5, 1993, pp. 3-4.

south.[226] There is no doubt that the airlift of food and medicine to the area created a draw for civilians. Many said they came to this and other food delivery locations to "pick seeds from the airstrip." This refers to scavenging by women of grains of maize that scatter when fifty-kilo bags are airdropped and a small percentage of them split open on the ground.[227] This has become a common survival strategy.

SPLA-Torit forces made a surprise sweep into Yuai on April 16, 1993. Right before the attack, Yuai's population was estimated at 15,000; over 7,000 people had just arrived, mainly from the food-deprived areas to the south.[228] Probably hundreds of civilians died in the attack, their huts burned, and their cattle looted. Their deaths are the direct responsibility of the SPLA-Torit attackers. Nevertheless, SPLA-Nasir/United was also in violation of the rules of war.

Under international diplomatic pressure, the two SPLA factions agreed to withdraw all their military personnel from an area encompassed by a forty-five-mile radius from the aircraft landing fields at Ayod, Kongor, Waat and Yuai, by June 5, 1993. This was done to create safe areas for delivery of food. This strategy did not work.

Civilians began to return to and rebuild Yuai. A Nuer man who fled Yuai after the April attack returned in May because relief was going in. "I feel safe when the U.N. is here," he reported, "because of the presence of expatriates."

On June 16, 1993, Garang's forces attacked Yuai again, despite the pullback agreement. Again, many civilians perished; some fled to the bush, and others ran to the river where they drowned, according to a witness. "After the second attack, many people died of hunger." Yuai was "burned to ashes."

---

[226]OLS (Southern Sector) Bi-Monthly Situation Report No. 35, February 21 - March 24, 1993, pp. 4-5 .

[227]Despite this loss, it is still more economical to air drop supplies than expend expensive fuel landing and taking off. WFP or other food monitors on the ground watch the airdrop and supervise movement of the bags of grain into a storage area. Obviously the spilled food does not go to waste.

[228]OLS (Southern Sector) Bi-Monthly Situation Report No. 35, February 21 - March 24, 1993, p. 4.

Yuai was then deserted. A relief assessment team reported in September 1993, that "[t]he situation in Yuai remains unchanged since the village was burned down during fighting. Only about 100 people remain in town; most have moved to rural areas."[229]

FORCED RECRUITMENT

The SPLA has conducted forcible recruitment campaigns (*kashas*, or forcible rounding up) since at least the mid-1980s. Because many soldiers go home when there is little or no fighting, kashas have coincided with military events and often occur before major battles. Hence, kashas often involve rounding up "deserters." There is little authority in international humanitarian law whereby a rebel army may engage in forcible recruitment. Rebel roundups of deserters are equally offensive.

Forced recruitment has long historical roots in Sudan and its practice by the SPLA has changed over time and varies from region to region. In Bahr El Ghazal and Upper Nile, where there has been a higher number of volunteers to fight the Sudan government, there have been fewer complaints of forced recruitment. In Equatoria, forced recruitment has been a more serious problem.

After the August 1991 split in the movement, the SPLA-Torit's reintroduction of forced conscription in some parts of Equatoria further alienated an already disgruntled population. SPLA-Torit recruitment occurred in Equatoria in late 1991 to early 1992, perhaps for the dry season counteroffensive against the SPLA-Nasir faction in Upper Nile and the expected government dry season campaign. Some "deserters" were rounded back up in August 1992 after the major SPLA-Torit thrusts into Juba. When Commander Willian Nyuon deserted from the SPLA-Torit in Pageri in September, 1992, and took his troops east through southern Torit, the SPLA-Torit rounded up men to chase him and perhaps to keep the locals from joining his band as well.

For example, in September 1991, SPLA Commander Abraham Akoye and the local chiefs held meetings in markets and other gathering places, encouraging people to join the SPLA. Later that month, further meetings took place with the SPLA and the chiefs to organize the kasha. A week later, groups of SPLA soldiers went into the villages and deceived

---

[229]OFDA Sudan Situation Report No. 6, September 10, 1993, p. 6.

some of the young men by asking them for "assistance with some work." When the young men complied, they were locked up in the chiefs' headquarters in Kinyiba, Mondikolok, and Jalimo villages.

Thirty men were taken in the first sweep, but the soldiers found fewer as time went on, as more people learned about the sweeps and hid in the forest. A witness told HRW/Africa that he hid in the forest by himself during the day and went home in the evening. Other men stayed full-time in the forest, and women brought food to them. Many young men fled to Uganda.

In all, ninety young men from Kinyiba were picked up, held together, and taken to a training camp at Pabanga, twenty-two miles from Kaya. Some escaped by breaking the door to one of the cells.

Also in September 1991, the village headmen from Mere, four miles from Kajo Kaji, were instructed to recruit five people each for the SPLA. When the SPLA saw that the headmen were not succeeding, they publicly stated that there would be no more recruiting, so "the people relaxed." Then, on November 5, 1991, SPLA soldiers went to the markets to arrest the young men. Some escaped, but seventy-two others were taken, the youngest fourteen years old. Ten of the people were from Mere; five escaped, but the other five have not been seen since.

A forty-year-old Kuku man from the Wudu area of Kajo Kaji described a major kasha from December 1991 to January 1992, at about the time of the SPLA-Torit counteroffensive into Upper Nile. The kasha was conducted within a three-mile radius of Kajo Kaji; the SPLA-Torit cordoned off the area and rounded up the young men. The forces took the property of some families to force them to produce their men.

In January 1992, SPLA-Torit Commander James Wanni Igga called a meeting in Kajo Kaji to end this kasha and apologize for the SPLA's actions. But, as a Kuku man told HRW/Africa, "The damage was done. They had continuously insulted the Kuku population, saying there is no room for anyone but soldiers in the 'New Sudan.' All of the professionals were told they were not valued or needed."[230]

Many Juba students fled to Uganda in January 1992 because of a school boycott. Some of the students were intercepted outside Juba by the SPLA-Torit and forcibly conscripted. The SPLA-Torit sent a group of them to Isoke, an SPLA-Torit military training camp south of Torit. The

---

[230]In other areas and at other times, the SPLA has specifically attempted to recruit or draft skilled workers.

SPLA tried to convince the boys to undergo military training. Some who refused were "punished or beaten," according to one of them. The rest, in fear, did not refuse. The boys were told that they would be trained and that after they completed the training they would be "free to go."

A training group which numbered 141 started training on February 26, 1992. After two-and-a-half months in training, the Catholic church interceded and fifty-seven seminarians in the group were freed.

In August 1992 after the battle for Juba, the SPLA-Torit initiated another kasha in Magwe in which they targeted a list of deserters. The soldiers beat people to force them to disclose the whereabouts of the alleged deserters. They also took belongings from people, which they would not return until the alleged deserters turned themselves in.

In early 1993 during the SPLA-Torit offensive into Upper Nile more recruits were sought in Equatoria.

In February 1993, the SPLA also came to Kansuk in the Kajo Kaji area looking for a list of deserters. If the deserter was not found, they would hold his wife or grown-up child until he reported. Also in February 1993, relief officials on a site visit to the Atepi camp were told that there were few people there because many young men fled to the bush after the SPLA-Torit began "rounding up" recruits for the eastern front.

In March 1993, the SPLA went looking for deserters in Kinyiba village near Kajo Kaji, located one deserter, looted two of his goats and five of his chickens, and took him, along with his gun, to be re-trained. After a month he escaped to his village.

Sensing (correctly) that a government offensive was imminent on the West Bank in July 1993, the SPLA-Torit faction undertook a kasha in the Nimule area and the Ame/Aswa/Atepi (Triple A) displaced persons camps. People reported seeing hundreds of "deserters" rounded up and held in Nimule before being moved to the front. A twenty-eight-year-old Ugandan refugee said that twenty-one Ugandans and a U.N. employee from a UNHCR refugee camp for Ugandans in the Nimule area were rounded up in this five-day kasha, during which hundreds of Sudanese men were similarly captured. The SPLA reportedly walked into the UNHCR camp and took the twenty-one Ugandans, and brought them to Kurki near Juba to identify whether they were deserters. The SPLA released those that were not deserters, but some were kept.

At midnight on July 3, 1993, SPLA-Torit forces broke into the U.N. compound in Nimule, beat up the guard, woke up and pointed their guns at U.N. relief workers (in violation of the agreed-upon on

U.N./SPLA-Torit guidelines for relief worker protection), and searched the compound for deserters. The International Rescue Committee compound in Nimule was similarly invaded, as was the nearby compound of the New Sudan Council of Churches, where a catechist was beaten up.

After receiving a prompt complaint about this breach of U.N. agreements by a visiting U.S. Congressional delegation led by Rep. Harry Johnston, SPLA-Torit local Commander Salva Kiir told OLS officials that the officer responsible for entering the U.N. and NGO compounds had been detained and would be punished.

Finally, according to Ugandan witnesses, the SPLA in 1985 and later gave some Ugandan refugees, primarily Ugandan army soldiers and officers, a choice: either join a Ugandan rebel force the SPLA was sponsoring, or be forcibly sent back to Uganda. This choice, if presented to refugees by a government adhering to the Convention Relating to the Status of Refugees and other refugee instruments or to the African Charter on Human and People's Rights, would be completely illegal.

A person with a well-founded fear of being persecuted for reasons of race, religion, nationality, membership of a particular social group or political opinion has a right to asylum under international law, and such a right may not be made contingent upon military service in a rebel army. Furthermore, under the African Charter, a person enjoying the right of asylum shall not engage in subversive activites against his country of origin, and the territory of a state adhering to the African Charter may not be used as a base for subversive activities against the people of any other State party to the African Charter.[231]

Therefore, there is no legal authority whatsoever permitting the SPLA to require would-be Ugandan refugees to serve in a rebel Ugandan army, on pain of refoulment.[232]

Forced Portering

Forcing civilians to porter supplies for the SPLA is a chronic abuse. A thirty-one-year-old man from Mere village was trading at the

---

[231]African Charter on Human and People's Rights, art. 23 (2) (a) and (b).

[232]Refoulement means return of a refugee back to the country of origin where his life or freedom would be threatened on account of his race, religion, nationality, membership in a particular social group or political opinion. Convention Relating to the Status of Refugees, art. 33.

Kansuk market when the SPLA arrived and forced him and twenty-four others to carry sorghum for the SPLA to a distant location. This happened to him on four occasions. Once, he and about one hundred others were forced to carry heavy artillery from the Nile to Kansuk. The terrain was very hilly, and it took a night and a day to reach their destination.

In October 1991, the SPLA forced a thirty-three-year-old man from Kinyiba village near Kajo Kaji to be a porter. He was traveling away from Kinyiba village when he was spotted by SPLA soldiers along the road. They ordered him to carry their luggage and threatened to beat him if he did not comply. Others traveling along the road were ordered to carry supplies, such as ammunition and food. On an evening in April 1993, the same man was riding a bicycle to Kinyiba, and again met SPLA soldiers, who were carrying bags of maize. They asked him why he did not get off his bike as a sign of respect when he saw them, and then ordered him to carry their three tins of maize for a distance of about three kilometers.

From 1988 until the overthrow of Mengistu in May 1991, several hundred Ugandan men originally trained by the SPLA in Ethiopia to be a Ugandan guerrilla force lived in Khor Shum (Pakok), Upper Nile, Sudan. There they were used by the SPLA to porter food from the refugee camp at Dima, Ethiopia, to Khor Shum because, as they put it, "there was little food in Sudan." The Ugandans said that they walked three days each way, traveling from 3 P.M. to 1 A.M., sleeping one to two hours, and then walking again until noon each day. The forced portering came to an end for the Ugandans when the government of Mengistu fell and the flow of food originating in the Sudanese refugee camps was cut off.

Historical Background

Almost all governments and many guerrilla organizations rely on involuntary recruitment or conscription. In northeast Africa, however, a history of military slavery underlies this practice.

> Military slavery in the Sudan is a product of state activity, and it predates the imperial ventures of either Egypt or Britain. States created and used slave armies; they defined, through the use of such armies, their relations with certain groups or categories of peoples. But those

> people continued to exist even after the state which first
> produced them had disappeared. Both the Egyptian and
> British empires made use of military slavery, and both
> changed it as they used it. But it cannot be said they
> completely controlled it.[233]

The Islamic institution of slave armies involved those who were alien to
the polity in which they served. "Military slavery involved systematic
acquisition of slaves who were trained and employed as soldiers."[234]
These slaves, captured in military campaigns scouring the hinterlands of
newly conquered Sudanic states, fought for the Turco-Egyptian army
throughout the world, sometimes on both sides of a conflict.[235]

The inherent weakness of the military slave system was
recruitment; the southern Sudan and the Nuba hills were seen by Anglo
Egyptian officials as the main reservoirs of recruitment of new slave
soldiers. In these areas, which remained largely unpacified until after the
First World War,"[236] slaves soldiers were captured in large well-
organized military campaigns and by requiring nomadic subjects to pay
their tribute in slaves.[237]

The status of a soldier was that of a slave. "He was not a soldier
because he was a slave; rather he was a slave because he was a
soldier."[238]

In addition to state military slavery, there was also private
military slavery. The zara'ib or armed camps in southern Sudan were
created by the independent commercial companies using private armies
from the 1850s to 1870s. These commercial companies, prospecting for
ivory, gold and other valuables, had two or three sources of soldiers:

---

[233]Johnson, "Military Slavery in Northeast Africa," p. 85.

[234]Ibid., p. 76.

[235]Ibid., p. 79.

[236]Ibid., p. 81.

[237]Ibid., p. 77.

[238]Ibid., p. 76.

recruited contractual soldiers[239] who often fell into debt bondage which they might escape by trading in slaves they captured on company raids; slaves captured by commercial companies to serve as soldiers;[240] and slaves recruited into the companies' armies from the "gun-boys."[241]

The *zara'ib* camps and often their armies were taken over by the Turco-Egyptian administration in the 1870s and later the Anglo-Egyptian government, which gradually extended itself out of these military/commercial centers, using an army founded on the old slave armies of the previous century. Very often they incorporated old *zara'ib* sites as new administrative posts, including present-day Nasir, Bor, Rejjaf, Rumbek, Shambe, Wau, and others[242] that have been fought over in the second civil war.

The current military practices of forced recruitment by the parties may be understood in this historical context, but violations of the rules of war are not justified or excused by history.

UNACCOMPANIED MINORS
AND RECRUITMENT OF CHILD SOLDIERS

Under the rules of war, recruitment, voluntary or involuntary, of soldiers under the age of fifteen is illegal;[243] under the Convention on

---

[239]The contractual soldiers (Nubians displaced from their own agricultural lands in the north) often were bound to the commercial companies by contract and debt. Douglas H. Johnson, "Recruitment and Entrapment in Private Slave Armies: The Structure of the *Zara'ib* in the Southern Sudan," *Slavery & Abolition* 13 (London: April 1992): p. 168.

[240]Johnson, "Military Slavery in Northeast Africa," p. 77.

[241]*Ibid.*, pp. 78-79.

[242]*Ibid.*

[243]Protocol II, article 4 (3) (c): "children who have not attained the age of fifteen years shall neither be recruited in the armed forces or groups nor allowed to take part in hostilities."

the Rights of the Child, those who recruit soldiers between the ages of fifteen and eighteen must endeavor to give priority to those who are oldest.[244] Although it is not yet in effect, the African Convention on the Rights of the Child prohibits recruitment of anyone under the age of eighteen.

The SPLA has engaged in recruitment of underage soldiers. It has maintained large camps of boys separate from their families and tribes, given them some education and military training, and from these camps has drawn fresh recruits.

Initially the SPLA encouraged many male minors to leave their parents and go to refugee camps in Ethiopia for education purposes starting in the mid-1980s; others went for safety reasons, many with their families as whole villages took flight from government army abuses.

In Ethiopia, the "SPLA was allowed to administer the 'minors' camps', where unaccompanied boys were kept separated from the main camp."[245] There were some 17,000 boys. In these camps, according to SPLA officers and the minors themselves, they were given military training. They were removed from the camps for military service when the needs of the SPLA demanded, including to fight with the Ethiopian army against the Ethiopian rebels; many who fought were under fifteen years of age. Other under fifteens were given military duties such as guarding checkpoints and prisoners.

When the Sudanese refugees fled Ethiopia, the unaccompanied boys were escorted back in large groups, still separated from their families, by the SPLA. In Sudan, more were trained and sent to the front. Others were held back in unaccompanied minors' camps, and from there were recruited into full time military participation.

Some 10,000 unaccompanied minors with adults fled the government capture of Kapoeta into Kenya, where they live in a refugee camp administered by the UNHCR and are no longer segregated. The rest of the boys have been absorbed into the SPLA but in 1994 there are

---

[244]Convention on the Rights of the Child, article 38 (3). This Convention applies to States Parties, and makes no mention of rebel groups, but does provide authoritative guidance for interpreting customary international humanitarian law applicable to rebels. Sudan has ratified the Convention.

[245]UNICEF, *Children of War: Wandering alone in southern Sudan* (New York: UNICEF, 1994), p. 15.

remnants of the original groupings in Laboni, Nasir, and perhaps elsewhere.

The presence of several thousand unaccompanied male Sudanese minors in segregated locations Sudan and over 10,000 such minors in a Kenyan refugee camp is the result of the SPLA's illegal policy of recruiting under-age soldiers.

All civilians in a region ravaged by war are at risk, but minors are among the most disadvantaged and need additional protection. In the second civil war in Sudan, even the adults are hard pressed to survive. Children separated from their families, where they might find a modicum of adult protection, supervision and concern, are at even greater risk than adults separated from their kin.[246]

Family reunification, an obvious solution, will not be indicated in each case; some boys have grown to adolescence and young manhood apart from their families and indeed from all adult discipline. Others have already been combatants and lived independently for too long. In these circumstances neither parents nor children may be able to make the adjustment to living together.

Family reunification, however, is the solution indicated for many by custom and well as law and expediency. The care and supervision the SPLA factions have provided have been much less than that which most family networks, even those displaced by war, could have provided.

SPLA-Torit Position on Recruitment of Minors

SPLA-Torit denied recruiting or arming young soldiers. John Garang stated, "Our cut-off age is eighteen and above."[247] When challenged on the use of boys as soldiers after the Nasir faction split in late 1991, Commander Garang denied that they even had enough guns to give to recruits above age eighteen, much less those under age.[248]

Others in the SPLA and its allies have advanced a variety of arguments to justify or explain away the practice of recruitment of

---

[246]UNICEF, *Children of War*, p. 29.

[247]Emma Sharp, "Child Soldiers in Southern Sudan," *Sudan Monitor*, vol. 2, issue 6 (London: December 1991), p. 4. John Garang made this statement on December 1, 1991.

[248]*Ibid.*

minors, and of the continued existence of large encampments of thousands of unaccompanied male minors that appeared first in Ethiopian refugee camps. Analizing these arguments throws light on the manner in which the phenomenon developed.

Rationale for Segregation of Unaccompanied Minors

These male minors first became "unaccompanied" when they undertook to go as refugees to Ethiopia in the mid-1980s. They usually left their homes in groups, together with adults. Some were orphaned by the war, but many were not.

While some started out their journey to Ethiopia enthusiastically, others were taken against their will, according to interviews. In late 1991, a journalist interviewed a chief of a village in the Sobat basin who said that in 1989, twenty-nine twelve-year-old boys had been taken from that village by force by the SPLA. Since then, none of their parents had heard from them.[249]

Some of the village women walked to the Itang refugee camp in Ethiopia on their own to find their boys but were told that the children had been taken to another place. The villagers found out that some of the larger children were sent to Kapoeta, for what they feared was military training.[250]

As to those who went voluntarily to Ethiopia, some SPLA supporters said that the unaccompanied boys were separated from their families when their cattle camps were raided by the government and government-aligned militias, and that they fled separate from their families. This might explain the fact that the unaccompanied minors were all boys, since girls' work did not include tending cattle in cattle camps away from the villages.[251]

Spontaneous flight across a nearby border certainly accounted for some of the unaccompanied minors, but it is not the only reason for the appearance of over 17,000 unaccompanied Sudanese boys in Ethiopia,

---

[249]*Ibid.*, pp. 2-4.

[250]*Ibid.*

[251]Some report, however, that girls may be found in cattle camps because children go there to be near a source of milk, or because girls go to prepare the food, traditionally female work, for their brothers and other male relatives.

most of whom came from areas hundreds of kilometers from the Ethiopian border.

The avenues of escape to Ethiopia developed over time. The safest route to Ethiopia, the only neighboring country that received refugees at the beginning of the war, through the SPLA networks, and the SPLA took increasing responsibility for organizing this flight, which then became routine. By 1988, large numbers of boys were being marched to Ethiopia, and in 1990 were observed by outsiders being transported by vehicle with adult supervisors.[252]

Often the boys left Sudan upon hearing from SPLA commanders of the educational opportunities available in the refugee camps in Ethiopia. Commander Riek described what he considered to be the initiation of the recruitment program:

> In 1988, five years after the start of the SPLA, I began to realize that we had no schools in the liberated areas. I was the commander of Upper Nile.[253] Garang sent a message that there were good schools in the refugee camps, if the children wanted to go there for school. This was a very noble idea.
>
> I started a campaign for them to go to school in the refugee camps. I vigorously pushed this in western and northern Upper Nile, my command, and also in areas bordering these zones.
>
> Kuol Manyang also sent children to the refugee camps from Bahr. We were competing with lost time, five years, 1983-88. It would affect our manpower in the future.

---

[252]Some, according to various reports, were even sent to Cuba for training. A journalist in Nasir as late as 1992 heard some of the minors speak proficient Spanish and sing songs in Spanish in praise of Fidel Castro. Sharp, "Child Soldiers in Southern Sudan," p. 3.

[253]In 1988, he was area commander of Western Upper Nile. He was appointed zonal commander of Upper Nile in late 1989.

As a Dinka leader close to the SPLA explained it, each chief was asked by the SPLA to send some children from his village for the schools in Ethiopia. Those had to be boys whose parents were prepared to release them. This leader's own brother and three nephews went to Ethiopia in this fashion. Often they were escorted in large groups. A Nuer commander from Bentiu told HRW/Africa that he had accompanied over one hundred boys from Bentiu region to Fugnido, Ethiopia, for education in 1986.

It was true that educational opportunities in southern Sudan were extremely limited, especially in the rural areas, even before the conflict broke out.[254] After SPLA advances in the mid-1980s the government cut off its services to the SPLA-controlled territory, which came to include all of southern Sudan except for a handful of garrison towns.

Most often, boys interviewed by social and relief workers routinely volunteered "education" as their reason for going to Ethiopia. Education continues to be a magnet. Today, Sudanese youth migrate to the Kenyan refugee camp at Kakuma for schooling. Equatorian youth, including those in besieged Juba, go to refugee camps in Uganda with the dream of education. They learn of these refugee schools by word of mouth, however, rather than from the SPLA.

While education may be a partial reason motivating the boys and the SPLA, it does not appear to be the sole reason.

Many explain the apparently anomalous and continuing segregation of male minors by pointing to two Sudanese precedents: boarding schools and the cattle camps.

In Sudan, southern youths who continued their schooling beyond a certain grade often lived in boarding schools distant from their family's

---

[254]Schools, even those built by community donations, were not staffed or supplied. One anthropologist who visited the Nasir area in 1983 remarked that most of the buildings (brick and zinc schools, medical dispensaries and veterinary offices) built to attract government services remained vacant. There were only fourteen primary schools and two junior secondary schools operating in the immediate Sobat region in 1983; Nasir had one of the intermediate schools. Throughout the 1970s and early 1980s, however, many of these schools were closed for weeks or months at a time due to shortages of textbooks, teachers, and other essentials. Sharon Hutchinson, "Potential Development Projects for the Sobat Valley Region; A set of Proposals Prepared for Save the Children Fund (U.K.)" (London: June 1993).

rural homes. These young people, however, usually returned home on vacations and continued to maintain ties with their families and to be brought up in the culture through initiation and marriage rites.

Others cited the cattle camp culture as an explanation for segregation of the boys. It is said that in the pastoral Nilotic culture, boys are sent to cattle camps at a young age, and there learn to fend for themselves and live apart from the family. The anthropologist Wendy James wrote that in some

> Nilotic communities, it was normal and traditional for boys and young men to form well-organized and independent groups, based upon age, which functioned as cattle-herding units and normally lived together in cattle camps for the dry season, on their own and away from their families. In the cattle camps they would depend largely on milk and other cattle products for subsistence. These bands of young men also had the duty of protecting herds from raids, and provided the framework for traditional forms of hostility and peacemaking. In some of the Nilotic groups, there is a formal and sophisticated system of age classes and grades, giving a coherent structure to the groupings and activities of boys and young men, and leading to their ceremonial initiation into the adult world. This is one factor in the social background against which the large groupings of unaccompanied boys found particularly in the former refugee camp of Fugnyido should be understood.[255]

This background is evoked, less subtly, by others to justify segregation of the unaccompanied minors as consistent with the culture. The cattle camp, however, was not a function of the war but a pre-existing economic phenomenon. In the cattle camp, boys performed a

---

[255]Wendy James, "Background Report and Guidelines for Future Planning: Nor Deng Centre for Sudanese Returnees, Nasir," WFP/Operation Lifeline Sudan, Southern Sector, Nairobi, Kenya, August 1991, p. 13.

seasonal economic function for the family and were accompanied by other family members, sometimes uncles, brothers, or grandfathers.[256]

Neither the boarding schools nor the cattle camps were intended to serve as the means of permanent separation of the boys from their families, such as has occurred for unaccompanied minors in the context of the conflict. Other, more directly military and war-related reasons provide a more plausible explanation for this modern phenomenon.

Historical Background for Boy Soldiers in Southern Sudan

Boy soldiers are part of a cultural pattern that is not offered as a justification for these unaccompanied minors. However, there is a history in northeast Africa of military slavery,[257] in which "gun-boys" were a source of soldiers.

Whereas the slaves captured for the Turco-Egyptian army before the twentieth century were mostly full-grown men, the commercial companies/armies formed to exploit the ivory and slave potential of the White Nile made use of young boys as well.[258]

These "gun-boys" were slave boys who, starting at the ages of about seven or ten, worked as gun bearers for individual soldiers. Every contractual soldier had at least one, some had two or more, and many slave-soldiers themselves had "gun-boys." The boys' service to the soldiers was part of their training, and when they grew older they became soldiers

---

[256]The war probably affected the movement of males to cattle camps; there is a good deal of testimony that men and boys tried to protect their cattle, their most valuable asset, from the raiders when it appeared a raid was on the way. Thus they would go to the cattle camp to move their cattle to a different location; many were killed trying to fend off cattle raiders who were either combatants or others taking advantage of the situation. In other cases the men and boys were safer from attacks away from the villages. Thus the existence of armed conflict and raiding done by organized military expeditions could have changed the rather temporary basis on which boys were sent to cattle camps.

[257]*See* above in this chapter.

[258]Johnson, "Military Slavery in Northeast Africa," p. 79.

themselves. They were the most regular though not the most numerous source of military slaves.[259]

> The gun-boys were observed as early as 1870, but they are a consistent feature of slave armies in the Nile Valley, and gun-boys turn up not only in the Uganda Rifles at the end of the last century, but in the King's African Rifles, the Sudanese army, and even the National Resistance Army and the Sudan People's Liberation Army of this century.[260]

This is not to say that the system that the SPLA follows today is a direct continuity from these earlier military slavery practices, but that conditions similar to those which fostered the expansion of military slavery in the nineteenth century now exist in the late twentieth century.

Colonial armies which grew out of the institution of military slavery in northeast Africa retained the legacy of having a reserve of boy soldiers who were regularly channeled into the army, whether as sons of soldiers or as hangers-on of soldiers, a regular feature even of the British army into the twentieth century. Both the Sudanese and Ugandan post-independence armies retained some form of boy soldiers, and in both countries the percentage of teenaged, and even younger, soldiers rose during the dislocation of prolonged civil wars, particularly in guerrilla armies.

At the start of the first civil war, 1,146 soldiers mutinied in Torit and later fled in August 1955. Among them were 380 boy soldiers.[261]

Change in Age at which Boys Become Adults

Historian Douglas H. Johnson suggests that the phenomenon of boy soldiers among the southern Sudanese today also is linked to another war-related phenomenon, a change in the age at which boys become adults.

---

[259]Johnson, "Recruitment and Entrapment in Private Slave Armies," p. 168.

[260]*Ibid.*, p. 168.

[261]Johnson, "Military Slavery in Northeast Africa," p. 86, n. 6.

Among the Nuer and those Dinka who practice facial scarification,[262] boys became adults when they are initiated into age-sets which are composed of groups of boys of roughly comparable ages. Earlier in this century initiation took place between the ages of fifteen and eighteen. Starting in the 1950s the age-sets have been initiated more frequently, and the age of initiatees has declined to ages thirteen and fourteen in the 1970s and 1980s, largely due to fears on the part of fathers that scarification would be banned.[263]

Once so marked, the boys are regarded as adults and are expected to take up adult duties, such as carrying spears and defending herds and homes from attack, and getting married. This applies to those societies which practice scarification at initiation for boys, most Nuer and many Dinka, which together make up perhaps half the population of south Sudan.

Although by international law standards these thirteen- and fourteen-year-olds remain underage for military recruitment purposes, many are considered by their own societies, and consider themselves to be, "adults" and thus old enough to serve in the military.

The historical and cultural background explains but does not excuse the recruitment of underage minors. The modern rules of war and Convention on the Rights of the Child were written to change just such practices in all societies.

Conditions in the Ethiopian Refugee Camps

When one international NGO first visited the Fugnido camp in Ethiopia in 1987, one staffer recalled they found "only naked bodies, very thin, of boys, as far as the eye could see. They did not even have tukls to live in." Later the boys built their own large sleeping quarters and schools, and NGOs helped recruit caretakers and teachers for them.

As the war progressed and flight into Ethiopia became more organized, a system of receiving refugees developed. After the boys reached Ethiopia, they were segregated into minors' sleeping and living quarters and there subjected to political and military training by the

---

[262]*See* above in this Chapter.

[263]Commander Riek tried to ban scarification by decree in the late 1980s in his jurisdiction of Western Upper Nile on medical grounds (lack of health service to treat infections resulting from scarification).

SPLA. The SPLA says that the boys were given military training in order to prepare them to defend their country in the event that the war lasted a long time, but denies that the boys were sent into combat. As explained below, that assertion is not true.

The SPLA instructed the minors in the camps in what to tell expatriate relief workers and other outsiders about their relations with the SPLA. Interviewers over the years remarked on the singular uniformity of answers to questions, such as why the minors went to Sudan ("education"). After the split in the SPLA in August 1991, a fuller picture began to emerge. HRW/Africa concludes that the SPLA recruited the boys for both education and military purposes, but attempted to conceal the military purpose.

Furthermore, many of the minors were not "unaccompanied." Surveys conducted in Ethiopian camps indicate that one-fifth of the unaccompanied boys in the Ethiopian camps had relatives in the camps. Many of these boys were required by the SPLA to live in segregated buildings with the other boys. This was possible because the SPLA, not international agencies, was delegated management authority in the camps by the Ethiopian government hosts.

Unfortunately, the schooling the boys received in Ethiopia was minimal, no doubt due to the difficult conditions under which they lived and the fact that they had to perform the whole range of feeding and housekeeping chores normally split up among family members according to age and sex. One 1989 survey of the unaccompanied minors in the camps in Ethiopia found that 90 percent of the unaccompanied minors were illiterate or in grade one.

One boy, a member of a small non-Nilotic tribe, told HRW/Africa that he left his family and village in 1989 to go to Ethiopia with his cousin. The reason he left was "because of the harassment of the system." Based on estimates of an adult who knew him in his village, he was about twelve or thirteen when he left for Ethiopia in 1989. The cousins traveled with a mixed group of 900 members of their tribe. Upon their arrival in the Itang refugee camp, the SPLA separated the boys among the 900 refugees by age. Those over sixteen or seventeen were sent for full-time military training, and his age group was sent to the housing for the other unaccompanied minors. He lived at the school at Tarpaam, in Itang, created in early 1990, where 5,000 unaccompanied male minors were registered.[264] He attended school in Tarpaam, where he estimated there were six schools. In his home village, he had gone to school up to grade four where the language of instruction was Arabic, which was not the language used in Tarpaam.

The Ethiopian refugee camps continued to receive refugees as the war in Sudan drove civilians out. By June 1990, there were three main Sudanese refugee camps in Ethiopia, Fugnido, Itang and Dima.[265] Not uncommonly, there is some dispute about the overall numbers of refugees and the numbers of minors. Conservative estimates were that Fugnido, with 76,204 refugees,[266] mostly Dinka, had the largest unaccompanied minor population: 10,000. Itang, the largest refugee camp with 150,000 mostly Nuer refugees,[267] had an unaccompanied minor population of 5,300. Dima, with a mixed population of 20,000,[268] had 2,000 unaccompanied minors.

The boys built the huts in which they lived. In Fugnido, they had access to the Gilo River, where they fished and bathed. They prepared their own food. They were assisted by caretakers and teachers, although

---

[264]UNICEF OLS, "The Return to Southern Sudan of the Sudanese Refugees from Itang Camp, Gambela, Ethiopia," Nasir, Southern Sudan, August 31, 1991, p. 4.

[265]A survey done in March 1988 indicated that in Itang camp 75.2 percent of the population was male, in Fugnido, 94.6 percent male, and in Dima, 97.8 percent male. de Waal, "Starving out the South," p. 161, n. 25.

[266]Office of UNHCR, "UNHCR activities financed by voluntary funds: Report for 1989-90 and proposed programmes and budget for 1991," Part I. Africa, A/AC.96/751 (Geneva: UNHCR), p. 33. Another source set the population of Fugnido (also written Panyido) at ·its height in 1991 at 86,000. Scott-Villiers, "Repatriation of Sudanese Refugees," p. 204.

[267]UNHCR, "Report for 1989-90," p. 33, gives a figure of 247,143 for Itang, but later studies concluded that the number was probably no more than 150,000. Scott-Villiers, "Repatriation of Sudanese Refugees," p. 204.

[268]UNHCR, "Report for 1989-90," p. 33, sets the number at 35,075 for Dima. Scott-Villiers estimates, based on later data, that the figure was closer to 20,000. Scott-Villiers, "Repatriation of Sudanese Refugees," p. 204.

the ratio of adults to children and adolescents was very small, much smaller than in the average Nilotic village.

The minors were assisted by international NGOs, although at no time were Ethiopian or expatriate relief workers allowed to live in or spend the night in the camps. The camp administration, which was in the hands of the SPLA and its designees, required relief workers to depart daily at 3 P.M. or 6 P.M., supposedly on safety grounds.

By 1989, the Sudanese refugee camp in Fugnido had exploded in size, far outstripping the nearby Anuak village of 5,000. In an armed incident in June 1989 sparked by conflicts between the unaccompanied Sudanese minors and Anuak youth, between fifty and one hundred Anuaks were killed by Sudanese refugees and SPLA cadre.[269]

Military Training for the "Red Army"

Some form of military training was admittedly given to all unaccompanied minors, regardless of age. A former SPLA commander told HRW/Africa that of the minors in Ethiopia the older boys (a relative term) received a full-time military training course of three or four months. The younger starting at age seven, received training during school holidays.

Minors were organized into separate military units which made up the "Red Army," according to another SPLA former commander. After he was wounded, this commander was transferred to a job as a teacher of the unaccompanied minors in a refugee camp with the rank of commander of the "Red Army."

Another former SPLA officer described the "Red Army" to HRW/Africa:

> The "Red Army" means the young people, ages fourteen through sixteen. They were organized as a separate army; the adults were in the SPLA. The Red Army was in battalions. Wherever SPLA had a stronghold, they had contingents of the Red Army.

---

[269]Commander Simon Mori was part of an investigation commission sent by John Garang to look into this incident. Its report was never published. Simon Mori is now affiliated with SPLA-Nasir/United.

In the first few years, the Red Army fought and was always massacred. Then they were taken off the front line. They were not good soldiers because they were too young. They were then assigned to menial jobs. In the last stage, they were in school in Itang and Fugnido, which was organized for them.

Others, not affiliated with the SPLA, observed that the Red Army boy soldiers were used as bodyguards for army officers and defense of "liberated" towns, which explains their armed presence in 1991 in Mongalla and Torit.[270] Some long-term prisoners of the SPLA said that their guards included these under age soldiers.

Military Deployment of Minors in Ethiopia

When the Ethiopian army began to collapse in late 1990 and early 1991, the Mengistu regime turned to the SPLA for reinforcements, and the SPLA provided troops to fight alongside its benefactor's army. Two former SPLA officers separately told HRW/Africa that at that time between 900 and 2,000 unaccompanied minors aged eleven and over were sent from the Ethiopian refugee camps for training and then sent into battle against the Ethiopian rebels in Dembidolo (February 1991) and in Gore (April-May 1991). Many died there.

HRW/Africa talked to one boy sent for military training at an SPLA base in early 1991. His group then was deployed to fight in SPLA units under SPLA command in Dembidolo, Ethiopia, against Ethiopian rebels. The boy was a private, he was armed, and he fired his rifle in the engagement. At the time he was probably fourteen.

Emergency Evacuation of Unaccompanied Minors Along With Sudanese Refugees from Ethiopia

When the Mengistu regime collapsed in May 1991, the SPLA prepared to move its troops and hundreds of thousands of civilian Sudanese refugees from Ethiopia. Although in some cases the minors were able to reunite with their families during the exodus, in most cases they were not.

A task force of minors, after their defeat in Dembidolo, Ethiopia, withdrew to Pochalla, on the Sudan side of the border. They stayed two

---

[270]Sharp, "Child Soldiers in Southern Sudan," p. 4.

weeks, then went to Boma, where they stayed for nine days. From there they went to Kapoeta, a fifteen-day walk. There may have been 1,000 boys on this march, according to one participant.

A former SPLA commander said that in May/June 1991, he was instructed by his SPLA commander to accompany another group of several thousand minors to Kapoeta for education "by the Kenyan government and NGOs." He took the boys from Tarpaam in Itang to Fugnido to join the larger group of unaccompanied minors, which he estimated then totaled 4,000. Once in Kapoeta, those who had already received military training were deployed to SPLA bases. Some 2,500 who had not been trained (ages eleven to sixteen) were trained less than three months in Kapoeta and then deployed.

The boy who had fought in Ethiopia and his 1,000 companions stayed one night in Kapoeta, then proceeded to Torit for twenty days, where they were idle. His account of his movements as part of the SPLA-Torit force was corroborated by others familiar with the period.[271]

Conditions for Unaccompanied Minors Repatriated to Sudan from Ethiopia

Those unaccompanied minors fleeing Ethiopia who were not yet incorporated into the SPLA appeared in large groups in the Sudanese towns of Nasir, Pochalla, and Pakok, all near the Ethiopian border. It was agreed by the agencies concerned that the ICRC would register and organize protection and assistance for the repatriated unaccompanied minors in Sudan. The ICRC registered 10,000 unaccompanied minors at Pochalla, 2,000 at Nasir and 2,000 at Pakok by the end of 1991.[272] This arrangement held until March 1992 when the ICRC was denied

---

[271]After Torit, the boy soldiers were taken to Magwe and stayed there for two months where they built their own huts. When the government's 1992 dry season offensive commenced this unit of boy soldiers moved to Ngangala where they fought with the Sudan government in April, 1992, and were defeated. The young witness' task force retreated to Lirya, north of Torit, and remained for forty days until they were ejected by the government. His company retreated south to the SPLA base in Lotukei, in Didinga territory. The rest of the task force left for the siege of Juba.

[272]*ICRC Annual Report 1991*, p. 39.

permission to continue operations in Sudan by the government, partly because of this very protection rule. UNICEF took over the job then.

Meanwhile, in August 1991, while the returning refugees were stalled in the three camps along the Ethiopian border, the Nasir faction broke from the SPLA. The rebel Nasir faction raised several human rights complaints against Garang--one was that the SPLA under Garang's leadership had recruited boys for its army. Riek later tried to explain how, even though he was a commander in that army, he disapproved of the practice:

> In 1990, after being in the field for five years, I decided to visit Itang. I found the children's camp there. They were receiving military training. It was the same in Fugnido.

> On April 1, 1990, I met Garang en route to operations. "Why are the children being militarily trained?" I asked him. "Those who succeed will go to school. This is our reservoir for the army," he said.

> I did not like it. I took a stand against the military training of children. I told Taban Deng Gai (the administrator of Itang) to stop the military training of the children. He was an ardent Garang supporter, but he stopped their training in Itang. The children left a few months later to Sudan. But there were actually more children being trained in Fugnido than in Itang.

Conditions in Nasir

The Nasir population of unaccompanied minors, which came from Itang and some from Dima, was originally estimated at 4,000-5,000. There were actually 3,500 boys in Nasir in June 1991 at a site called Pandanyang. Some 1,500 left Nasir in June and July, probably walking to their accessible home areas.[273] The minors in Nasir were mostly Nuer, with some Dinka, Nubans, and others.

---

[273]UNICEF OLS, "Return to Southern Sudan of the Sudanese Refugees," p. 4. Pandanyang had been an Anya-Nya II base prior to the fall of Nasir to SPLA siege in January 1989. *Ibid.*, p. 19.

Due to government intransigience, relief flights were not able to land in Nasir, and because the returned refugees were not able to cultivate, a severe food shortage developed. The minors set up a separate camp. A nutritional survey in August 1991 by relief agencies found 60 percent moderate malnourishment among these boys.

A study of the repatriation and the international relief efforts in Nasir in 1991 found that the SPLA-Nasir manipulated the remaining 1,500-2,000 unaccompanied minors and other repatriatees to secure more aid for themselves. This study found that significant relief was required for the refugees returning to Nasir from Ethiopia, that the Sudan government was doing everything in its power to block the needed relief, and that the international community was not responding to the need. The SPLA-Nasir "directed the focus of relief on to the severely malnourished unaccompanied minors,"[274] and this focus helped to generate what little assistance was brought, although in the end, the minors did not receive the needed assistance. The study concluded:

> A fair proportion of the special food distributed to the unaccompanied minors never reached their mouths, but instead went to feed other more powerful individuals. The minors therefore remained, for a long time, in a state of near starvation, and this helped ensure the continuation of relief assistance.[275]

Those Passing Through Pochalla and Their Flight from Pochalla to Avoid Government Attack

One study found one in three of the 2,000 unaccompanied minors in Nasir suffered from severe malnutrition.[276] Some 10,000 unaccompanied minors in Fugnido fled to Pochalla, where they set up a

---

[274]Scott-Villiers, "Repatriation of Sudanese Refugees," p. 209.

[275]*Ibid.* The other group manipulated and prevented from leaving Nasir in order to attract more relief was the Uduk. *Ibid.*, p. 210. *See generally*, Wendy James, "Uduk Asylum Seekers in Gambela, 1992," Report for UNHCR (Addis Ababa: October 31, 1992).

[276]OFDA, "Sudan - Drought/Civil Strife, Situation Report no. 52," December 5, 1991 (Washington, D.C.: U.S.AID), cited in Burr, *Genocide*, p.45, n. 190.

separate camp apart from the large displaced persons' camps for families fleeing Ethiopia. Crossing the Gilo River in Ethiopia, many drowned. Other minors went to Khor Shum (Pakok), where in November 1991 a nutritional survey showed 66 percent moderate malnourishment.

After unsuccessful militia attacks on Pochalla, the Sudan government launched a cross-border attack on Pochalla from Ethiopian soil in early 1992 as part of its 1992 dry season offensive. The offensive had been expected, and tens of thousands of the former refugees, including the minors, were evacuated before the government reached Pochalla.

The ICRC assisted the minors and others in evacuating Pochalla and traveling south, providing food and medical assistance at stations along the long route. The ICRC was expelled from Sudan in March 1992 by the government, in part because of this humanitarian assistance. Some relief workers suspected that part of the government motivation for the Pochalla attack was to kill or capture large groups of the minors whom the Sudan government viewed as combatants or at least a military reserve force.

The minors' journey, from February to the end of April 1992, led them across very difficult marshy and desert terrain as well as an area controlled by the hostile Toposa militia. The OLS reported an attack by Toposa bandits at Magos, northeast of Kapoeta, on March 19, 1992 that killed five minors.[277]

SPLA-Torit Commander Salva Kiir, Garang's chief of military operations, accompanied the minors. Interviewed with them before they arrived in Kapoeta, he said that the plan was to settle the boys in a new camp at Narus near the Kenyan border, for which large-scale international assistance would be required.[278]

---

[277]SEPHA Bi-Monthly Report no. 14 on OLS Emergency and Relief Operations in the Southern Sector for the period March 21 to April 5, 1992, p. 2.

[278]"Long March," *Sudan Update*, vol. 3, no. 15 (London: March 30, 1992), p.1, quoting Peter Biles in *The Guardian* (London).

A headcount of unaccompanied minors in Narus completed on April 22, 1992[279] showed 12,241 minors and 6,600 "teachers and dependents." Narus was to be a temporary place for the minors. Some 850, the OLS noted, could have been reunited with their families immediately if there were government flight clearance to Ler.[280]

The Flight from Sudan to Refuge in Kenya

A month later, on May 28, 1992, the nearby town of Kapoeta unexpectedly fell to the government. Many fled from Kapoeta south to Narus, and those in Narus quickly fled to Kenya. The hasty exodus was not coordinated or directed by the SPLA, according to relief officials directly across the border in Lokichokio, Kenya at the time.

After the minors arrived in Lokichokio in late May 1992, their numbers were estimated at 12,000. A later, more leisurely headcount of the minors at the Kakuma refugee camp just set up one hundred kilometers south of Lokichokio found only 10,500 minors, prompting the accusation that the SPLA-Torit had kidnapped some 1,500 to 3,000 of the minors and sent them back to fight or receive military training in Sudan. At the time, a UNHCR spokesperson said that at least 1,000 unaccompanied minors apparently had left the Lokochokio camp in Kenya in one night, and that a U.S.-based relief organization, World Vision, had reported seeing a sudden increase in the number of boys mainly in their late teens back in Narus.[281] Some believed that these boys were deployed in the major SPLA-Torit assaults on Juba that

---

[279]The headcount was conducted jointly by the U.N., NGOs, and the SRRA, the relief wing of the SPLA-Torit.

[280]SEPHA Bi-Monthly Report no. 16 on OLS Emergency and Relief Operations in the Southern Sector for the period April 19 to May 5, 1992, p.6.

[281]Jane Perlez, "1,000 Boys Return to Camp in Sudan," *The New York Times*, August 19, 1992.

occurred in June and July 1992.[282] The discrepancy in numbers was never fully explained,[283] and the SPLA-Torit denied the charges.

The minors who remained in Kenya were moved to a newly created refugee camp at Kakuma, Kenya, which, as of late June, 1993, had 28,000 Sudanese refugees, 10,500 of them unaccompanied minors, a disproportionate share of that population. Some 95 percent of the Sudanese were Dinka.[284]

At Kakuma, the UNHCR established a foster care family program for approximately 2,500 unaccompanied minors, who live in groups of four or five with refugee families who are given incentives to take them in.

The refugee camp operated eighteen schools with 318 headmasters for 12,500 students.[285] Further evidence of the difficulty Sudanese children have faced over the war years in receiving an education is the fact that, in the camp in Kakuma, where the average age of all Sudanese students was fourteen to fifteen, only fifty or sixty Sudanese attended secondary school, according to camp administrators.

The school itself may attract unaccompanied minors from the Sudan. In one week in June 1993, one hundred Dinka minors, average age fourteen, arrived from Lotukei, a Didinga (Equatorian tribe) border area where an SPLA base is located.

Unaccompanied Minors Remaining in SPLA-Torit Areas, Including Palataka

There were unaccompanied minors in several locations inside Sudan even before the fall of Mengistu and the evacuation of the Sudanese refugee camps in May 1991.

In 1989-1990 the SPLA proposed creation of schools that also would function as self-sustaining economic enterprises, to be run by its

---

[282]Ibid.

[283]Relief workers in this region tend to view all numbers with skepticism and regard most as educated estimates, at best.

[284]The total refugee population in Kakuma camp was 35,000. UNHCR Camp Profile -- Kakuma, Kenya (updated June 28, 1993).

[285]Ibid.

Friends of African Children Educational (FACE) Foundation. Industrial and agricultural enterprises would draw their labor from schoolchildren working in shifts who would thereby generate enough income to make the educational system self-supporting. Funding agencies did not find the FACE proposal attractive because it would have directed too many resources to a small group, would not serve all children in the population, and seemed more like an agricultural project for children than an educational project.[286] Nevertheless, the SPLA established a FACE school along these lines on the grounds of a large Catholic mission and farm at Palataka, south of Torit. Other schools were set up north of Nimule, in Molitokuro and Borongolei.

A visitor to the Palataka school in late 1991 observed that the "situation is shocking, but not because military training is going on. It is shocking because the boys are dying of starvation and easily preventable diseases, such as malaria and diarrhoea . . . . Observers say that military training has gone on in the past, but most of the children are too weak and small to make effective soldiers."[287] Other visitors agreed that the conditions were deplorable.[288]

In 1992 an estimated 4,100 boys from seven to fourteen years were in Palataka; most were ten and eleven years old.[289] A Norwegian journalist who visited Palataka in February 1992 saw these very young boys with weapons; one, fully armed and in uniform, told her that he was thirteen and had been a soldier for three years. She observed that the children were "undernourished, some are losing their hair, others can hardly stand." The boys "often have no other food than the leaves from the trees."[290]

---

[286]"Boys starve to death in F.A.C.E. Foundation schools," *Sudan Monitor*, vol. 2, no. 7 (London: January 1992), p. 3.

[287]Sharp, "Child Soldiers in Southern Sudan," p. 4.

[288]"Boys starve to death in F.A.C.E. Foundation schools," *Sudan Monitor*, pp. 1, 3.

[289]UNICEF, *Children of War*, p. 25.

[290]Tove Gravdal, "They Don't Cry, but Their Eyes are Full of Tears," translation from Norwegian supplied by author to HRW/Africa (London, 1992).

She observed that the principal was an officer in the SPLA, and she received eyewitness accounts of daily military drills, tough discipline including beatings and exposure to the sun for some who tried to escape, and reports that many were taken by force from their families.[291] Other foreigners in the area also received complaints from Acholi villages that SPLA cadre recruited boys for these boarding schools from the surrounding area and that some were taken against the will of their parents.

An OLS report for the March/April 1992 period noted, "The health, nutritional and educational situation of 6,000 boys who are in 3 boarding schools in Palataka, Molitokuro, and Borongolei is said to be deplorable."[292] Evacuees from Torit to Palataka in May 1992 saw 3,000 boys, some as young as five to eight years old, living there in terrible conditions, with no latrines. The minors were entering into conflicts with the Acholi who lived in the area because the boys raided the fields around Palataka in a desperate search for food.

By July of 1992, health workers were in each of the three FACE "boarding schools" and feeding centers had been opened there as well. The total population of three schools was 7,750, with fifty-three health workers, some 602 children were in the feeding centers.[293]

The WFP determined a monthly food distribution schedule for the three FACE schools, population then grown to 9,000, in September 1992.[294] This schedule was interrupted, however, by the killing of three relief workers in the area that same month, causing the U.N. to pull out of this south Torit region. The provision of food to these schools fell to Catholic Relief Services, which in December 1992 began operations in the area unprotected by the U.N. umbrella. Bringing relief to Palataka

---

[291]*Ibid.*

[292]SEPHA Bi-Monthly Report no. 14 on OLS Emergency and Relief Operations in the Southern Sector for the period March 21 to April 5, 1992, p. 4.

[293]OLS (Southern Sector), Bi-Monthly Situation Report No. 21, July 4-20, 1992, p. 8.

[294]OLS (Southern Sector), Bi-Montly Situation Report No. 25, September 5-22, 1992, p. 6.

involved two problems: Palataka is twenty-two kilometers over a bad mountain road from Magwe, and the Magwe area was the scene of several clashes between SPLA-Torit and the breakaway William Nyuon faction in late 1992.

Conditions did not improve in 1993. A visitor to Palataka in July 1993 reported about 2,500 to 3,000 boys in the facility. He reported a serious food shortage there, due in part to the transportation and coordination difficulties. The children were cared for by eighty caretakers and thirty teachers. The boys in the school were aged five to fourteen. They lived in the thirty to forty unrepaired brick buildings of the Catholic Mission, in poor health and deplorable hygenic conditions. In short, Palataka remained a scandal.

Security in the area due to factional fighting continued to be poor in August and September 1993, causing the parish at Palataka to relocate to Nimule. Not all security problems were attributable to the combatants: some land mines, for example, were believed to have been laid by the local Acholi people, who were hostile to the mainly Dinka minors.

Increasing military clashes in the area led to the evacuation in early 1994 of the boys from Palataka to Laboni, an almost inaccessible site to which tens of thousands of displaced from the Triple A camps were also moved.

In Molitokuro school in early 1991, there were only 800 boys, all from the area around Torit and Kapoeta. In mid-1991, some 2,300 arrived from Ethiopian refugee camps and later from the Bor Massacre. Education was provided up to seventh and eighth grades.[295] By late 1992 there were about 3,100 boys from seven to seventeen years old, most in the fourteen- to fifteen-year-old group.

The 1,250 boys in Borongolei came almost entirely from the Dima refugee camp in Ethiopia. In Borongolei school, classes went up to fifth or sixth grades.

As described below, most of the boys from both Molokoturo and Borongolei schools, who were slightly older than the Palataka boys, were "evacuated" and disappeared in mid-1992.

Other reported locations of unaccompanied minors include Chukudum in Didinga territory south of Torit. There, in 1991, U.S. AID

---

[295]SEPHA Bi-Monthly Report no. 19 on OLS Emergency Operations in Southern Sudan for the period June 7-22, 1992, p. 3. An assessment done in June 1992 noted 150 malnourished minors at this school. *Ibid.*

personnel observed an Oxfam/U.S. agricultural project for 6,000 displaced, including some 500-800 unaccompanied minors who were being given military training by the SPLA.[296]

Military Training and Forced Recruitment of Boys Inside Sudan

One location where boys were trained by the SPLA inside Sudan was a training camp in Kapoeta that was marked with a sign "Jesh Amer" (Red Army) until August 1991, according to a journalist who wrote: "Eyewitnesses saw boys as young as 11 years old being trained there. It was quite an open practice until all the adverse publicity in July, after which time the sign was removed."[297] Many relief workers in southern Sudan at that time reported seeing very young boys armed with Kalashnikovs, en route to battle with the SPLA-Nasir faction after the split occurred.[298]

Several thousand boys are believed to have been recruited into the SPLA-Torit from the two FACE boarding schools established for them in Borongele and Molitoko in the vicinity of the "Triple A" displaced persons camps on the east bank of the White Nile. In late 1992 or early 1993, the SPLA closed the Borongolei and Molitokuro schools and evacuated the minors, on the pretext that the area was under military threat from the government. Nevertheless, only the unaccompanied minors were moved, not the over 100,000 displaced persons in the nearby "Triple A" camps. The estimated 4,350 boys from these two camps were walked first to Palataka, about 200 kilometers away; they arrived tired and weak. Some 700 stayed in Palataka and the rest, about 3,650, were taken to the Narus area, where, it is suspected, they were given military

---

[296]Burr, *Food Aid*, p. 20.

[297]Sharp, "Child Soldiers in Southern Sudan," p. 4.

[298]*Ibid.* Sharp saw dozens of twelve-year-old boys on the night of November 25, 1991, being transported towards the front line on the road from Torit to Ngangala. Another witness told this reporter of seeing 150 trucks of SPLA-Torit troops passing the Juba turn-off on the Ngangala-Mongalla road on November 19, 1991; one-third of the soldiers in those trucks were children under fifteen, and some as young as eleven.

training and were deployed in the SPLA-Torit offensive against the Nasir faction in Kongor in March 1993.[299]

No family reunification efforts have been undertaken by the SPLA-Torit through any agencies.

Conditions in Nasir and Status of Family Reunification Program and Schooling

Efforts at family reunification for the minors were part of the ICRC's work in Sudan in 1992. The ICRC picked up from Radda Barnen's work in Ethiopia, attempting to document the social history of each individual minor who returned to Sudan. The Radda Barnen personal history files in Addis Ababa, however, were destroyed during the uprising that overthrew Mengistu.

In an agreement signed in Nairobi on June 19, 1992, between the two SPLA factions, point number 3 (c) states that the two factions shall "Promote the voluntary reunion of divided families and shall take measures to resolve other humanitarian issues."[300] The SPLA-Torit faction has apparently done nothing to promote such voluntary reunion, and the SPLA-Nasir/United faction, while making a start on such efforts, backtracked in 1993.

The SPLA-Nasir group was cooperative with early attempts at family reunification for the minors settled in Nasir. Agencies administered a questionnaire to the boys, including the question, "Do you want to see your mother?" The minors routinely answered no, or said that they did not care. Commander Riek, made aware of this response, announced that the minors should be free to talk. The answers to this question, and others, were then reversed: the minors replied that indeed they did want to see their mothers and fathers.

In February 1992, 150 Nuer minors were reunified with their families in Ler, Upper Nile, after interviews to locate the families and assure the voluntary nature of the reunification. After that, the Sudan government, as part of its dry season offensive in 1992, refused further flight permission and the reunification program was suspended.

---

[299]One report said that these boys were sent to Natinga, just north of the Kenyan border. UNICEF, *Children of War*, p. 27.

[300]Signed by Commander William Nyuon Bany for SPLA-Torit and Commander Lam Akol Ajawin for SPLA-Nasir/United.

UNICEF registered some 1,456 unaccompanied minors in Nasir in May 1992, of whom about 800 were considered appropriate for reunification with their Upper Nile families. Some had been rejoining their families without assistance; some seventy walked hundreds of kilometers to Ler, arriving in October 1992.[301]

In June 1992, those minors who stayed behind in Nasir were observed in poor condition. The grass houses the minors had constructed for themselves could not possibly withstand a series of heavy rains and were already on the verge of collapse. The school had not yet been opened, allegedly because promised school supplies had not been delivered;[302] the tent intended to serve as the school was severely ripped and leaking. The boys, to ensure their own survival, were walking three hours each way to a fishing pool, but had no proper fishing nets or materials, nor mosquito nets. When food aid became erratic, due to Sudan government obstructionism, their situation visibly deteriorated.[303]

The reunification program in Nasir recommenced in December 1992, after flight permission was reinstated by the government, and another 300 minors were reunited with their families in Ler.[304] UNICEF took over the effort when the ICRC was expelled by the Sudan government in March 1992. Although the reunification was largely successful, a small percentage of the older boys did not want to stay with their families and returned on their own to Nasir.

In early 1993, the reunification program operating out of Nasir had to be suspended due to an outbreak of relapsing fever in the boys' living area in Nasir. Before it could be diagnosed and treated with

---

[301]OLS (Southern Sector) Bi-Monthly Situation Report No. 29, November 6-21, 1992, p. 4.

[302]School materials such as blackboards and a mimeograph machine were provided in 1991 but were diverted for use in Riek's headquarters, according to one former U.N. representative with personal knowledge.

[303]OLS (Southern Sector) Bi-Monthly Situation Report No. 22, July 21 to August 5, 1992, p. 3.

[304]OLS (Southern Sector) "Situation Assessment 1992/93," February 1993, p. 23.

tetracycline, some seventeen children died, according to officials. A medical officer noted that the disease is transmitted through lice, and because of their poor hygiene the minors were the first to be affected.

By the time the outbreak was controlled, SPLA-Nasir was having second thoughts. It refused permission for further reunification, on the grounds that there were no schools in the areas to which the boys were being taken, while the school at Nasir went up to grade six. Commander Riek told HRW/Africa that this measure was taken in part to bring pressure on UNICEF to open up schools in south Sudan. "Some of the boys who were taken to Ler walked back to Nasir since there was no school for them in Ler. I am telling the U.N. to provide schools for them in their home areas and in Nasir," he added.

The agency questionnaire administered to the minors in Nasir in January 1992 asked if they wanted to go home if there was no school at home. Fifty percent responded that they did, indicating that lack of schools in the home areas is not an adequate reason for suspending the entire reunification program.

In the schools in the two Nasir minors locations, most of the children were in grades one through three in June, 1993.[305] At Ketbek minors' camp, there were only fifty students in grade four, thirty in grade five, and thirty in grade six, of a total of 1,100 students.

It is not accurate to say that there were no schools outside of Nasir. UNICEF's education program reached 930 schools throughout southern Sudan in 1993 with 730 education kits benefiting 1,940,000 pupils. An NGO trained 112 teachers in southern Sudan in 1993, and forty teachers attended a basic course in trauma treatment in Nasir organized by UNICEF.[306]

In early 1994, twenty minors walked from Nasir to Ler, which took one month, to rejoin their families. UNICEF prepared a new reunification program for about 3,000 boys from Nasir to Ler,[307] the

---

[305]The two locations were Ketbak (1,273 minors of whom 1,100 were enrolled in school) and Brjoc (114 minors in their own farming community) in June 1993.

[306]OLS (Southern Sector) Situation Report No. 52, January 16-31, 1994, p. 3.

[307]OLS (Southern Sudan) Situation Report No. 53, February 1-15, 1994, p. 2.

SPLA-Nasir/United having withdrawn its objections to the reunification program. Several hundred youth were reunified with their families before fighting between Nuer tribes in early 1994 led to the burning of all huts in Nasir and the population scattering. About 600 unaccompanied minors settled temporarily in a displaced persons camp in Malual village.[308]

Minority Minors

The segregation of students in the refugee camps in Ethiopia and the evacuation the unaccompanied minors separately from the rest of the refugee community had an inevitable result: many minors have since lost touch with family members. Family reunification has become all but impossible.

This is especially hard on ethnic and tribal groups that are not in the majority in the Dinka or Nuer areas where the concentrations of unaccompanied minors are located, because they may be subject to different treatment and even discrimination when they have Arabic names or are Muslims. They also tend to lose their culture since they grow up away from the adults who could teach them tribal customs and traditions.

Although most of the minors in Nasir are Nuer, there are several hundred minors from other groups, such as Dinka (perhaps eighty) and Nuba. The Dinka minors' families have been traced mostly to the Kakuma refugee camp in Kenya. Although it is against UNHCR policy to transport people out of their country and make them refugees, the interests of child welfare and family reunification expressed in the Convention on the Rights of the Child[309] should override that policy in this case.

---

[308]OLS (Southern Sector), "Weekly Update, May 31, 1994," Nairobi, Kenya, p. 2.

[309]The Convention on the Rights of the Child, art. 10 (1) states, "applications by a child or his or her parents to enter or leave a State Party for the purpose of family reunification shall be dealt with by State Parties in a positive, humane and expeditious manner."

The Nuba boys speak Arabic[310] and have Arabic names, and some of them are Muslims. They have been the object of jokes or comments by others and are in need of family reunification, which is difficult because the Nuba Mountains are too militarily conflicted to permit such an effort. Should their families or even fellow villagers be located in refugee camps or elsewhere, the minors' relocation should be permitted if desired, regardless of borders.

In SPLA-Torit territory, HRW/Africa interviewed an eighteen-year-old boy, born in Blue Nile province, a member of a small non-Nilotic tribe. As of July 1993, he had been separated from his family for over three years.

The boy originally attended school in Blue Nile province, where the classes were in Arabic, his second language. He managed to complete grade three at age eleven, before the war reached his village.

Government forces burned the village to the ground in 1986, and villagers scattered to various places. He, his family, and others walked eight days to Ethiopia, to a camp near Asosa town. He had to start in grade one at the refugee school because the instruction was in English, not a language he understood. The Sudanese government attacked this refugee camp inside Ethiopia on January 4, 1990. The refugees fled to Itang, but in Itang, he "had no time to go to school." He and a male cousin were separated from their parents and sent to live with the unaccompanied minors. In May 1991, when Mengistu fell, and he and the other unaccompanied minors were taken to Fugnido, where they stayed a week. With a group of sixty-three boys from his tribe and other minors with whom he had been living in Itang, he was taken from Fugnido to Pochalla, a four-day walk. In Pochalla they remained from July 1991 to March 1992, and left when the Sudan government launched an attack.[311]

They arrived in Kapoeta, and his ethnic group of sixty-three was divided. He remained with thirty-three who stayed in the Catholic Mission compound; there was no other room. After a series of evacuations the thirty-three boys were moved in July 1992 to the "Triple A" camps where

---

[310]Nuba often speak Arabic to each other, since there are many different dialects in the Nuba Mountains.

[311]From Pochalla he, his ethnic group of sixty-three, and other minors proceeded to Kapoeta, a journey of sixteen days.

they were split up among the three camps. He and what remained of his group settled near a few elders and women from their tribe who had fled to the "Triple A" displaced persons camps from Ethiopian camps.

The boys spoke their own language to each other but instruction in the "triple A" school was in English, a language none of them spoke. A teacher who spoke Arabic apparently interpreted the classes for them. They studied math, English, geography, and science, but had no books. The boys expressed a desire to see their parents, but "there is no chance." They lost all contact with their parents when they were separated in Itang, and now do not know where the parents are.

SUMMARY EXECUTIONS, DISAPPEARANCES, AND TORTURE

Both SPLA factions have committed abuses such as summary executions, disappearances, and torture and mistreatment of prisoners. The SPLA-Torit has held prisoners in long-term arbitrary detention. These abuses have persisted over several years.

Summary Executions

Executions without due process are no more than murder, which is prohibited by common article 3. Examples of summary executions appear throughout this report. Amnesty International also has gathered many examples of summary executions; for instance it found that in May 1992 the SPLA-Torit instituted a policy of "deliberate and arbitrary killing of civilians of Toposa ethnicity in villages around Kapoeta . . . in retaliation for the involvement of Toposa pro-government militia in the capture of Kapoeta and subsequent attacks on refugees fleeing the town."[312]

Disappearances

Disappearance of a person while in the custody of a government or rebel group a particularly distressing phenomenon. It often involves unacknowledged detention, which provides the detaining authority with deniability should that authority later decide to summarily execute the detainee. Thus the detainee may be tortured or subjected to other abuse and/or executed during the time of unacknowledged detention.

---

[312]Amnesty International, "Patterns of repression," pp. 9-10.

In Sudan, many have disappeared after they have been openly detained, but they do not reappear and the authorities seem to feel under no obligation to account for the disappearance of a detainee while in their custody. Often, in the case of the SPLA factions, they deny that the prisoner has been summarily executed and claim that he has escaped and is in Europe or the U.S. In these cases, the detaining authorities never acknowledge the deaths of which they are the cause, nor are the bodies turned over to the families.

Some prisoners have escaped. Often they reappear in refugee camps and reestablish contact with their friends, political allies, and fellow tribesmen. Others have been killed while escaping. Since many escapes are made in groups because of the rough terrain, there are often witnesses to those killed during the course of an escape (by ambush, wild animals, or thirst). Others have been summarily executed secretly, without ever having made an escape attempt.

If a person remains missing, despite family and other efforts to locate him while others who have "disappeared" turn up in exile or elsewhere, the presumption that the missing person has died at the hands of the detaining authorities in whose custody he was last seen alive is almost irrebuttable. The burden is on the detaining authority to show otherwise. Therefore, HRW/Africa cannot accept the simple claim that the person has "escaped" and is no longer the responsibility of the authorities. The burden is on the authorities to establish the fact of escape alive.

In one case, the circumstances point to summary execution but not conclusively. Three long-term political prisoners were held by SPLA-Torit in Morobo:[313] Martin Majier Gai, Martin Makur Aleu, and Martin Kajiboro. They reportedly had been released by SPLA-Torit after several other prisoners escaped in September 1992[314] from their prison near Morobo, but were rearrested and jailed in Morobo two months later. When the government started its offensive in this area in late July 1993, they were in jail. The government bombed the area and witnesses reportedly saw the three alive, fleeing with their guards towards the Zaire border. They were not seen again.

---

[313]Morobo is close to the Uganda border, in a hilly area in which Anya-Nya I had a guerrilla camp.

[314]*See* accounts of Commanders Faustino and Kerubino, below.

Another case is that of a Nuer doctor who had attended medical school in Ethiopia and was an SPLA officer performing medical duties in Kapoeta until it fell in May 1992, when he fled with others to Narus. In June or July 1992, he was accused of being a follower of a Nuer commander who defected. The doctor was captured in the presence of many witnesses in the officers' mess, where a senior officer announced to everyone that the doctor was under arrest. Two days later, a witness to the arrest heard one bullet fired. He was later told, unofficially, that the doctor had been shot by the SPLA-Torit. He did not see the body, but the man never reappeared, in exile or otherwise. There was no court martial; the ordinary procedure in a court martial followed by a death sentence is to publicize the investigation, court martial, and sentence among the troops, and to conduct the execution by a firing squad before the troops. The lack of any such procedure led the witness to conclude this was a summary execution.

Torture

The right to humane treatment while in custody is one of the core human rights; common article 3 to the four Geneva Conventions of 1949 forbids "at any time and in any place whatsoever mutilation, cruel treatment, and torture."[315] In addition, "outrages upon personal dignity, in particular humiliating and degrading treatment" are prohibited.

"Torture became the norm," according to one assigned to judicial duties in Eastern Equatoria in the late 1980s and early 1990s. "It was not possible to control torture," he claimed. He learned of many cases in his jurisdiction where people died under military torture, usually those accused of political or security offenses.

Some, usually the a security or spying detainees, were kept in a hole in the ground for many days on end. The hole in the ground was two or three by one or one-and-a-half meters, surrounded by thorns. "People left there would die from heat and diseases." This pit was used for serious political crimes, before a hearing, to bring pressure on the captive.

People were also tied very tightly by the arms and wrists. He saw one prisoner who thereafter lost the ability to move his arm. People accused of spying sometimes had their fingernails removed; the same

---

[315]*See* Appendix A.

judicial officer saw many in this condition, with no fingernails on several fingers.

Although this officer tried to intervene with senior officers[316] on behalf of these tortured men, he was brushed off with the excuse that "we were in war and things will change gradually over time." Even when the accused were not tortured, it became the custom to administer twenty lashes when anyone was detained, even before any questions were asked. The conditions of detention were sometimes very harsh. The place of custody sometimes was inside garrisons. More often people were held outdoors, fenced in with thorns like cattle, exposed to the elements, with no roof or cover.

The abusive treatment occurred also in Ethiopia. An officer detained in 1989 saw and heard the sounds of other SPLA prisoners being very badly treated by SPLA guards under the eyes and ears of the Ethiopian state security in Gambela. Some prisoners were in a hole, under the rain and sun. When they were allowed to climb out of the hole to go to the toilet, an armed guard followed them. They were beaten daily, including beatings with a rifle butt. The officer heard their cries as they received between fifty to a hundred lashes, until they were unconscious. They were beaten more if they made any noise. Cold water was poured over them to revive them; their underwear was red with blood. They were tied with their hands behind with a rope from the wrists up the back to the mouth to hold a gag.

As to the SPLA-Nasir/United, HRW/Africa received several credible testimonies of similar types of torture and conditions of detention that occurred in 1992 at the hands of that faction's security police.

One displaced man reported that in 1992 he was held by SPLA-Nasir in terrible conditions of detention (in the open, behind a thorn fence, "like cattle," with little food and water) for weeks near Nasir, without any charges brought against him, along with forty other men.

The SPLA-Nasir/United's only prison is said to be in Fangak, in the middle of a malarial swamp. Other SPLA-Nasir/United prisons may exist, even though Commander Riek did not mention them to HRW/Africa. Relief workers in the area said that prisons similar to

---

[316]Almost all persons serving in the civil administration of the SPLA are or have been SPLA officers or soldiers assigned to civilian duties.

Fangak existed on islands in the rivers when Riek was Area Commander of Western Upper Nile.

In mid-1993, four persons were said to be jailed in Fanjak. Two civilians were jailed after being convicted by the General Court Martial of homicide and sentenced to three years and payment of compensation. A third Fangak prisoner, an SPLA-Nasir/United soldier, was tried in 1993 in Nasir for "security" offenses, indisicipline, and disobedience. He was found guilty, dismissed from the SPLA-Nasir/United army, and sentenced to two years in Fangak prison. A fourth man was convicted in Nasir for security offenses, dismissed, and is serving a two year sentence in Fangak.

The ICRC was able to visit 190 detainees held by the SPLA in southern Sudan in January 1992. Sixty-seven of them had been registered by the ICRC before and 123 were seen for the first time. Follow-up visits were carried out in March, 1992 before the suspension of ICRC work in Sudan.[317] It appears that these detainees were Sudan army soldiers held by SPLA-Torit. It does not appear that SPLA-Nasir/United conducts operations against the government or holds any Sudan army prisoners.

Prolonged Arbitrary Detention and Torture of Long-Term Prisoners

The SPLA has, over the years, detained SPLA officers alleged to be plotting coups against or challenging the leadership of Chairman and Commander-in-Chief John Garang. Few have been charged formally with violations of the SPLA Code or given an opportunity to defend themselves or have their day in court. At least forty SPLA officers have been in this situation; they have rotted in jail, until negotiations led to their release, or until they died or escaped. Some are still in jail.

HRW/Africa interviewed two former long-term prisoners, Commanders Kerubino Kuanyin Bol and Faustino Atem Gualdit, whose testimony is consistent with written testimony of other former long-term prisoners.[318] Their treatment by the SPLA-Torit violated the absolute ban in common article 3 on "cruel treatment and torture" as well as "outrages upon personal dignity, in particular humiliating and degrading

---

[317]*ICRC, 1992 Annual Report*, p. 51.

[318]"For a Strong SPLM/A: What Is To Be Done? By a Group of Former Political Detainees," Amon Mon Wantok, Chol Deng Alak, Ater Benjamin, Deng Bior Deng, Ajiing Adiang, Nairobi, Kenya, June 11, 1992.

treatment." The fact that they were never tried violated the ban on prolonged arbitrary detention.[319]

The SPLA attempted to justify this denial of due process by calling it a less severe penalty than execution, which is required for such crimes under the SPLA Code. Not trying persons who were clearly guilty meant sparing their lives, Garang supporters maintained. They also claimed that the SPLA deserves credit for not summarily executing coup plotters, a practice followed in numerous other liberation movements and by the government of Sudan.

These justifications are not to the point. The long-term detention without trial of political opponents represents a serious deviation from the rule of law, especially for a movement whose political agenda is democracy. Keeping prisoners four to eight years in jail without any charges or trial violates the prohibition on prolonged arbitrary detention. The assumption that they would have been found guilty after trial makes a travesty of the presumption of innocence.

These detainees are not prisoners of war, that is, captured enemy combatants. They are officers of the rebel army taken into custody by their own commander. Rebels in an internal armed conflict have no authority to jail anyone indefinitely, without trial, as would be permitted in an international armed conflict for states capturing foreign enemy combatants and treating them as prisoners of war whereby they may be held without trial until the end of the hostilities. While the rebels and the government in an internal armed conflict may elect to treat captured enemy combatants as prisoners of war, and not try them, these rebel officers, jailed by their own army, do not fall into the category of captured enemy combatants. Their capture was inspired by their political, not military, activities.

Commander Kerubino, at the time the second in command of the SPLA, was arrested in mid-September 1987 by Ethiopian President Mengistu Haile Mariam, who summoned Kerubino from his command in the South Blue Nile front to the palace in Addis Ababa. Kerubino was accused of being a "reactionary," but the main allegation was that he was

---

[319]*See* Theodor Meron, *Human Rights and Humanitarian Norms as Customary Law* (Oxford, England: Clarendon Press, 1989), pp. 49-50.

plotting a coup against Garang.[320] After Kerubino's arrest, his forces based in Assosa, Ethiopia, near the Sudan border, were disarmed by the Ethiopian army and the SPLA, which besieged them at the SPLA base in Assosa with artillery. Three days later, some forty of Kerubino's supporters, all officers, were arrested there, including Faustino.[321]

When Faustino was arrested, he was told that the investigation would only take a few days. He and the others were tied up and taken to an open area at the SPLA base. In front of the assembled SPLA soldiers, Garang denounced the captives, calling them "reactionaries" and declaring them "enemies of the people." There was never any hearing or trial.

In jail, Faustino was tortured and accused of instigating the coup plot. During the first seven days his hands and legs were tied behind him. For four days, he was held naked in a pit filled to his neck with cold water. Only when he was near death was he brought out of the pit. He was tied up again when he recovered.

Faustino and the others were in jail at the SPLA base in Assosa for seven months. Kerubino was held separately. For six months he was in Walega, Ethiopia, in a military barracks prison. He was not questioned or tried. An Ethiopian army officer told him he was held on orders of Garang "for security reasons." While in Ethiopian custody, Kerubino was not beaten or tortured, and he was fed.

After six months, Kerubino was sent to Gambela for three days and then to another SPLA Ethiopian base he called Aman. Commander

---

[320]"I met with Mengistu for six hours. He accused me of wanting to spoil the SPLA movement. The Ethiopians had their own experience of faction fighting," Kerubino said. Kerubino also had disagreements with Garang over whether the SPLA should participate in the civil war in Ethiopia; the Ethiopian government wanted the SPLA to fight Ethiopian secessionist movements, which had in turn been aided by the Sudanese government. "I refused to fight against the Oromo [the largest Ethiopian tribe] with the Ethiopian army. They asked me to do this in early 1986," Kerubino said. "Garang said we were all one team and we should fight the Oromo."

[321]Later, many of these soldiers were released "with orders to fight the Oromo with the Ethiopian government." The Oromo Liberation Front eventually won. In Kerubino's account, "the Oromo and the Sudan government conducted a joint attack on South Blue Nile and forced us out in 1990, capturing Assosa in October, 1990. They captured Walega and their forces came to Addis and they were the end of Mengistu" in May 1991.

Arok Thon Arok, another one of the SPLA high command, had been arrested in the meantime and brought to the same place. Kerubino and Arok were kept in isolation in separate tukls and not allowed to talk to each other. Here Kerubino was badly mistreated.

> I could not leave the hut except to go to the toilet and sometimes not even for that. They gave me a bucket. I was tortured by soldiers, young soldiers, ages fourteen, seventeen, eighteen, who were given orders to torture us.
>
> I was tied with rope on my wrists and legs. I was flogged with a leather whip for a long time, on my back. They also tied my eyes, so I could not see who was lashing me. They did not ask questions, they just lashed.
> They have orders not to talk to you.

He was given little food and was denied medical treatment for a preexisting condition.

Kerubino and Arok Thon Arok were in that prison for more than two years, from 1988 until mid-1991. Arok noted that there were other Sudanese prisoners at this facility who were subjected to worse torture, such as mock executions.[322]

At about the same time in 1988 that Kerubino and Arok Thon Arok were moved to this prison at an SPLA base in Ethiopia, Faustino and seven other SPLA officer-prisoners were transferred to Boma, Sudan.[323] One prisoner calculated the date as May 26, 1988.[324] A total of forty-three Sudanese SPLA officer prisoners from different areas

---

[322]The SPLA apparently gave blankets to Commanders Kerubino and Arok, the highest-ranking detainees, but not to the others.

[323]First they were moved in an Ethiopian army helicopter to Gambela, Ethiopia, tied hand and foot and blindfolded for the journey. After one night in Gambela, they were sent by plane to south Ethiopia, almost at the Sudan border, where they were put into grain sacks (two sacks to cover each man) and tossed into vehicles. They were taken on a rough road across the border to Boma.

[324]"For a Strong SPLM/A, By a Group of Former Detainees," p. 13.

were held there.[325] Some had been freshly beaten. Among them were very senior SPLA officers. All the prisoners were kept in a small room, some five by seven meters. All remaining possessions were removed from them, leaving them with only a shirt and a pair of pants each. They were each given a ground sheet and a blanket. The guards brought a bucket for everyone, saying, "If you want to urinate, defecate, wash your face, use this bucket." The guards only removed the bucket when it was overflowing (one prisoner estimates this was every seven days). For four months they did not move outside the room. "This was the worst period of my detention," Faustino said. Another prisoner said they did not bathe for ninety-seven days.[326] Maggots and lice were everywhere, and the smell was very bad.

The prison roof was of corrugated iron, and the walls were of the same material. The building held the heat of the equatorial sun. Some of the prisoners became ill from insects at a location where they were taken to dig a well. They received very little food, mostly just maize in water. They survived by organizing themselves; most were educated men so they gave lectures to each other to pass the time, each in his field of study.

After several months in Boma (perhaps in January 1989), the prisoners were removed to a hut about six hours on foot from Boma. They believed they were moved in order to prevent anyone from discovering their detention place.[327] In the new location, prisoners lived in a hut, under guard at all times. The conditions were terrible--the grass roof did not protect them from rain, and they sat close to their belongings to try to keep them dry. They were locked inside the hut for one year, after which their shelter improved but their minimal food

---

[325] Others say all the detainees from Bilpam, Blue Nile and Bonga were taken to Gambela, helicoptered to Raad, and driven to Boma. They list twenty-four officers who were so transferred. "For a Strong SPLM/A, By a Group of Former Detainees, p. 12.

[326] Ibid., p. 13.

[327] Cars from Torit passed by Boma. The prisoners' friends and relatives were trying to find them and there was a chance they might discover the Boma prison.

rations did not. They remained there until 1991. Another fifteen prisoners were brought to the area but kept in a separate hut.[328]

They were videotaped by security men while in this jail; they were in very bad condition. "If you had seen me, you would not have believed I was human," Faustino said, adding

> You could count all my ribs, you could see every artery in my legs. We lost weight. We had no medicine, no treatment. Three or four of the prisoners died. When they died, we did not see where they were buried. We could only put the body outside the hut.

They had little food and lived on the leaves from the cassava plant. Later on, they had no food and remained that way "for a long time." Faustino continued:

> Once we did not eat, in protest. They decided if we were not going to eat, we would not drink, either. We protested to make them try and sentence us or free us. We asked for our wives to be given to us. We heard that our wives were given to others on the orders of Garang.

After the hunger strike started the guards withheld the water, usually brought in cans, leaving the prisoners all day without water. When they were taken out to get water, they were taken to dirty water. Faustino described beatings:

> How we survived is a miracle. They even had a graveyard set up. They expected us to die. Sometimes when we wanted to call a guard they would reply by shooting at us. Many times we were lashed with a whip made from the hide of a hippopotamus, very hard leather. It was ordinary to be given a hundred lashes. I protested the lashing of an older man, a pilot and my

---

[328]They believed that "Garang arrived one or twice in an Ethiopian helicopter with the Cuban and East German ambassadors in another helicopter, and hovered over the place." When they were arrested, other officers told them that the Cubans and East Germans were cooperating with Garang.

teacher, Manyar. They told me I was talking only because I had a high rank; they tied me up and took me to a senior officer and he gave me a hundred lashes, no questions asked.

They continued to lash him to make him run, but "I lay down and refused to move. They only stopped lashing me when I was about to die. Then I got up and fell down two times."

When Mengistu's government was overthrown by the Ethiopian rebels in May 1991, the prisoners Kerubino and Arok Thon Arok were removed from Ethiopia to Boma, Sudan, where they were kept in isolation.

When Riek defected from the SPLA three months later, the SPLA-Torit feared that the Riek forces would try to release these prisoners, so they removed them in November 1991 to a place between Torit and Kapoeta, where Kerubino and Arok were no longer in isolation. At this time there were negotiations between the two SPLA factions on a possible reconciliation. An agreement was reached through church mediation and signed on December 17, 1991. Forty prisoners were to be released as a step toward reuniting the factions, and many were released in early 1992 in Torit.[329]

At least four long-term prisoners, however, were not to be released: Kerubino, Arok, John Kulang Puot, and Martin Makur Aleu, who were all left in detention pending further negotiations.

Several of the released prisoners were jailed again twenty-four hours later. Faustino was among those jailed again, on the grounds that Garang had wanted to talk to them before they were released. They were taken to Kidepo, sixty miles from Torit, near Garang's headquarters. The others detained again with him were Malath Joseph Luath, Martin Kajiboro, Thomas Kerou Tong, Atem Zacharia Dut, and Mabior Marier. While still in Kidepo, the prisoner Thomas Kerou Tong[330] was

---

[329]Some of those who were released as a result of the late 1991 agreement between the factions feared rearrest and, when Kapoeta fell, fled with others to Kenya, where they sought UNHCR and Kenyan protection. "For a Strong SPLM/A, By a Group of Former Detainees," p. 28.

[330]He was a captain and an SPLA pilot, a graduate of the flying school at Kidlington, England.

removed from the cell. The guards told them that Thomas escaped to the U.S. or Europe. They later heard that Thomas's body was found with his hands tied and a bullet in his temple. He has never reappeared.[331]

After Kapoeta fell to the government in late May, 1992, the prisoners were moved several times before being taken to Morobo, described as a former Anya Nya I camp in Western Equatoria, west of Kaya near the Ugandan border. On September 5, 1992, a group of seven guards and five prisoners escaped from that prison to Uganda. The prisoners were Mabior Marier, Malath Joseph Luath, Arok Thon Arok, Faustino Atem Gualdit, and Kerubino Kuanyin Bol. One, Malath Joseph Luath, was shot dead in a SPLA-Torit ambush during the flight to Uganda.

Word of the escape leaked out, and international appeals prevailed upon the Ugandan government not to return the prisoners to the SPLA-Torit, pursuant to refugee law.[332] The Sudan government sent a representative to visit them in Ugandan detention. The Ugandans kept them in almost complete incommunicado detention for about five months before turning them over to the UNHCR, effectively freeing them.

Prolonged Arbitrary Detention and Torture of Ugandan Prisoners by SPLA-Torit

Perhaps as many as fifty Ugandans have been held in prolonged arbitrary detention for some years in Ethiopia and Sudan by the SPLA acting in coordination with a Ugandan guerrilla movement sponsored by the SPLA. Their imprisonment illustrates the enormous powers delegated to the SPLA by the Mengistu government of Ethiopia, and the complexity of cross-border tribal and insurgent relations. HRW/Africa considers the detentions to be highly illegal since these persons were refugees. Treatment meted out to them also violated the ban on torture.

---

[331]*Ibid.*, p. 27.

[332]On September 18, 1992, the SPLA-Nasir issued a press release regarding the escape, which it said occurred on September 7. "Escape of SPLA Detainees," *Sudan Update*, vol. 4, no. 1, (London: September 22, 1992), p.3.

In 1985, a group of about 600 Ugandan army officers and soldiers fled Uganda across the border into SPLA territory.[333] Led by Peter Otai,[334] the men were on the wrong side of a recent Ugandan coup that brought Tito Okello to power, prior to current President Museveni's January 1989 takeover.[335] The SPLA told the would-be refugees that they could join a nascent Ugandan guerrilla organization to fight against the Ugandan government. The Ugandans felt they had no other option and went to Ethiopia for military training. None ever returned to Uganda as a guerrilla.[336]

The 600 Ugandans were first held at Dima, an SPLA base fifteen minutes from the Dima refugee camp in Ethiopia. They lived at the SPLA base but were not registered as refugees since they were "not supposed to be" in Ethiopia. They were told they had to pass as Sudanese if they encountered any expatriates at the refugee camp. Conditions at the base were bad: of the 600 Ugandans there, one quarter to one half died of sickness and lack of food, one of the Ugandans said.

Seven were arrested at Dima in July 1987, after Peter Otai announced the formation in Nairobi of a splinter Ugandan resistance movement, the Uganda People's Army. Some detainees were members of Otai's tribe, the Iteso. Thirty-three Ugandans in all were detained in Dima in 1987 by Ugandan guerrilla Commander Ben Odiek, with the assistance of the SPLA.

The prisoners were held in a corral, exposed to the sun, rain, and cold. There were no sanitation facilities. Medicine was difficult to come

---

[333]"Sudan/Uganda: Border control," *Africa Confidential*, vol. 34, no. 16 (London: August 13, 1993), p. 4.

[334]Otai was Minister of State for Defense in Uganda under President Milton Obote. *Ibid.*

[335]*Ibid.*

[336]The motivation for training such an army was never stated by the SPLA but its opponents and observers believed that Garang wished to have a Ugandan guerrilla group under his control with which to threaten Museveni, the President of Uganda, if Museveni did not cooperate with the SPLA. "For a Strong SPLM/A, By a Group of Former Detainees," pp. 21-22; "Sudan/Uganda: Border Control," *Africa Confidential*.

by. One victim said he was tortured by the SPLA at the direction of Commander Ben Odiek, and beaten with sticks to pressure him to "confess."

In February, 1988, the Ugandans, prisoners and non-prisoners, were escorted by the SPLA on foot to the SPLA base in Khor Shum (renamed Pakok when thousands of Sudanese repatriating refugees arrived in 1991), Upper Nile, Sudan, on the Ethiopian border. The Ugandans who ran the camp kept the prisoners in a thorn-enclosed corral, beat them with sticks and fists, and tortured them. The prisoners received no medicine, little food, no visits from their family or anyone else and were isolated from the other Ugandans. Three prisoners died in that detention.

Unlike the case of the SPLA commanders held for years without trial or court martial, however, a court martial was convened for the Ugandan detainees in February 1988 in Khor Shum (Pakok) to judge those arrested in 1987. They were charged with violations of the SPLA Code, including charges of violation of section 29 (1) (d), being an "enemy of the people."[337] Why the SPLA Code applied to these Ugandan guerrillas was not clear, nor of which "people" they were "enemies."

The result was the same as if they had never been tried, however. The six Ugandan officers who were members of the court martial worked, with breaks due to paper shortages, from February, 1988, to April, 1989, when the court martial ended in a stalemate, three for conviction and three for acquittal. The accused remained jailed. They were joined in jail, in April, 1989, by their former torturer, Commander Ben Odiek. He and others were arrested with the help of the SPLA on unrelated charges.

The Ugandans stayed in Khor Shum (Pakok) from February, 1988, until November, 1992,[338] when in anticipation of a government attack on nearby Boma they were ordered to move. The Ugandan prisoners were taken to a prison in Narus, where they were housed with thirty SPLA prisoners. The Narus prisoners were seriously underfed.

---

[337]*See* below in this Chapter for a description of the SPLA Code and this crime.

[338]*See* above in this Chapter for an account of the forced portering the SPLA required the Ugandans to do there, and their recruitment as rebels by the SPLA.

Initially, they were kept in the open, exposed to rain, then required to build a cell for themselves. Some fourteen Ugandan prisoners were transferred to this "Ugandan" cell on December 25, 1992. When government planes bombed the area, the prisoners were not allowed to find shelter away from the cell, and bombs often fell nearby.

The prisoners began to resist because they were tired of being whipped "for minor things." Another platoon of thirty Ugandan soldiers was added to the sixteen Ugandan military police already in Narus as prison guards. In January, 1993, six more Ugandans were arrested and put in the SPLA-Torit cell in Narus when they refused orders to fight alongside the SPLA-Torit.

At least twelve Ugandan prisoners in two groups escaped from the Ugandan and SPLA-Torit cells in Narus, joined by a young guard. The first group escaped in early 1993; it took them five days to reach Kenya, and one died of thirst on the way. The second group, including a guard, escaped two days later; although they reached the Kenyan border in two days, on the way one died of thirst. "The rest of us drank our urine."

Until the prisoners escaped from Sudan did their relatives know if they were alive or dead. Of the estimated fifty Ugandans held under SPLA authority in Ethiopia and Sudan from 1985-1993, over half may still have been in detention in Sudan in SPLA-Torit-controlled areas in mid-1993.

Other Arbitrary Detention

There are other cases of prolonged or arbitrary detention of less well-known persons. A court official visited detainees and found cases where people were in custody for fifteen days "just because of a family quarrel; there was no legal justification for their detention." In his experience, a soldier could send the military police to capture his wife because of family matters, and cause her to be kept in military detention without a hearing. There were many people in custody for two or three years with no accusation against them. "It was up to the whim of the commander or the person who got them thrown in custody."

Local chiefs were imprisoned sometimes for being "stubborn." One local chief in the Kajo Kaji area, Juma Lukolo, used to skip many of the SPLA meetings, and when he attended, he was very argumentative. According to a resident, the SPLA put him in jail for a week in 1991 for "arguing," an arbitrary reason for imprisonment.

SPLA ADMINISTRATION OF JUSTICE

Despite an eleven-year history of controlling a large population and territory, the SPLA has not developed anything approaching a system of justice and due process. For a guerrilla army, the difficulties of administering a judicial system are considerable. Under international rules of war, however, rebels have certain human rights obligations that the SPLA factions are ignoring.[339] The absence of the rule of law is evident in reports of torture, summary executions, arbitrary and prolonged detentions, denial of due process, and the failure of military accountability for human rights abuses.

HRW/Africa focuses on these legal issues in part because both factions have indicated an interest in improving their legal systems. This chapter does not address the government's extensive violations of international law. The issues facing the government are different and deserve separate treatment which they have received from HRW/Africa and other human rights organizations; they include and go far beyond the abuses of the rules of war described herein.[340]

Customary Southern Sudanese Law

It is difficult to generalize about the administration of justice throughout southern Sudan. What can be said is that neither shari'a nor the penal code of Sudan is applied outside of government-controlled garrison towns. In their place are customary southern Sudanese law and the SPLA Code.

---

[339]*See* Appendix A.

[340]*See* Africa Watch, "Sudan: Violations of Academic Freedom," vol. IV, issue no. 12 (New York: Human Rights Watch, November 7, 1992); "Sudan: The Ghosts Remain," vol. no. 4, issue no. 6 (New York: Human Rights Watch, April 27, 1992); "Sudan: New Islamic Penal Code Violates Basic Human Rights," vol. no. 3, issue no. 9 (New York: Human Rights Watch, April 9, 1991); "Sudan: Inside Al Bashir's Prisons: Torture, Denial odf Medical Atten and Poor Conditions" (New York: Human Rights Watch, February 11, 1991); "Sudan: Suppression of Information, Curbs on the Press, Attacks on Journalists, Writers and Academics," vol. no. 2, issue no. 28 (New York: Human Rights Watch, August 30, 1990); "Sudan: Threat to Women's Status from Fundamentalist Regime," vol. no. 2, issue no. 12 (New York: Human Rights Watch, April 9, 1990).

Customary south Sudanese law,[341] varying from tribe to tribe,[342] is applied by chiefs in tribal courts in much the same way as it was under the Anglo-Egyptian Condominium government (1899-1956), run by the British. That government recognized three codes of law by which Sudanese peoples were to be governed: the Sudan Penal Code, which covered offences against persons and property; the Islamic shari'a law, which regulated the personal and family life of Muslims; and tribal or customary law, which was not a single code but a recognition of the different varieties of customary law that existed throughout the rural areas of the country.[343]

In south Sudan, disputes among the Nilotic tribes were settled by negotiations between ad hoc groups of mediators drawn from the heads of opposing social or family units. In feuds, where strong feeling inhibited groups from meeting together, a neutral arbitrator who could impose additional sanctions, usually the land priest, was brought in. He was able to persuade groups to meet and to agree on a settlement.

The British government was drawn into the traditional system when, in attempting to end Nuer-Dinka fighting, it acted as an arbitrator and negotiated settlements according to customary law. The British mediation of external disputes was facilitated by their gradual creation of

---

[341]Early British officials sometimes wrote about a "tribal code" or "tribal law" but in general they adopted the legal category of "customary law" to cover all such codes, and to distinguish it from the written codes of civil, criminal and shari'a law. We refer to it as customary southern Sudanese law to distinguish it from other areas of the country.

[342]For instance, Nilotic (Dinka, Nuer, Shilluk and Anuak) women have fewer rights to divorce than do Equatorian women. Customary law is very public: HRW/Africa had the opportunity to watch part of a trial for adultery under Dinka law. Several hundred people observed these proceedings, which lasted three days.

[343]Douglas H. Johnson, "Judicial Regulation and Administrative Control: Customary Law and the Nuer, 1895-1954," *Journal of African History* 27 (London, 1986): p. 62.

chiefs' courts among the Nuer and Dinka, grafting a system of executive chief and court president onto the system.[344]

At the same time, the British did not abandon their attempts to introduce clear categories of crime and punishment, of "law" and deterrence,[345] and by 1930 government policy had seriously weakened traditional forms of justice.

This British system did not satisfy the customary requirement of reconciliation and compromise or the traditional linking of different segments of the community together by a willingness to share, give, loan, and accept compensation for wrongs.[346]

Customary law continued to be applied in the rural areas of southern Sudan after independence in 1956, without interruption. It was evoked to convene inter-tribal meetings after the settlement of the first civil war in 1972; the southern regional government spent years fostering these meetings to sort out the claims and feuds which grew up during the war.

Today customary southern Sudanese law continues to be applied in SPLA areas. Candidates from chiefly families continue to be elected to fill the court offices. The SPLA supervised a number of elections which have brought younger men into office,[347] but many of the chiefs interviewed by HRW/Africa were older men, who retained an emblem of office, the sash.

Local negotiations along traditional lines were successful in calming factional feuds along the border between Bahr El Ghazal/Lakes and Upper Nile provinces after the faction fighting of 1991-92. The Nuer prophet, Wut Nyang, tried to support such arbitration along the

---

[344]Johnson, "Judicial Regulation," p. 72. "The court president looked after the functioning of the courts in his area, the executive chief (also a member of the court) supervised the execution of judgments." *Ibid.*

[345]*Ibid.*, p. 62.

[346]"To fulfill one's obligations completely is to sever a link; to repay one's full debt ends a form of relationship." *Ibid.*, p. 74.

[347]Commander Riek complained that the SPLA officers used to interfere with and sit as judges in the customary courts because they liked to collect the fines, paid in cows. He claimed to have put a stop to this practice.

Ayod/Duk border following the looting and massacres in Kongor and Bor in 1991, but without success.

The SPLA-Nasir/United has utilized the traditional means of negotiations and payment of compensation to settle some disputes. For example, in 1993, two Nuer tribes escalated their dispute over fishing rights in the Ulang area of the Sobat River basin to fighting, including village burning, retaliatory killings, and cattle raiding. The SPLA-Nasir/United intervened and pressured both sides to enter into negotiations. The dispute was settled by payment of cattle.

The SPLA Code

The SPLA's initial political goal was a "united secular Sudan," in contrast to prior southern rebel demands for a separate state and also in contrast to the aim of northern political parties to make some form of shari'a the law of the land.[348] The SPLA drew up a legal code, the "Sudan People's Revolutionary Laws, SPLM/SPLA Punitive Provisions 1983" (SPLA Code) that both factions say they follow.

The SPLA Code is basically secular. It lists substantive offenses that are military in nature: mutiny, disobedience of lawful orders, drunkenness on duty, desertion, and theft of firearms.[349]

The code, however, also attempts far-reaching regulation of civilian life, criminalizing for civilians the following actions: posing as a soldier, murder, robbery, theft, criminal breach of trust, forgery, rape, traffic in and kidnapping of minors. (Most of these acts are crimes for the military also.) The Code also punishes failure to produce food, to observe sanitation and dress standards, and indolence, and provides for game preservation.[350]

In a more serious class than any of these offenses, however, forbidden to civilians and military alike, is that of being an "enemy of the people." The offense, which reflects the Soviet/Cold War origins of the 1983 SPLA Code, provides the greatest opportunity for abuse since its

---

[348]In recent negotiations for settlement of the war, Sudan government officials expressed a willingness to exempt the south from the application of shar'ia by providing for local options in areas of non-Muslim populations.

[349]SPLA Code §§ 26-34.

[350]*Ibid.*, §§ 35-50.

provisions are vague and overly broad. An enemy of the people includes "[m]embers of Sudan People's Liberation Movement that may break away from the principles of the people's socialist movement" and "[i]ndividuals or groups of people who propagate or advocate ideas, [ideologies], or philosophies, or organize societies and organizations that tend to uphold or [perpetuate] the oppression of the people or their exploitation by the Khartoum or similar bourgeois system."[351]

In other areas of life, customary south Sudanese law still applies to civilians.[352]

The actual extent and rigor of the application of the SPLA Code is hard to determine. According to a former officer, the code was given to each commander, who was expected to explain the law to his soldiers as part of his responsibility to lead and control his troops. However, a copy of the code is extremely hard if not impossible to come by in the field. Many say it is ignored; it obviously cannot be followed if it is not available to those who should be administering it.

It is difficult to know how the rudimentary judicial system functions in all parts of southern Sudan under the control of the two factions. The formality of the administrative system seems to have declined since 1992 when the SPLA-Torit lost control to the government of several towns that were the locales of its embryonic government.

Due Process Lacking in Procedure and Investigations

A major defect in the SPLA Code is its lack of procedural guarantees or any procedural guidelines at all. For instance, there is no limit on the time any accused person may be held for investigation and no requirement to bring him to trial within a certain time period.[353] Prolonged arbitrary detention -- for years -- of dozens of political

---

[351]*Ibid.*, § 10, 10 (c), 10 (f).

[352]Under the SPLA Code, similar to the British system, the customary courts do not have the power to sentence defendants to death nor to long-term imprisonment.

[353]Commander Riek said that in his territory limits are imposed on time spent in detention, unlike in the SPLA Code. He claimed that investigations are completed with twenty-four hours. If a General Court Martial is required, that is done "immediately," he said, but former SPLA-Nasir detainees contradict this.

prisoners has been the result. Nor is there any rule of law available to guarantee a fair trial. The lack of procedural guidelines gives absolute discretion to military officers and others untrained in the law. "In the absence of a code of procedure, laymen cannot apply the law," said an attorney who had practiced in the Sudan judicial system before joining the SPLA.

As for procedure during investigations, under the code the battalion commander or his deputy has the power to direct any officer or other person on his force to investigate an offense.[354] No other provisions, guidelines, or procedures for investigation exist in the code, with two exceptions. First, the military police have the "duty" to discover crimes and report them to the commander. The military police, however, are not regulated or regular. The commander, including the commander of a platoon, designates soldiers to serve in a "police" capacity on an ad hoc basis to keep order in the camp and in the force.

The second exception is that on appeal or confirmation of a sentence, the written investigation as well as a summary of the proceeding is to be provided to the confirming or appellate authority.[355]

HRW/Africa was told by a former officer who served on several boards of investigation that in practice, investigations of military personnel are performed when they are ordered by the commander. A board of investigation, consisting of three officers, is formed, one of whom must be from the security service. The board's work is similar to that of an ordinary prosecutor: to collect evidence and take statements of witnesses. The board gives its report to the commander, who decides if the matter will be tried by a court martial.

In practice, also absent from the SPLA Code, there is a "combat intelligence unit" whose duty includes investigating reports of spying. This unit reports directly to the "leader of the movement" and has a separate chain of command from the regular army units.

The one exception to the procedural void for investigations in the code is for investigations of "enemies of the people." When such suspects are captured, the code provides that the officer in charge shall investigate "the truth of that suspicion." When the charge is proved "beyond a

---

[354]SPLA Code, § 51.

[355]*Ibid.*, §52 (1).

reasonable doubt," the particulars are to be reported to the next superior officer, unless the "military situation is one of grave urgency," in which case the investigating officer may administer the death penalty on the spot.[356]

No Independent Tribunal

A specific due process requirement in common article 3 (1) (d) is a "regularly constituted court." Later expert opinion[357] redefined this as "a court offering the essential guarantees of independence and impartiality."[358] A U.N. proposal defined these requirements of independence and impartiality to include:

> 1. individual guarantees that allow every judge to "decide matters before him in accordance with his assessment of the facts and his understanding of the law without any improper influences, inducements, or pressures, direct or indirect, from any quarter or for any reason;" and
> 2. membership in a judiciary which is "independent of the executive and legislature, and has jurisdiction, directly or by way of review, over all issues of a judicial nature."[359]

The court system set forth in the SPLA Code is not independent. Violations of the SPLA Code are to be tried in three tiers of military

---

[356]*Ibid.*, § 12.

[357]The opinion was that "it was unlikely that a court could be 'regularly constituted' under national law by an insurgent party." ICRC, *Commentary on the Additional Protocol*, p. 1398.

[358]Protocol II, article 6 (2).

[359]Draft Principles on the Independence of the Judiciary, UN Doc. E/CN.4/Sub. 2/481/Add. 1 at 3 (1981); Americas Watch, "Violations of Fair Trial Guarantees by the FMLN's Ad Hoc Courts" (New York: Human Rights Watch, May 1990).

courts;[360] first mentioned is the highest court, the People's General Courts Martial, which has personal jurisdiction over high-ranking officers and officials of the SPLA and subject matter jurisdiction over offenses requiring the death penalty and life imprisonment, and appeals therefrom.[361]

The SPLA Code confers on the People's District Courts Martial jurisdiction over all civil suits; appeals from People's Summary Courts Martial for less serious offenses; and appeals from People's Regional Courts in cases traditionally tried by local courts.[362]

As contemplated in the code, all these courts lack independence from the military. They are not standing courts, and their personnel are appointed on an ad hoc basis, with no tenure in office. In the case of the General Court Martial, the three members are appointed by the chairman of the SPLA; the chair must have a rank of captain or higher.[363] The District Court Martial consists of three members, all appointed by a battalion commander, with the chair being a first lieutenant or higher rank.[364] The three to five members of the People's Regional Courts are to be appointed by the battalion commander; the members need not be military.[365] Finally, the district judicial officer, who has the powers of a District Court Martial in "purely civilian trials," is to be appointed by the battalion commander and should

---

[360]Section 16 of the SPLA Code refers to "Three tiers of military courts" which are the People's General Courts Martial, The People's District Courts Martial, and the People's Summary Courts Martial.

[361]SPLA Code, §17.

[362]Ibid., §§ 16-19, 21.

[363]Ibid., § 17 (1). According to Riek, a General Court Martial in his area is formed by zonal commanders, not solely by Riek as chairman.

[364]Ibid., § 18 (1).

[365]Ibid., § 21.

be a military officer "or suitable experienced and educated" citizen "working in the movement."[366]

The creation of a military court system to judge military crimes and offenses committed by military personnel is not objectionable. HRW/Africa objects to military control of a judicial system that is to judge civilians as a violation of the requirement that the court be independent and impartial.

The SPLA factions, like most guerrilla armies, lack trained judicial personnel. From 1983 to the present, there were less than twenty attorneys in the SPLA, and most of them were not doing legal work, according to one. In the philosophy of the SPLA movement, one must first be a soldier, lead forces, and know how to fight, according to an attorney who received SPLA military training in Ethiopia and commanded SPLA troops. The concept was that everyone should make a military contribution. Prior education, even advanced education, is not as highly regarded as military rank.

The courts have been subject to pressure from military commanders. "There is no clear line between civilian and military," a man who served in a civilian court told HRW/Africa. In his experience, the commanders sometimes tried to influence the outcome of the judicial proceedings. One commander even threatened him with a firing squad if he did not dispose of a case as ordered.

Capital Punishment

Common article 3 requires that the courts afford "all the judicial guarantees which are recognized as indispensable by civilized peoples," which include as a matter of customary law the principles that the penalty shall be proportionate to the offense and that no sentence shall be pronounced by a court except after a regular trial.[367]

Other due process rights that are almost certainly included under customary international humanitarian law include the right to presumption of innocence, the right not to testify against oneself or to be compelled to confess guilt (the right against self-incrimination), the right to be tried in one's presence (no trials in *absentia*), the right to defend oneself in person or through legal assistance of one's own choosing, the

---

[366]*Ibid.*, § 20 (1)-(3).

[367]Meron, *Customary Law*, pp. 49-50.

right to examine witnesses against oneself, the right to have one's
conviction and sentence reviewed by a higher tribunal, and the right not
to be tried or punished again for an offense for which one has already
been convicted or acquitted.[368]

Capital punishment, a common penalty under the SPLA Code, is
a disproportionate penalty for almost every offense for which it is
permitted, and thus a violation of customary international law.[369]
HRW/Africa opposes the application of the death penalty in all
circumstances because of its irreversibility and inherent cruelty.

Execution is a punishment permissible under the SPLA Code for
being an "enemy of the people,"[370] mutiny,[371] disobedience of
lawful orders,[372] desertion from the SPLA (with a gun or other
military equipment),[373] abetting the theft of military equipment,
criminal breach of trust in respect of military equipment, breach of trust
in respect of state property,[374] bribery,[375] murder,[376] theft of
property valued at more than one million Sudanese pounds, criminal
breach of trust,[377] criminal misappropriation, cheating or extortion of

---

[368]*Ibid.*, pp. 95-97, 134.

[369]In the twelve months from mid-1992 to mid-1993, Commander Riek
claimed, the death penalty had been imposed in his territory only once, for
homicide, on a soldier who shot his commander in Nasir in 1993.

[370]SPLA Code §§17 (1), 37.

[371]*Ibid.*, §16 (3).

[372]*Ibid.*, §27 (1).

[373]*Ibid.*, §29 (1).

[374]*Ibid.*, §§30-32.

[375]*Ibid.*, §33.

[376]*Ibid.*, §38.

[377]*Ibid.*, §40 (1).

property valued more than one million Sudanese pounds,[378] forgery of an official document,[379] rape with fire arms,[380] traffic in minors, and kidnapping of minors.[381]

The death penalty has been administered at times with rigor for military offenses such as mutiny. A participant in a court martial told HRW/Africa of a trial in 1991 of thirty-three soldiers, an entire platoon, for mutiny. They had been ordered to ambush a government convoy, which they had refused to do, and they then had resisted arrest. At the court martial they pleaded that the order was not clear and in addition that it was unlawful, since ambushes were not in their mission, which was to directly attack the enemy. Four of the soldiers alleged an alibi: they were absent from the ambush because they were sick. All thirty-three were found guilty and executed by firing squad.

The military has great leeway, especially in applying the death penalty to one accused of being an "enemy of the people." The officer in charge of the army unit that captures a person suspected of being an "enemy of the people" may be the judge, jury, and executioner. Such an officer's investigation must prove "beyond reasonable doubt that the prisoners are in fact enemies of the people."[382] How such a burden of proof might be met is not clear. If the officer is satisfied with his own investigation, he may execute the accused. He is authorized to:

> Summarily dispose of some of the more notorious enemies of the people by firing squads if the military situation is one of grave urgency . . . .[383]

---

[378]*Ibid.*, §41 (1).

[379]*Ibid.*, §42 (1).

[380]*Ibid.*, §43 (1).

[381]*Ibid.*, §44, 45.

[382]*Ibid.*, §12 (2).

[383]*Ibid.*, §12 (2) (a).

These provisions also violate the principle that no sentence shall be imposed without a regular trial that conforms to due process. The potential for abuse is obvious.

Under quieter conditions, those accused of being "enemies of the people" are to be tried by a People's Court Martial, made up of three members by written order of the chairman of the SPLA.[384] Usually a death sentence must be confirmed by the chairman, unless "communications with the headquarters are difficult because of enemy action, or if morale and discipline dictate."[385] What constitutes morale and discipline is entirely at the discretion of the Court Martial, effectively removing the right of appeal in a death sentence. A death sentence also may be carried out without appeal or approval of the Chairman "whenever enemy action makes it necessary to decamp in flight."[386]

Accountability

Military discipline for abuses by soldiers and officers is known to occur, but the frequency and regularity of such discipline is difficult to ascertain. Many claim that discipline is applied in an ethnically discriminatory fashion.[387]

As described above, punishment for the most egregious and widespread human rights abuses is profoundly lacking in both factions. Some observers rate the SPLA factions as more disciplined than many other African insurgents, but this is not an acceptable standard. It is clear that neither faction demands that its soldiers and officers be held responsible for wrongful acts committed during combat, including indiscriminate shooting of civilians, looting and burning civilian property,

---

[384]*Ibid.*, §§14 (2) and 17 (2).

[385]*Ibid.*, § 17 (4).

[386]*Ibid.*, § 17 (5).

[387]"There were orders that if you rape you will be executed," one Maban (Equatorian) soldier said, complaining that in practice, the Dinka soldiers were simply transferred as a punishment for rape, but Equatorians and other non-Dinka were executed. He claimed that fourteen SPLA soldiers from the Maban tribe were executed for various reasons from 1986 to 1991.

and, in most cases, abduction and rape. Ethnically targeted attacks on civilians are clearly part of a command decision in some incursions into factional enemy territory.

Accountability for combat-related abuses and violations of the rules of war is discussed above in this chapter for the SPLA-Torit (for the 1992 killing of relief workers and its 1993 campaign) and for the SPLA-Nasir (for the 1991 Bor Massacre).

Reports of SPLA-Torit accountability for non-combat-related abuses of civilians are mixed. In June 1992, an SPLA-Torit soldier raped a girl he encountered at the river at Palataka. The girl's father, accompanied by his daughter, confronted the soldier's commander, who arrested the soldier but released him when the father left, according to another soldier who was present.

In some areas, commanders have been more strict with their soldiers, often following local protests. A local man observed that if the people complained to the commander of Kajo Kaji that the SPLA soldiers "came as thieves and just took whatever they wanted," the soldiers involved sometimes would be lashed a hundred times and jailed. These punishments were instituted following local dissatisfaction with the SPLA prior to its capture of Kajo Kaji in 1990. During that period, women from nearby Mere were so often sexually abused by the soldiers, and their cattle, goats, and chickens so often looted by the soldiers, that the population organized and confronted the SPLA commanders. The situation thereafter improved. Later in 1990, a soldier was publicly executed for raping a woman from the area.

In 1991, an officer accused of killing a detainee was said to be court martialed. The Toposa militia had attacked an SPLA base near Kapoeta. After the attack, a fifteen-year-old boy was apprehended, suspected of working with the Toposa. While he was in custody, the officer killed him, alleging that the boy had tried to escape. The officer was found guilty, sentenced to death, and executed by firing squad.

As for SPLA-Nasir accountability for non-combat-related abuses, Commander Riek cited the case of Commander Thomas Tot Bangaong of Waat as an example of military discipline. According to Riek, the commander shot a prisoner, Commander Kuol Ajak (a Dinka from the Kongor area who belonged to SPLA-Nasir), in custody. The Dinka prisoner was accused of the tribally motivated murder of two Nuer (a RASS official and a radio operator) in Kongor when they went there in December 1992 to prepare that outpost, then unoccupied, for U.N. relief operations.[388] Commander Thomas Tot Bangaong arrested the Dinka suspect and then summarily executed him.[389] Commander Thomas was tried by SPLA-Nasir court martial for executing a captive, found guilty, dismissed from the army, and sentenced to three years in jail--a disproportionately light punishment.

---

[388]One murder was discovered when relief workers flew in and found a dead body but no RASS staff in Kongor.

[389]Initially an SPLA-Nasir press release claimed that Garang forces captured Commander Kuol Ajak. Department of Information and Culture, Press Release, January 14, 1993. Several other details of this account are not consistent, either.

V. RECOMMENDATIONS

UNITED NATIONS

HRW/Africa recommends that the U.N. Security Council:

- institute an arms embargo on the warring parties in Sudan, with special attention to bombs and airplanes used to deliver them.
- authorize a contingent of full-time U.N. human rights monitors to observe, investigate, bring to the attention of the responsible authorities, and make public violations of humanitarian and human rights laws by all parties. The monitors should have access to all parts of Sudan and be based in southern Sudan because the conflict is at its most extreme there.
- establish a civilian-directed and -staffed program of human rights education for all regions of and all parties in Sudan. This program should be a supplement to, not a substitute for, the human rights monitors.

HRW/Africa recommends that UNICEF and UNHCR :

- conduct voluntary family reunification; where small groups of minors are separated from their larger tribe, efforts should be made to reunite them in the safest location, even if that means reuniting them outside of Sudan or from one country of refuge to another. This task should receive the cooperation of all U.N. and NGO agencies.

UNITED STATES, UNITED KINGDOM, AND OTHER CONCERNED COUNTRIES

HRW/Africa recommends that the U.S., U.K., and other concerned countries:

- support an arms embargo.
- support the creation of a full-time U.N. human rights monitoring team.
- maintain pressure on the Sudan government to respect human rights and humanitarian law and permit access to relief operations.

- pressure all parties to improve their human rights performance by 1) instituting due process, 2) abolishing political detention, torture and summary executions, 3) abolishing the death penalty, 4) halting attacks on civilians, 5) ceasing abuse of civilian access to food, 6) ceasing to draft minors or to permit them to participate in hostilities, and 7) facilitating relief access, voluntary family reunification, and access for human rights monitors.

Until the human rights performance of the Sudan government is substantially improved, other governments should not provide any assistance except for humanitarian assistance.

Until the human rights performance of the SPLA factions is improved, there should be no consideration given to any assistance to the SPLA factions by any government.

The recommended U.N. human rights monitors and educational program should not be funneled through the government, the SPLA factions or their agencies.

The concerned countries of Kenya, Uganda, Ethiopia, Zaire and other refugee-receiving countries should permit those unaccompanied minors in Sudan or in other countries to be reunited with their parents or closest surviving relatives who are refugees in their territories pursuant to their obligations under the Convention of the Rights of the Child, article 10.

SUDAN GOVERNMENT

HRW/Africa calls on the Sudan government to:
- respect international humanitarian and human rights law, particularly the prohibitions on targeting civilians, indiscriminate bombardment, and destruction or looting of civilian property.
- cease using aerial bombardment in southern Sudan except where the bombs can be precisely aimed at military objectives.
- abolish political detention, torture and summary executions.
- institute due process.
- abolish the death penalty.
- permit the International Committee of the Red Cross to visit persons detained in connection with the conflict according to its specific criteria.

- facilitate access to all parts of the country, particularly the Nuba Mountains and the south, for human rights monitors, human rights educators, and relief workers.
- disarm and disband tribal militias and Popular Defence Forces created from them.
- facilitate voluntary family reunification.
- refrain from involuntarily recruiting anyone; refrain from drafting those under the age of fifteeen or permitting them to participate in hostilities. If persons under eighteen and older than fourteen participate voluntarily in the hostilities, those who are older should be given priority in assignments.
- refrain from taking food or non-food items, directly or indirectly, from those at or below the subsistence level.

SPLA-TORIT AND SPLA-NASIR/UNITED

Africa Watch calls on SPLA-Torit and SPLA-Nasir/United to:
- respect international humanitarian and human rights law, particularly the prohibitions on targeting civilians, indiscriminate attacks on civilians, and destruction or looting of civilian property.
- institute due process.
- abolish political detention, torture and summary executions.
- abolish the death penalty.
- permit the International Committee of the Red Cross to visit persons detained in connection with the conflict according to its specific criteria.
- cooperate with relief efforts and human rights monitors and educators, and facilitate their access to all parts of the country.
- facilitate voluntary family reunification.
- refrain from involuntarily recruiting anyone; refrain from drafting those under the age of fifteeen or permitting them to participate in hostilities. If persons under eighteen and older than fourteen participate voluntarily in the hostilities, those who are older should be given priority in assignments.
- refrain from taking food or non-food items, directly or indirectly, from those at or below the subsistence level.

Both factions claim to respect human rights. At least one, the SPLA-Nasir/United, has sought funding for training for its cadre to protect and promote human rights.[1] We believe this is a worthwhile effort, provided the training is not funded through the SPLAs' organizations.

Nongovernmental organizations play a vital role in the delivery of food and non-food relief to the needy in south Sudan, and several are attempting development projects. In the course of their work, they should not hesitate to discuss international standards of humanitarian law and human rights with the parties to the conflict and to urge them to adhere to these norms.

---

[1]Sudan People's Liberation Movement and Sudan People's Liberation Army United, "Request for Support from the international Community Government, Non-Governmental Organisation (NGOs) and Others," Nairobi, Kenya, January 12, 1994.

APPENDIX A
APPLICATION OF THE RULES OF WAR
TO THE CONFLICT IN SUDAN

The conduct of government armies and insurgent forces fighting an internal conflict is governed not by human rights laws such as the International Covenant on Civil and Political Rights but by the rules of war, also called international humanitarian law, which comprise the four 1949 Geneva Conventions, the two 1977 Protocols to those Conventions, and the customary laws of war. Unlike human rights law, the rules of war ordinarily apply during armed conflicts and their basic provisions are not derogable nor capable of suspension. The rules are primarily intended to protect the victims of armed conflicts.

Despite their separate origins and fields of application, human rights and international humanitarian law share the common purpose of securing for all persons a minimum standard of treatment under all circumstances. For example, both human rights and humanitarian law conventions absolutely prohibit summary executions, torture and other inhuman treatment and the application of ex post facto law.

THE SUDAN: A NON-INTERNATIONAL ARMED CONFLICT

International humanitarian law makes a critical distinction between international and non-international (internal) armed conflicts. Since the rules governing each type of conflict vary significantly, a proper characterization of the conflict is necessary to determine which aspects of humanitarian law apply.

For the past eleven years, the government of the Sudan has been engaged in an armed conflict with the dissident SPLA forces. Over the years the government has requested and received military assistance, advisers and training from various countries in its efforts to fight the SPLA.

Since no state has either declared war against Sudan or directly intervened with its armed forces against the government, the requisite preconditions for the existence of an international armed conflict are not satisfied at this time.[1]

The nature of hostilities between the government Sudan People's Armed Forces and SPLA forces in the Sudan, and of one SPLA faction against the other, therefore is that of a non-international armed conflict. As such, government and insurgent forces' conduct is governed by common article 3 of the Geneva Conventions and customary international law applicable to internal armed conflicts. The 1977 Protocol II to the Geneva Conventions contains rules providing authoritative guidance on the conduct of hostilities by the warring parties.[2]

THE APPLICATION OF ARTICLE 3

Article 3 common to the four Geneva Conventions[3] is virtually a convention within a convention. It is the only provision of the Geneva Conventions that directly applies to internal (as opposed to international) armed conflicts.

Common article 3, section 1, states:

> In the case of armed conflict not of an international character occurring in the territory of one of the High Contracting Parties, each Party to the conflict shall be bound to apply, as a minimum, the following provisions:
>
> (1)   Persons taking no active part in the hostilities, including members of armed forces who had laid down their arms

---

[1]Under article 2 common to the four 1949 Geneva Conventions, an international armed conflict must involve a declared war or any other armed conflict which may arise "between two or more of the High Contracting Parties" to the Convention; it is also described as any difference between two states leading to the intervention of armed forces. Only states and not rebel groups may be "High Contracting Parties."

[2]Sudan has not yet ratified Protocol II.

[3]Sudan acceded to the four Geneva Conventions on September 23, 1957.

and those placed *hors de combat* by sickness, wounds, detention, or any other cause, shall in all circumstances be treated humanely, without any adverse distinction founded on race, colour, religion or faith, sex, birth or wealth, or any other similar criteria.

To this end the following acts are and shall remain prohibited at any time and in any place whatsoever with respect to the above-mentioned persons:

(a)   violence to life and person, in particular murder of all kinds, mutilation, cruel treatment and torture;

(b)   taking of hostages;

(c)   outrages upon personal dignity, in particular humiliating and degrading treatment;

(d)   the passing of sentences and the carrying out of executions without previous judgment pronounced by a regularly constituted court, affording all the judicial guarantees which are recognized as indispensable by civilized peoples.

Article 3 thus imposes fixed legal obligations on the parties to an internal conflict to ensure humane treatment of persons not, or no longer, taking an active role in the hostilities.

Article 3 applies when a situation of internal armed conflict objectively exists in the territory of a State Party; it expressly binds all parties to the internal conflict, including insurgents although they do not have the legal capacity to sign the Geneva Conventions.[4] In the Sudan, the government and the two SPLA factions and possibly a third SPLA faction, that of William Nyuon, are parties to the conflict.

The obligation to apply article 3 is absolute for all parties to the conflict and independent of the obligation of the other parties. That

---

[4]As private individuals within the national territory of a State Party, certain obligations are imposed on them. ICRC, *Commentary on the Additional Protocols*, p. 1345.

means that the Sudan government cannot excuse itself from complying with article 3 on the grounds that the SPLA is violating article 3, and vice versa.

Application of article 3 by the government cannot be legally construed as recognition of the insurgent party's belligerence, from which recognition of additional legal obligations beyond common article 3, would flow. Nor is it necessary for any government to recognize the SPLA's belligerent status for article 3 to apply.

Unlike international conflicts, the law governing internal armed conflicts does not recognize the combatant's privilege[5] and therefore does not provide any special status for combatants, even when captured. Thus, the Sudan government is not obliged to grant captured members of the SPLA prisoner of war status. Similarly, government army combatants who are captured by the SPLA need not be accorded this status. Any party can agree to treat its captives as prisoners of war, however.

Since the SPLA forces are not privileged combatants, they may be tried and punished by the Sudan government for treason, sedition, and the commission of other crimes under domestic laws.

CUSTOMARY INTERNATIONAL LAW
APPLICABLE TO INTERNAL ARMED CONFLICTS

United Nations General Assembly Resolution 2444,[6] adopted by unanimous vote on December 19, 1969, expressly recognized the

---

[5]The combatant's privilege is a license to kill or capture enemy troops, destroy military objectives and cause unavoidable civilian casualties. This privilege immunizes members of armed forces or rebels from criminal prosecution by their captors for their violent acts that do not violate the laws of war but would otherwise be crimes under domestic law. Prisoner of war status depends on and flows from this privilege. See Solf, "The Status of Combatants in Non-International Armed Conflicts Under Domestic Law and Transnational Practice," *American University Law Review* 33 (1953): p. 59.

[6]U.N. General Assembly, *Respect for Human Rights in Armed Conflicts*, United Nations Resolution 2444, G.A. Res. 2444, 23 U.N. GAOR Supp. (No. 18), p. 164, U.N. Doc. A/7433 (New York: U.N., 1968).

customary law principle of civilian immunity and its complementary principle requiring the warring parties to distinguish civilians from combatants at all times. The preamble to this resolution states that these fundamental humanitarian law principles apply "in all armed conflicts," meaning both international and internal armed conflicts. Resolution 2444 affirms:

> . . . the following principles for observance by all government and other authorities responsible for action in armed conflicts:
>
> (a)   That the right of the parties to a conflict to adopt means of injuring the enemy is not unlimited;
>
> (b)   That it is prohibited to launch attacks against the civilian populations as such;
>
> (c)   That distinction must be made at all times between persons taking part in the hostilities and members of the civilian population to the effect that the latter be spared as much as possible.

PROTECTION OF THE CIVILIAN POPULATION UNDER THE RULES OF WAR

In situations of internal armed conflict, generally speaking, a civilian is anyone who is not a member of the armed forces or of an organized armed group of a party to the conflict. Accordingly, "the civilian population comprises all persons who do not actively participate in the hostilities."[7]

Civilians may not be subject to deliberate individualized attack since they pose no immediate threat to the adversary.[8]

---

[7]R. Goldman, "International Humanitarian Law and the Armed Conflicts in El Salvador and Nicaragua," *American University Journal of International Law & Policy* 2 (1987): p. 553.

[8]Bothe, *New Rules for Victims of Armed Conflicts*, p. 303.

The term "civilian" also includes some employees of the military establishment who are not members of the armed forces but assist them.[9] While as civilians they may not be targeted, these civilian employees of military establishments or those who indirectly assist combatants assume the risk of death or injury incidental to attacks against legitimate military targets while they are at or in the immediate vicinity of military targets.

In addition, both sides utilize as part-time combatants persons who are otherwise engaged in civilian occupations. These civilians lose their immunity from attack for as long as they directly participate in hostilities.[10] "[D]irect participation [in hostilities] means acts of war which by their nature and purpose are likely to cause actual harm to the personnel and equipment of enemy armed forces," and includes acts of defense.[11]

"Hostilities" not only covers the time when the civilian actually makes use of a weapon but also the time that he is carrying it, as well as situations in which he undertakes hostile acts without using a weapon.[12] Examples are provided in the United States Army Field Manual which lists some hostile acts as including

> sabotage, destruction of communication facilities, intentional misleading of troops by guides, and liberation of prisoners of war. . . . This is also the case of a person acting as a member of

---

[9]Civilians include those persons who are "directly linked to the armed forces, including those who accompany the armed forces without being members thereof, such as civilian members of military aircraft crews, supply contractors, members of labour units, or of services responsible for the welfare of the armed forces, members of the crew of the merchant marine and the crews of civil aircraft employed in the transportation of military personnel, material or supplies. . . . Civilians employed in the production, distribution and storage of munitions of war . . . ." *Ibid.*, pp. 293-94.

[10]*Ibid.*, p. 303.

[11]ICRC, *Commentary on the Additional Protocols*, p. 619.

[12]ICRC, *Commentary on the Additional Protocols*, p. 618-19. This is a broader definition than "attacks" and includes at a minimum preparation for combat and return from combat. Bothe, *New Rules for Victims of Armed Conflicts*, p. 303.

a weapons crew, or one providing target information for weapon
systems intended for immediate use against the enemy such as
artillery spotters or members of ground observer teams. [It]
would include direct logistic support for units engaged directly in
battle such as the delivery of ammunition to a firing position. On
the other hand civilians providing only indirect support to the
armed forces, such as workers in defense plants or those engaged
in distribution or storage of military supplies in rear areas, do
not pose an immediate threat to the adversary and therefore
would not be subject to deliberate individual attack.[13]

Once their participation in hostilities ceases, that is, while
engaged in their civilian vocations, these civilians may not be attacked.

Persons protected by article 3 include members of both
government and SPLA forces who surrender, are wounded, sick or
unarmed, or are captured. They are *hors de combat*, literally, out of
combat, until such time as they take a hostile action such as attempting
to escape.

DESIGNATION OF MILITARY OBJECTIVES

Under the laws of war, military objectives are defined only as
they relate to objects or targets, rather than to personnel. To constitute
a legitimate military objective, the object or target, selected by its nature,
location, purpose, or use, must contribute effectively to the enemy's
military capability or activity, and its total or partial destruction or
neutralization must offer a definite military advantage in the
circumstances.[14]

Legitimate military objectives are combatants' weapons, convoys,
installations, and supplies. In addition:

an object generally used for civilian purposes, such as a
dwelling, a bus, a fleet of taxicabs, or a civilian airfield or
railroad siding, can become a military objective if its

---

[13]*Ibid.*, p. 303 (footnote omitted).

[14]Protocol I, art. 52 (2).

location or use meets [the criteria in Protocol I, art. 52(2)].[15]

Full-time members of the Sudan government's armed forces and SPLA are legitimate military targets and subject to attack, individually or collectively, until such time as they become *hors de combat*, that is, surrender or are wounded or captured.[16]

Popular Defence Forces (PDF), government-sponsored militia, are proper military targets while they directly participate in hostilities, which includes guard and patrol duties. Part-time PDF members may not be individually attacked when they are not directly participating in hostilities or performing military duties.

Unofficial paramilitary tribal militias, often organized by political parties or operating with impunity and/or equipped by the Sudan military, like other civilians lose their immunity from attack whenever they assume a combatant's role. Thus, when they prepare for, actively participate in and return from combat or raiding (while carrying a weapon or committing hostile acts without using a weapon), they are proper military targets for the SPLA.

Policemen without combat duties are not legitimate military targets, nor are certain other government personnel authorized to bear arms such as customs agents.[17] Policemen with combat duties, however, would be proper military targets, subject to direct individualized attack.

Those mujahedeen participating in hostilities in Sudan, whether as part of a Holy War or for financial motives, are legitimate military targets.

---

[15]Bothe, *New Rules for Victims of Armed Conflicts*, pp. 306-07.

[16]Killing a wounded or captured combatant is not proper because: it does not offer a "definite military advantage in the circumstances" because the fighter is already rendered useless or *hors de combat*.

[17]Report of Working Group B, Committee I, 18 March 1975 (CDDH/I/238/Rev.1; X, 93), in Howard S. Levie, ed., *The Law of NonInternational Armed Conflict*, (Dordrecht, Netherlands: Martinus Nijhoff, 1987), p. 67. *See* Rosario Conde, "Policemen without Combat Duties: Illegitimate Targets of Direct Attack under Humanitarian Law," student paper (New York: Columbia Law School, May 12, 1989).

PROHIBITED ACTS

While not an all-encompassing list, customary and conventional international law prohibits the following kinds of practices, orders, or actions:

- Orders that there shall be no survivors, such threats to combatants, or direction to conduct hostilities on this basis.

- Attacks against combatants who are captured, surrender, or are placed *hors de combat*.
- Torture, any form of corporal punishment, or other cruel treatment of persons under any circumstances.
- Desecration of corpses.[18] Mutilation of the dead is never permissible and violates the rules of war.
- The infliction of humiliating or degrading treatment on civilians or combatants who are captured, have surrendered, or are *hors de combat*.
- Hostage taking.[19]
- Shielding, or using the presence of the civilian population to immunize areas from military operations, or to favor or impede military operations. In addition, the parties may not direct the movement of civilians in order to attempt to shield legitimate military objectives from attack, or to favor militiary operations.[20]

---

[18]Protocol II, article 8, states:

> Whenever circumstances permit, and particularly after an engagement, all possible measures shall be taken, without delay, . . . to search for the dead, prevent their being despoiled, and decently dispose of them.

[19]The ICRC, *Commentary on the Additional Protocols*, p. 874, defines hostages as persons who find themselves, willingly or unwillingly, in the power of the enemy and who answer with their freedom or their life for compliance with the orders of the latter and for upholding the security of its armed forces.

[20]*See* Protocol I, article 51 (7).

•   Pillage and destruction of civilian property. This prohibition is
      designed to spare civilians the suffering resulting from the
      destruction of their real and personal property: houses, furniture,
      clothing, provisions, tools, and so forth. Pillage includes
      organized acts as well as individual acts without the consent of
      the military authorities.[21]

TAXATION OR REQUISITION OF FOOD

There is little authority in international law for a rebel army
fighting in an internal conflict to requisition property from the civilian
population, or to impose taxes upon them. Such are usually powers of
States over their own citizens and others residing in their territory. A
rebel army is not a State and does not have all the powers of States vis
a vis those who reside under its military jurisdiction.

In an international armed conflict, a State army that occupies
territory of another State has certain limited powers to requisition food
from the population in that territory. That occupying power has the duty
first to ensure the food and medical supplies of the population, however,
and must bring in the necessary food and other articles if the resouces of
the occupied territory are inadequate. The occupying power may only
requisition food if the requirements of the civilian population have been
taken into account. Then the occupying power must make arrangements
to pay fair value for the requisitioned goods.[22]

A noted authority comments, "During recent conflicts thousands
of human beings suffered from starvation during the occupation of the
country. Their destitution was made still worse by requisitioning."[23] The
above provisions in the 1949 Geneva Conventions were designed to
prevent such destitution.

---

[21]International Committee of the Red Cross (ICRC), *Commentary, IV Geneva
Convention* (Geneva: ICRC, 1958), p. 226.

[22]IV Geneva Convention of 1949, art. 55. These limitations and restrictions
were specifically not imposed on the relations between a State party and its own
residents or citizens.

[23]ICRC, *Commentary, IV Geneva Convention*, p. 309.

Common article 3 to the four 1949 Geneva Conventions and Protocol II, which are relevant to internal armed conflicts, do not specifically empower the rebel army to requisition food or other articles, or to tax civilians.

Even if such authority to requisition or tax existed, however, there is no reason it should be superior to the authority conferred on occupying powers under IV Geneva, article 55. In almost every respect, a rebel army and its combatants in an internal conflict have fewer humanitarian law rights than does a State party to an international conflict.[24]

If the rebel army does have rights comparable to those of the occupying power to requisition food from the civilian population as described in IV Geneva, article 55, then the SPLA's requisition of food from the civilian population of southern Sudan is a violation of article 55. The occupying power may under no circumstances take food from the population without taking the needs of the civilian population into account, and, for a large portion of the southern Sudan population, simply no surplus food at all. There are pockets of famine throughout this population, and many other areas where there is nothing beyond a minimal subsistence. The situation is as bad as or worse than anything in World War II, on which experience the IV Geneva Convention was based.

PROHIBITION OF INDISCRIMINATE ATTACKS: THE PRINCIPLE OF PROPORTIONALITY

The civilian population and individual civilians general are to be protected against attack.

As set forth above, to constitute a legitimate military object, the target must 1) contribute effectively to the enemy's military capability or activity, and 2) its total or partial destruction or neutralization must offer a definite military advantage in the circumstances.

---

[24]For example, in an internal conflict there is no combatant's privilege and thus captured combatants do not have the status of prisoners of war. In an international conflict, captured combatants have extensive rights and protections detailed in III Geneva Convention.

The laws of war implicitly characterize all objects as civilian unless they satisfy this two-fold test. Objects normally dedicated to civilian use, such as churches, houses and schools, are presumed not to be military objectives. If they in fact do assist the enemy's military action, they can lose their immunity from direct attack. This presumption attaches, however, only to objects that ordinarily have no significant military use or purpose. For example, this presumption would not include objects such as transportation and communications systems that under applicable criteria are military objectives.

The attacker also must do everything "feasible" to verify that the objectives to be attacked are not civilian. "Feasible" means "that which is practical or practically possible taking into account all the circumstances at the time, including those relevant to the success of military operations."[25]

Even attacks on legitimate military targets, however, are limited by the principle of proportionality. This principle places a duty on combatants to choose means of attack that avoid or minimize damage to civilians. In particular, the attacker should refrain from launching an attack if the expected civilian casualties would outweigh the importance of the military target to the attacker. The principle of proportionality is codified in Protocol I, article 51 (5):

> Among others, the following types of attacks are to be considered as indiscriminate: . . .
>
> (b)   an attack which may be expected to cause incidental loss of civilian life, injury to civilians, damage to civilian objects, or a combination thereof, which would be excessive in relation to the concrete and direct military advantage anticipated.

If an attack can be expected to cause incidental civilian casualties or damage, two requirements must be met before that attack is launched. First, there must be an anticipated "concrete and direct" military advantage. "Direct" means "'without intervening condition of agency.' . .

---

[25]Bothe, *New Rules for Victims of Armed Conflict*, p. 362 (footnote omitted).

A remote advantage to be gained at some unknown time in the future would not be a proper consideration to weigh against civilian losses."[26]

Creating conditions "conducive to surrender by means of attacks which incidentally harm the civilian population"[27] is too remote and insufficiently military to qualify as a "concrete and direct" military advantage. "A military advantage can only consist in ground gained and in annilihation or weakening the enemy armed forces."[28]

The "concrete and direct" military advantage surpasses the "definite" military advantage required to qualify an object or target as a "legitimate military target."[29]

The second requirement in the principle of proportionality is that the foreseeable injury to civilians and damage to civilian objects not be disproportionate, that is, "excessive" in comparison to the expected "concrete and definite military advantage."

Excessive damage is a relative concept. For instance, the presence of a soldier on leave cannot serve as a justification to destroy the entire village. If the destruction of a bridge is of paramount importance for the occupation of a strategic zone, "it is understood that some houses may be hit, but not that a whole urban area be levelled."[30] There is never a justification for excessive civilian casualties, no matter how valuable the military target.[31]

Indiscriminate attacks are defined in Protocol I, article 51 (4), as:

---

[26]*Ibid.*, p. 365.

[27]ICRC, *Commentary on the Additional Protocols*, p. 685.

[28]*Ibid.*, p. 685.

[29]As set forth above, to constitute a legitimate military objective, the object, selected by its nature, location, purpose or use must contribution effectively to the enemy's military capability or activitiy, and its total or partial destruction or neutralization must offer a "definite" military advantage in the circumstances. See Protocol I, art. 52 (2) where this definition is codified.

[30]ICRC, *Commentary on the Additional Protocols*, p. 684.

[31]*Ibid.*, p. 626.

a) those which are not directed at a specific military objective;
b) those which employ a method or means of combat which cannot be directed at a specific military objective; or
c) those which employ a method or means of combat the effects of which cannot be limited as required by this Protocol; and consequently, in each such case, are of a nature to strike military objectives and civilians or civilian objects without distinction.

PROTECTION OF CIVILIANS FROM DISPLACEMENT FOR REASONS RELATED TO THE CONFLICT

There are only two exceptions to the prohibition on displacement, for war-related reasons, of civilians: their security or imperative military reasons. Article 17 of Protocol II states:

1. The displacement of the civilian population shall not be ordered for reasons related to the conflict unless the security of the civilians involved or imperative military reasons so demand. Should such displacements have to be carried out, all possible measures shall be taken in order that the civilian population may be received under satisfactory conditions of shelter, hygiene, health, safety and nutrition.

The term "imperative military reasons" usually refers to evacuation because of imminent military operations. The provisional measure of evacuation is appropriate if an area is in danger as a result of military operations or is liable to be subjected to intense bombing. It may also be permitted when the presence of protected persons in an area hampers military operations. The prompt return of the evacuees to their homes is required as soon as hostilities in the area have ceased. The evacuating authority bears the burden of proving that its forcible relocation conforms to these conditions.

Displacement or capture of civilians solely to deny a social base to the enemy has nothing to do with the security of the civilians. Nor is it justified by "imperative military reasons," which require "the most meticulous assessment of the circumstances"[32] because such reasons are so capable of abuse. One authority has stated:

> Clearly, imperative military reasons cannot be justified by political motives. For example, it would be prohibited to move a population in order to exercise more effective control over a dissident ethnic group.[33]

Mass relocation or displacement of civilians for the purpose of denying a willing social base to the opposing force is prohibited since it is a political motive as described above.

Even if the government were to show that the displacement were necessary, it still has the independent obligation to take "all possible measures" to receive the civilian population "under satisfactory conditions of shelter, hygiene, health, safety, and nutrition."

STARVATION OF CIVILIANS AS A METHOD OF COMBAT

Starvation of civilians as a method of combat has become illegal as a matter of customary law, as reflected in Protocol II:

> Article 14 -- Protection of objects indispensable to the survival of the civilian population
>
> Starvation of civilians as a method of combat is prohibited. It is prohibited to attack, destroy, remove or render useless, for that purpose, objects indispensable to the survival of the civilian population, such as foodstuffs, agricultural areas for the production of foodstuffs, crops, livestock, drinking water installations and supplies and irrigation works.

What is prohibited is using starvation as "a weapon to annihilate or weaken the population." Using starvation as a method of warfare does

---

[32]*Ibid.*, p. 1472.

[33]*Ibid.*

not mean that the population has to reach the point of starving to death before a violation can be proved. What is forbidden is deliberately "causing the population to suffer hunger, particularly by depriving it of its sources of food or of supplies."

This prohibition on starving civilians "is a rule from which no derogation may be made."[34] No exception was made for imperative military necessity, for instance.

Article 14 lists the most usual ways in which starvation is brought about. Specific protection is extended to "objects indispensable to the survival of the civilian population," and a non-exhaustive list of such objects follows: "foodstuffs, agricultural areas for the production of foodstuffs, crops, livestock, drinking water installations and supplies and irrigation works." The article prohibits taking certain destructive actions aimed at these essential supplies, and describes these actions with verbs which are meant to cover all eventualities: "attack, destroy, remove or render useless."

The textual reference to "objects indispensable to the survival of the civilian population"

> does not distinguish between objects intended for the armed forces and those intended for civilians. Except for the case where supplies are specifically intended as provisions for combatants, it is prohibited to destroy or attack objects indispensable for survival, even if the adversary may benefit from them. The prohibition would be meaningless if one could invoke the argument that members of the government's armed forces or armed opposition might make use of the objects in question.[35]

Attacks on objects used "in direct support of military action" are permissible, however, even if these objects are civilian foodstuffs and other objects protected under article 14. This exception is limited to the immediate zone of actual armed engagements, as is obvious from the examples provided of military objects used in direct support of military action: "bombarding a food-producing area to prevent the army from

---

[34]*Ibid.*, p. 1456.

[35]*Ibid.*, p. 1458-59.

advancing through it, or attacking a food-storage barn which is being used by the enemy for cover or as an arms depot, etc."[36]

The provisions of Protocol I, article 54 are also useful as a guideline to the narrowness of the permissible means and methods of attack on foodstuffs.[37] Like article 14 of Protocol II, article 54 of Protocol I permits attacks on military food supplies. It specifically limits such attacks to those directed at foodstuffs intended for the sole use of the enemy's armed forces. This means "supplies already in the hands of the adverse party's armed forces because it is only at that point that one could know that they are intended for use only for the members of the enemy's armed forces."[38] Even then, the attacker cannot destroy foodstuffs "in the military supply system intended for the sustenance of prisoners of war, the civilian population of occupied territory or persons classified as civilians serving with, or accompanying, the armed forces."[39]

Proof of Intention to Starve Civilians

Under article 14, what is forbidden are actions taken with the intention of using starvation as a method or weapon to attack the civilian population. Such an intention may not be easy to prove and most armies will not admit this intention. Proof does not rest solely on the attacker's own statements, however. Intention may be inferred from the totality of the circumstances of the military campaign.

Particularly relevant to assessment of intention is the effort the attacker makes to comply with the duties to distinguish between civilians and military targets and to avoid harming civilians and the civilian

---

[36]*Ibid.*, p. 657. The *New Rules* gives the following examples of direct support: "an irrigation canal used as part of a defensive position, a water tower used as an observation post, or a cornfield used as cover for the infiltration of an attacking force." Bothe, *New Rules for Victims of Armed Conflicts*, p. 341.

[37]Article 54 of Protocol I is the parallel, for international armed conflicts, to article 14, Protocol II in its prohibition on starvation of civilians as a method of warfare.

[38]Bothe, *New Rules for Victims of Armed Conflict*, p. 340.

[39]*Ibid.*, pp. 340-41.

economy.[40] If the attacker does not comply with these duties, and food shortages result, an intention to attack civilians by starvation may be inferred.

The more sweeping and indiscriminate the measures taken which result in food shortages, when other less restrictive means of combat are available, the more likely the real intention is to attack the civilian population by causing it food deprivation. For instance, an attacker who conducts a scorced earth campaign in enemy territory to deprive the enemy of sources of food may be deemed to have an intention of attacking by starvation the civilian population living in enemy territory. The attacker may not claim ignorance of the effects upon civilians of such a scorched earth campaign, since these effects are a matter of common knowledge and publicity. In particular, relief organizations, both domestic and international, usually sound the alarm of impending food shortages occurring during conflicts in order to bring pressure on the parties to permit access for food delivery and to raise money for their complex and costly operations.

The true intentions of the attacker also must be judged by the effort it makes to take prompt remedies, such as permitting relief convoys to reach the needy or itself supplying food to remedy hunger. An attacker who fails to make adequate provision for the affected civilian population, who blocks access to those who would do so, or who refuses to permit civilian evacuation in times of food shortage, may be deemed to have the intention to starve that civilian population.

Sieges

Proportionality is an important principle in the context of sieges and other methods of war directed at combatants comingled with civilians. While starvation of the civilian population is forbidden, starvation of combatants remains a permitted method of combat, as in siege warfare or blockades.[41]

---

[40]Civilians are not legitimate military targets; this is expressly forbidden by U.N. General Assembly Resolution 2444, above. The duty to distinguish at all times between civilians and combatants, and between civilian objects and military objects, includes the duty to direct military operations only against military objectives.

[41]ICRC, *Commentary on the Additional Protocols*, p. 1457.

A blockade consists of disrupting the maritime trade of a country; a siege "consists of encircling an enemy location, cutting off those inside from any communication in order to bring about their surrender."[42]

Siege is the oldest form of total war, in which civilians have been attacked along with soldiers, or in order to reach soldiers. A siege may occur when an army takes refuge inside city walls, or when the inhabitants of a threatened city seek the most immediate form of military protection and agree to be garrisoned.[43]

Both blockades and sieges are theoretically aimed at preventing military materiel from reaching the combatants. Both are considered low-cost alternatives to frontal assaults.[44]

Under the rule of proportionality and the duty to distinguish, besieging forces may not close their eyes to the effect upon civilians of a food blockade or siege. It is well recognized that, in reality, "in case of shortages occasioned by armed conflict, the highest priority of available sustenance materials is assigned to combatants".[45] In other words, "Fed last, and only with the army's surplus, [civilians] die first. More civilians died in the siege of Leningrad than in the modernist infernos of Hamburg, Dresden, Tokyo, Hiroshima, and Nagasaki, taken together."[46] The besieging forces therefore are deemed to know that, in any besieged area where civilians as well as combatants are present, the civilians will suffer food shortage long before the combatants.

---

[42]*Ibid.*, 1457.

[43]Michael Walzer, *Just and Unjust Wars* (New York: Basic Books, 1977).

[44]One historian notes that "the capture of cities is often an important military objective -- in the age of the city-state, it was the ultimate objective -- and, frontal assault failing, the siege is the only remaining means to success. In fact, however, it is not even necessary that a frontal assault fail before a siege is thought justifiable. Sitting and waiting is far less costly to the besieging army than attacking, and such calculations are permitted by the principle of military necessity." *Ibid.*, p. 169.

[45]Bothe, *New Rules for Victims of Armed Conflicts*, p. 680.

[46]Walzer, *Just and Unjust Wars*, p. 160.

Historically, sieges have been used as weapons to bring pressure through civilians on the military leadership.

> When a city is encircled and deprived of food, it is not the expectation of the attackers that the garrison will hold out until the individual soldiers, like Josephus' old men, drop dead in the streets. The death of the ordinary inhabitants of the city is expected to force the hand of the civilian or military leadership. The goal is surrender; the means is not the defeat of the enemy army, but the fearful spectacle of the civilian dead.[47]

One authority notes that soldiers "are under an obligation to help civilians leave the scene of a battle." In the case of a siege, "it is only when they fulfill this obligation that the batttle itself is morally possible.

> But is it still militarily possible? Once free exit has been offered, and been accepted by a significant numbers of people, the besieging army is placed under a certain handicap. The city's food supply will now last so much longer. It is precisely this handicap that siege commanders have in the past refused to accept.[48]

Under the prohibition on starving the civilian population as a method of combat, sieges are a form of starvation by omission. One ICRC Commentary notes that

> Starvation can also result from an omission. To deliberately decide not to take measures to supply the population with objects indispensable for its survival in a way would become a method of combat by default, and would be prohibited under this rule.[49]

---

[47]*Ibid.*

[48]*Ibid.*, pp. 169-70.

[49]ICRC, *Commentary on the Additional Protocols*, p. 1458.

It is therefore incumbent upon the attackers, in sieges and blockades as well as in other methods of combat, to take actions to ameliorate the effects upon civilians. The Protocols suggest various alternatives, among them permitting relief supplies to the civilian population.[50]

Failure to take any action to relieve the threat of civilian starvation leads directly to the inference that the intention of the besieging forces is to starve civilians.

RIGHTS OF THE CHILD

Recruitment of Child Soldiers

Military recruitment of those under the age of fifteen is forbidden.[51] This principle also prohibits accepting voluntary

---

[50]*See* Protocol I, articles 68-71.

[51]Protocol II, article 4 (3) provides:
Children shall be provided with the care and aid they require, and in particular:
(a) they shall receive an education, including religious and moral education in keeping with the wishes of their parents or, in the absence of parents, of those responsible for their care;
(b) all appropriate steps shall be taken to facilitate the reunion of families temporarily separated;
(c) children who have not attained the age of fifteen years shall neither be recruited in the armed forces or groups nor allowed to take part in hostilities;
(d) the special protection provided by this Article to children who have not attained the age of fifteen years shall remain applicable to them if they take a direct part in hostilities despite the provisions of sub-paragraph (c) and are captured;
(e) measures shall be taken, if necessary, and whenever possible with the consent of their parents or persons who by law or custom are primarily responsible for their care, to remove children temporarily from the area in which hostilities are taking place to a safer area within the country and ensure that they are accompanied by persons responsible for their safety and well-being.

enlistment. The child should not be allowed to take part in hostilities, that is, to participate in military operations including gathering information, transmitting orders, transporting ammunition and foodstuffs, or acts of sabotage.[52]

The reason for these special rules for children in warfare is that "[c]hildren are particularly vulnerable; they require privileged treatment in comparison with the rest of the civilian population."[53]

In addition to the rules of war, other authoritative guidance is provided by the Convention on the Rights of the Child.[54] The provisions of Protocol II are echoed in article 38 (2) of the Convention on the Rights of the Child, stating that the parties "shall take all feasible measures to ensure that persons who have not attained the age of fifteen years do not take a direct part in hostilities." The parties to the Convention also agreed that in "recruiting among those persons who have attained the age of fifteen years but who have not attained the age of eighteen years, [we] shall endeavor to give priority to those who are oldest."[55]

Article 9 of the Convention states as a matter of principle that a child shall not be separated from his or her parents against their will except where such separation is deemed necessary in the best interests of the child after judicial review. Forced recruitment of children violates these principles as well as the rules of war.

Although it has not yet come into effect, the African Convention on the Rights of the Child prohibits recruitment of those under eighteen years of age.

------

[52]ICRC, *Commentary on the Additional Protocols*, p. 1380.

[53]*Ibid.,*, p. 1377.

[54]Sudan ratified this convention on August 3, 1990. It came into force on September 2, 1990. This Convention applies to States Parties, and makes no mention of rebel groups, but does provide authoritative guidance for interpreting customary international humanitarian law applicable to rebels.

[55]Convention on the Rights of the Child, art. 38(2).

Family Reunification

Article 10 of the Convention on the Rights of the Child addresses the need for family reunification across national borders.

1. In accordance with the obligation of States Parties under article 9, paragraph 1, applications by a child or his or her parents to enter or leave a State Party for the purpose of family reunification shall be dealt with by States Parties in a positive, humane and expeditious manner. . . .

2. A child whose parents reside in different States shall have the right to maintain on a regular basis save in exceptional circumstances personal relations and direct contacts with both parents. Towards that end . . . States Parties shall respect the right of the child and his or her parents to leave any country, including their own, and to enter their own country. . . . .

Kenya, Uganda, Ethiopia, Zaire, and other countries host Sudanese refugees. These named countries have ratified the Convention on the Rights of the Child.[56] Under the above mentioned article 10, they have an obligation to permit the unaccompanied minors now in Sudan or even in refugee camps in other countries, whose parents or families are refugees in their countries, to be reunified with their families, even if it means taking in additional refugees.

---

[56]Kenya ratified the Convention on the Rights of the Child on July 30, 1990; Uganda ratified it on August 17, 1990; Ethiopia acceded to it on May 14, 1991; and Zaire ratified it on September 27, 1990.